BANKRUPTCY
INVE$TING
HOW TO PROFIT FROM
DISTRESSED COMPANIES

BANKRUPTCY INVE$TING

HOW TO PROFIT FROM DISTRESSED COMPANIES

BY BEN BRANCH AND HUGH RAY

BeardBooks

WASHINGTON, DC

Library of Congress Cataloging-in-Publication Data

Branch, Ben, 1943–
    Bankruptcy investing : how to profit from distressed companies /
Ben Branch, Hugh Ray.
        p.   cm.
    Originally published: [Chicago, Ill.] : Dearborn Financial Pub., c1992.
    Includes bibliographical references and index.
    ISBN 1-893122-06-9 (paper)
      1. Bankruptcy—United States. 2. Investments—United States.
3. Business failures—Law and legislation—United States.
4. Business enterprises—United States—Finances. I. Ray, Hugh.
II. Title
HG3766.B73   1999
332.6—dc21   98-52215
                                                          CIP

Printed in the United States of America

CONTENTS

PREFACE

A casual reader of today's financial pages will have noticed an increase in the number of corporate reorganizations occurring under Chapter 11 of the Bankruptcy Code. A more careful reader will have noticed a number of instances in which substantial dividends were paid to certain classes of creditors of large organizations. Because people seldom recall minute details (such as isolated bond prices over a period of years), the investors' holding period returns may have gone largely unnoticed. In fact, many investors in distressed companies are reaping huge profits by carefully timing their investments in companies that others refused to touch simply because these companies were in public financial disgrace.

The active participants in major bankruptcy cases have long observed the investment opportunities available to the knowledgeable bottom fisher who understands that the investment quality of today's Chapter 11 debtor (in bankruptcy) is vastly different from the public failure of a decade ago. We have studied the results of careful examinations of companies in Chapter 11 reorganizations and well-timed investments in those companies. To lose money in this area is quite possible. *But* if the investor (apprentice vulture) is willing to take the time to study the materials that follow and apply his or her common sense, substantial rewards can be achieved.

Buying out-of-season goods has long been known to produce bargains for the customers willing to wait to use them. Patience is the key. The average Chapter 11 reorganization case takes 25 months to confirm a reorganization plan. Some take longer, some less. Quick turnarounds are rare. Also rare is complete financial optimism. What is common is enough gloomy press and public proclamations to scare away the boldest of contrarians.

What is unusual is the opportunity created by the interreactions of economic theory and the legal entanglements of social legislation. Concepts of equality of distribution and price efficiency diverge and cross at several points. Fundamental concepts of risks and reward are skewed. At times, they are skewed in favor of you, the risk taker. At other times, the bias runs in the opposite direction. Our purpose is to advise you regarding when each of those times is present. We are not giving specific legal advice, nor are we giving specific investment advice. We hope only to set out for you some of the more important rules of the contest.

No single place now exists for the investor to look for advice regarding how to participate in bankruptcy investments. The current crop of players—as have most traditional pioneers—gained their experience and made their money by actually feeling their way as they went along from case to case. Much of what they learned came from trial and error, much from sheer luck. Almost all of the experience has been acquired since the "rules of the game" changed in 1979 with the enactment of the revised Bankruptcy Code. The public perceptions of bankruptcy gained in previous decades became inapplicable at that time. In the years that followed, certain factors have become more clearly defined. In the years to come, those factors will become clearer. At this point we feel a structure and theme exists on which the reader can frame an investment program with some understanding of the substantial risks involved.

The pages that follow are the only extensive source material available that effectively melds the legal and financial processes of bankruptcy investing into a coherent structure. Both areas must be generally understood if the bankruptcy investor can hope to succeed. Many new funds are moving into this post–junk bond era of vulture investing. Hopefully, this resource material will provide both the beginning investor and the experienced fund manager with a "Rosetta stone" for translating the often confusing lexicon of bankruptcy into a profitable investment program.

This book is designed for serious—though not necessarily large-scale—investors who would like to participate in the risky but potentially lucrative game of investing in the securities of troubled companies. Investments in both debt and equity securities are considered. Most of the discussion will focus on publicly traded instruments, but nonpublic securities also will be discussed.

Depending on the degree of distress, troubled companies may or may not go through any or all of the following: informal workout, formal workout, Chapter 11 bankruptcy or Chapter 7 bankruptcy. The investment implications for the securities of firms in each of these stages of financial distress are considered in this book.

No specialized background is required to read and understand the material presented here. Although the book ultimately treats a number of rather advanced topics, everything needed to understand the issues is contained within these pages. Starting at an elementary level, the discussion moves on to whatever level of complexity is required to understand the concepts. Each step of that process is carefully explained. Additionally, an extensive glossary of relevant terms is included in the book. This glossary constitutes a handy general reference as well as a help source for the reader who needs a refresher on the meanings of some relevant terminology introduced earlier.

The coauthors have a unique combination of knowledge and experience about bankruptcy and bankruptcy investing law and finance.

Ben Branch is a professor of finance at the University of Massachusetts. He has written books and articles (both popular and academic) on investing and has personally invested in the securities of a number of troubled companies. He is a well-known and respected academician in the areas of economics and finance and has served on a number of creditors' committees, including the chairmanship of the First Republic Senior unsecured creditors' committee. He recently (1991) was elected Chapter 7 trustee for the Bank of New England Corporation, as well as chairman of the board of the reorganized First Republic Bank Corporation.

Hugh Ray is a senior partner in the law firm of Andrews & Kurth. In that capacity, he has played a significant role in the legal proceedings of most major bankruptcy cases that have occurred over the past 25 years (e.g., Braniff Airways, Continental Airlines, Storage Technology, Dockocil [Wilson Foods], Smith International, Commonwealth Oil, Zale Corporation, Hunt Brothers, First Republic Bank, Columbia Gas, Bank of New England, etc.). He is a recognized expert in the field of bankruptcy law and litigation and has been certified as a Business Bankruptcy Specialist by the Texas Board of Legal Specialization.

ACKNOWLEDGMENTS

We wish to thank numerous people for their help in producing this book. Glenn Atkins of Garner Asset Management read and made helpful comments on every part of the book. Moreover, parts of chapters five and six were adapted with permission from "High-Yield Bonds," by Glenn E. Atkins and Ben Branch, *AAII Journal* (October 1991), © American Association of Individual Investors, 625 N. Michigan Ave., Suite 1900, Chicago, IL 60611. Kathy Welton has served effectively as editor. The Word Processing Center at the University of Massachusetts (Rebecca Jerome, Supervisor) has done its usual excellent word-processing job. In addition, we would like to thank Jeff Spiers, Jim Donnell and Crawford Moorefield for their assistance in chapters one and three.

While the authors have sought to verify the accuracy of the information contained herein, no warranties expressed or implied are given. Investing is an inherently risky endeavor. Investing in the securities of bankrupt companies is particularly risky. The book should help one reduce the risks, but nothing is guaranteed. Nothing in this book should be construed to constitute specific legal advice.

CHAPTER 1

Inside the Bankruptcy Process

Often, you will hear references to Chapter 10s, Chapter 7s, Chapter 11s and the like. You also will hear references to the Bankruptcy Code or the Bankruptcy Act. Actually, all of this technical jargon can be simply explained so that an investor with absolutely no legal training can understand the bankruptcy process sufficiently well to make intelligent decisions.

The Bankruptcy Act of 1898 (commonly referred to as the Bankruptcy Act) no longer exists. It was replaced by the Bankruptcy Reform Act of 1978, which applies to all bankruptcies filed since October 1, 1979. This current law is called the Bankruptcy Code. Whenever we refer to a section number, the reference is to the Bankruptcy Code. Coincidentally, and confusingly, the Bankruptcy Code is codified at 11 United States Code, beginning at §101. Your primary interest as an investor will be in Chapter 11 bankruptcy proceedings. The 11 United States Code (11 U.S.C.) includes a number of bankruptcy chapters only one of which is called Chapter 11. In other words, 11 U.S.C. divides up the substantive law of bankruptcy into several different chapters. Chapters 1, 3 and 5 generally are applicable to all bankruptcy cases (e.g., 7s and 11s), unless specific reference is made to a particular problem. The specific chapters are: Chapter 7 (liquidation), Chapter 9 (municipalities), Chapter 11 (reorganization), Chapter 12 (family farmers) and Chapter 13 (wage earners). Each of these chapters specifies particular treatments for specific types of cases. You can line up the chapters that make up part of 11 U.S.C. as shown in Figure 1.1.

In addition, Chapter 15 provides for a United States Trustee (U.S. trustee). Most districts have a U.S. trustee; he or she is one of the three

FIGURE 1.1   Chapters of 11 United States Code (11 U.S.C.)

Generally applicable	Chapter 1 —	Generally provisions and definitions
	Chapter 3 —	Case administration
	Chapter 5 —	The relationship between creditors, the debtor and the estate in certain situations
Specific treatments	Chapter 7 —	Liquidations
	Chapter 9 —	Municipalities
	Chapter 11 —	Reorganizations
	Chapter 12 —	Family farmers with regular annual income

different types of trustees that may be encountered in a typical bankruptcy proceeding. The U.S. trustee is an employee of the Department of Justice charged with attending to some of the administrative matters as will be explained in more detail later in this chapter. The other two types of trustees, the bankruptcy trustee and the indenture trustee, will be discussed shortly.

The United States Supreme Court has promulgated specific procedural bankruptcy rules. Most of these rules are well beyond the scope of your interest. Certain local rules differ from district to district. Thus, each judge is able to govern that particular district's practice and procedure so long as such rules are consistent with the bankruptcy rules.

State laws also are incorporated into the bankruptcy laws. While the states are unable to supersede federal bankruptcy laws in most instances, the Bankruptcy Code often expressly recognizes the state laws where they can be incorporated in a nonconflicting fashion.

State laws approach bankruptcies differently from federal bankruptcy laws in several respects. Most state laws are designed to reward fast action by creditors. In other words, the first creditor to attach the debtor's property is the one most likely to be paid. Federal bankruptcy laws, on the other hand, are social legislation that tries to emphasize equality of treatment and promote the opportunities for debtors to obtain fresh starts. The overall federal theme seeks to prevent an individual creditor from improving its position (relative to other creditors) by acting with alacrity, once the debtor files for bankruptcy. In addition, federal bankruptcy laws place severe limitations on a creditor's ability to collect or secure repayment of its debts in the time periods just before the bankruptcy.

Probably the unique and most valuable feature of U.S. bankruptcy laws is the ability the laws afford a debtor to receive a "discharge," or the equivalent of a discharge from its debts, thus giving the debtor the chance to get a fresh start.

Theoretical Approaches

The Two Types of Bankruptcies:
Liquidations and Reorganizations

Chapter 7 provides for liquidations. In most other countries when a person seeks protection under the insolvency laws, a receiver simply collects and liquidates all the debtor's assets and then distributes the proceeds to the ever-hungry creditors. The debtor often gets a discharge and walks away without being legally responsible for most of the debts that were incurred prior to bankruptcy. Rehabilitation of the debtor is not especially important in most other countries. A U.S. Chapter 7 bankruptcy is conceptually similar to the bankruptcy procedures followed in most other countries. The Chapter 7 debtor's assets are placed in the hands of the appointed bankruptcy trustee (different from the U.S. trustee described previously) who liquidates them for the best price available and distributes the assets. This bankruptcy trustee is charged with administering the estate as the liquidation process proceeds. He or she performs the duties that the debtor would have performed had the estate remained outside of bankruptcy. The trustee may be elected by the creditors and must be a qualified disinterested person. This individual is customarily awarded a fee of 1 to 3% of the estate for his or her services. More will be said on this subject later.

By contrast, rehabilitation is usually the theme of Chapter 11 reorganization. Chapter 11 provides an opportunity for the reorganization of a debtor, rather than a liquidation of its assets. The social policy of fresh start is incorporated in this chapter. U.S. Chapter 11 reorganization cases are distinguished from the way insolvencies are handled in Chapter 7 and in most of the rest of the world in one primary way: In Chapter 11 reorganization, the debtor retains control of its assets and continues its operations. While under this protection, the debtor seeks to pay off creditors (often at a discount) over a period of time pursuant to a plan approved by a bankruptcy court. In other words, the creditors by law can be forced to look solely to the endeavors of the debtor for repayment. A cynic would criticize the social policy implications of this approach: It appears to allow the person who led the company into its present difficulties to continue doing whatever he or she was doing to run the company into the ground. On the other hand, many bankruptcies, particularly after the heady leveraged buyout (LBO) days of the 1980s, resulted from piling too much debt onto too few assets. The core business and its management may be potentially quite viable. Because Chapter 11 allows this fresh start, jobs may be saved and productive resources kept operating efficiently rather than being scrapped or put to a less productive use. The credit system in the United States appears to be wealthy enough to afford this fresh-start concept. Nonetheless, statistically only one out of every eight cases that file for Chapter 11 reorganization has been able to reorganize successfully according to the Administrative Office of the U.S. courts. A debtor's estate also may be liquidated under Chapter 11 of the Bankruptcy Code, for it frequently is less expensive and more efficient than liquidating through the use of Chapter 7 and a trustee.

The Bankruptcy Arena's Seven Key Players

1. *The judge of the bankruptcy court.* This is the judge who presides over the case. He or she is referred the case by the relevant U.S. District Court and is a judicial officer operating under that referred authority.
2. *The debtor.* This is the entity seeking relief in the bankruptcy court. This unlucky entity used to be referred to as "the Bankrupt." As a part of the Bankruptcy Reform Act that became effective in 1979, the phrase "the Bankrupt" was expunged from the statute because of negative connotations. The cognomen lives on, however.
3. *Secured/unsecured claimant.* A creditor that holds a lien on property that belongs to the debtor or has the right of setoff against property of the debtor holds what is called a secured claim. The party that has no lien on any of the debtor's property holds an unsecured claim. If property owned by the debtor on which the secured creditor holds the lien is not at least equal in value to the amount of the claim, then the claim can be partially secured (the value of the collateral) and unsecured (the difference between the value of the collateral and the amount of the claim). A creditor may be either senior or subordinated to other creditors. Indeed, several layers of subordination may exist.

4. *The bankruptcy trustee or trustee of the estate.* Unlike the U.S. trustee, a bankruptcy trustee is not an employee of the federal government. Rather, he or she is a private citizen who often is also a lawyer. Every Chapter 7 has a trustee, and sometimes a trustee is appointed in Chapter 11 cases, although not often. The trustee is appointed by the U.S. trustee, and at the initial meeting (the 341 meeting, so named because §341 of the Bankruptcy Code requires the U.S. trustee to convene a meeting of creditors at which time the debtor is required to appear and submit to an examination under oath), creditors can elect a trustee to replace the appointed trustee. The trustee is charged with liquidating the assets of the debtor and overseeing their equitable distribution.

5. *The U.S. trustee.* This is the aforementioned government employee who, as an employee of the Department of Justice, appoints bankruptcy trustees and creditors' committees and performs other administrative tasks that contribute to the smooth operation of the bankruptcy case.

6. *Debtor in possession.* The debtor in a Chapter 11 case, and still in possession of the company's property (no trustee has been appointed), is called a debtor in possession. This debtor in possession has certain fiduciary duties akin to those of a trustee that require it to operate its business in a manner that is fair, equitable and in the best interest of the creditors.

7. *The creditors' committee.* These are the representatives of the creditors in Chapter 11 cases that are appointed by the U.S. trustee or the bankruptcy judge to oversee the debtor in possession and assist in the formulation and confirmation of a plan.

In addition to the previously mentioned individuals, a number of legal representations generally play an important part in the case. Specifically, the debtor in possession or bankruptcy trustee usually will retain counsel to represent it in the proceedings before the court. Similarly, the creditors' committees almost certainly will, and individual creditors also may engage their own separate counsel. Each creditors' committee usually will retain separate legal counsel. Other professionals such as accountants and investment bankers also may be retained by the various parties at interest. The fees of these professionals are one of the costs that make bankruptcies so expensive. A bankruptcy lawyer, for example, can easily cost $200 to $400 per hour plus expenses. One interested party (e.g., the senior creditors) may retain one law firm to achieve one objective (maximum recovery for the seniors), while a second group (e.g., the junior creditors) may have its lawyer pursue a conflicting objective (maximum recovery for the juniors). For a Chapter 11 case, the estate pays both lawyers' fees. Moreover, the claims for fees are administrative claims and as such have the highest priority in settling the affairs of the estate. The professionals do not want to take on bankruptcy work unless they are relatively sure that they will get paid. Generally, they are not only paid but paid quite well.

Chapter 7.   As previously mentioned, in Chapter 7, the debtor's property is collected and sold, and the proceeds are distributed to creditors by a trustee. Additionally, the debtor is normally discharged from its liabilities.

The independent bankruptcy trustee collects and liquidates the property of the estate in Chapter 7. This trustee is charged with selling the assets of the debtor. He or she is the source of information concerning what property the debtor has for sale and how it is to be sold. The bankruptcy clerk's office can furnish the name of a trustee for an individual debtor. You need only call the bankruptcy clerk's office for the district in which the bankruptcy case is pending to learn the name of the trustee. While this trustee can operate the business of the debtor for a limited period, his or her primary responsibility is to see that the assets are sold. Frequently, no equity remains for property of the debtor on which a lien has been placed. Accordingly, the secured creditor may be permitted simply to take the property back. When this type of settlement occurs, you should contact the secured creditor if you wish to purchase what had been the debtor's property.

Chapter 11.   A Chapter 11 typically involves a business that the debtor hopes can be rehabilitated via a plan of reorganization. This process requires persuading the creditors to accept, and the court to approve, the proposed plan. A Chapter 11 case can begin either voluntarily by a debtor or involuntarily by certain of the debtor's creditors or their indenture trustee taking action. This indenture trustee is the third of the three types of trustees that may be involved in a bankruptcy case. The indenture trustee (usually a bank, trust company or other secure, highly respected institution) is named in the indenture agreement (the contract between the bondholders and the bond issuer) as the bondholder's agent that is charged with enforcing the terms of the indenture.

With an eye toward rehabilitation, generally under Chapter 11 reorganization, the business will be allowed to continue to operate with the debtor operating the business. Court supervision usually is restricted to transactions out of the ordinary course of business. Although optional provisions for bankruptcy trustees are provided in Chapter 11 reorganization, they seldom are utilized. The debtor itself, as debtor in possession, has all the rights and responsibilities of a trustee. Usually, an unambiguous abuse of those duties is required before a trustee is appointed.

In most Chapter 11s, the debtor will work with its creditors to formulate a plan of reorganization. This plan sets out for the creditors who will be paid how much and over what period of time. An exclusivity period occurs at the beginning of each case during which time only the debtor can file a plan of reorganization. This period often is extended by the judge on a request of the debtor. After that exclusivity period finally expires, any party in interest can file a plan proposing how the debtor's creditors are to be repaid.

Typically, any plan will divide the various creditors into several classes of claims, including the classes of unsecured claimants and secured claimants. As a general requirement, any claim in a particular class must be treated the same as other claims in that class.

After a Chapter 11 plan is filed, the creditors and stockholders of the debtor frequently will be solicited to obtain their approval of the plan. As part of obtaining this approval, a full disclosure of pertinent facts must be made by filing a formal disclosure statement in the court. The statement must be approved by the court as containing adequate and accurate information prior to being sent out to the creditors for their vote to approve or disapprove the proposed plan. The disclosure statement is your best source of information outside of, or possibly including, an original prospectus, with respect to any particular company in which you may choose to invest.

The final stage of a Chapter 11 reorganization is the confirmation of a plan. Even if the creditors approve the plan (by their vote), the bankruptcy judge still can refuse to confirm a plan because of a failure to meet certain other conditions: The plan must be proposed in good faith, and each creditor must receive no less than he or she would receive in a Chapter 7 liquidation. Moreover, the plan can be confirmed by the bankruptcy judge even though every class does not accept the plan. This judicial overruling of a dissenting class is called a "cramdown." If one class of noninsider creditors does accept a plan, the court still can confirm the plan if it is "fair and equitable" and accordingly provides that no class of claims that is junior to a nonassenting impaired class receives anything until the nonassenting impaired class has been fully compensated. Noninsider creditors are those not classified as insiders by the Bankruptcy Code. "Insiders" are defined to include a corporate debtor's officers and directors; a debtor partnership's partners; and an individual debtor's relatives.

Why would a debtor that has a choice in the matter agree to go through this process? The answer is that the debtor gets a fresh start. Corporations do not technically receive a discharge in the traditional sense. Nonetheless, the confirmation of the plan effectively discharges the successful Chapter 11 debtor from its prepetition debts except for those set out in the plan or in the order of confirmation. Chapter 11 is a unique creation often taken for granted in the United States. Do not assume that it necessarily makes economic sense. The statistical data would indicate that its sole justification is as social legislation. The United States is hardly the only country in the civilized world that has a credit system healthy enough to afford placing its legal system behind a statute that allows the people who ran a company into the ground to continue to control the company. Recall, however, that creditors in the aggregate must consent legally or actually to any successful plan of reorganization. True, the debtor in possession manages the estate in Chapter 11 reorganization (at least at the outset). However, the creditors, particularly if they are assertive, eventually tend to gain the upper hand. Only a reorganization plan that is acceptable to the creditor groups (especially the senior creditors) is likely to be confirmed. Still, a confirmed plan may or may not provide a favorable outcome for the creditors. Do not try to superimpose your investment decision with any assumptions that the legal system will either guarantee the success or failure of your investment judgment. The social motivation of the debtor and its lawyer has little to do with your decision. Their ability to "pull off" a successful reorganization does.

How Cases Begin

A bankruptcy case may commence in either of two general ways: voluntarily and involuntarily. Voluntary cases start when a debtor files a petition requesting relief in the appropriate district: the one in which for the 180 days or the majority thereof immediately preceding the commencement of the case, the domicile, residence, principal place of business or principal assets of the debtor were located.

Involuntary cases are commenced under either Chapter 7 or Chapter 11 of the Bankruptcy Code by creditors having claims that are not contingent. Generally, three unsecured creditors with claims totaling at least $5,000 must join in the filing of the involuntary petition. In the rare case of a debtor having fewer than 12 creditors, a single creditor with an unsecured claim of $5,000 or more is adequate to file.

A great deal of confusion exists over what happens when creditors file an involuntary bankruptcy petition against an obligor. In very simple terms, all that really has happened is that a lawsuit has been filed. The debtor is not automatically put straight into bankruptcy. The debtor has the right to file an answer and litigate the issue of whether or not the debtor should be in bankruptcy. While this litigation proceeds, the debtor receives the benefits of the automatic stay, yet gets to operate the business without having to file bankruptcy schedules or come to court for permission to conduct the business's usual affairs. The issue that generally is litigated is whether the debtor is paying its debts as they mature. The petition is likely to succeed if a creditor can establish that the debtor generally has failed to pay its valid debts when due (allowing for the passage of the grace period). An involuntary petition also will succeed if a receiver or custodian has taken possession of substantially all of the debtor's assets. While this litigation wears on, the debtor continues to operate its business without a trustee unless a court finds that one is necessary to prevent the loss of the estate's property. Despite the legal freedom of operation that exists after a filing of an involuntary petition, the filing spells disaster for many businesses. Their reputations are severely impaired by the stigma of being forced into bankruptcy. For this reason, creditors who file unwarranted petitions may be held liable for serious consequential damages and attorneys' fees.

A debtor against whom an involuntary Chapter 7 is filed has a right to convert the case to a Chapter 11 proceeding. A Chapter 7 debtor that filed a voluntary petition also can convert the case to a Chapter 11 proceeding. In addition, the bankruptcy court can convert a Chapter 11 case to a Chapter 7 case or dismiss the case for cause. One such cause would be the inability of the debtor to effectuate a plan.

The bankruptcy court also may, at its discretion, abstain from hearing a bankruptcy case even though all the technical requirements for a bankruptcy case have been met. The bankruptcy judge's decision to abstain cannot be appealed. Courts have been known to dismiss bankruptcy petitions when debtors have shown substantial progress in reaching out-of-court workouts of their problems.

A bankruptcy court also may dismiss a Chapter 11 case for cause, generally considering the action to be in the best interest of the creditors and the estate. Such a dismissal can occur at any point in the case.

How Cases Operate:
Administering the Assets of a Chapter 11 Debtor

Understanding the boundaries of how a debtor operates its business and disposes of its assets is critical to understanding the other chapters of this book that deal with the timing of investments. The prime immediate benefit that a debtor receives by filing Chapter 11 is an automatic stay of the acts of creditors to collect from the debtor. At the time that this stay becomes effective, an "estate" of sorts is created. This bankruptcy estate is conceptually much like a probate estate. All the debtor's property passes into this estate upon the filing. Not surprisingly, the use and sale of the property of this estate is subject to court supervision.

The stay is designed to give a Chapter 11 debtor time to prepare and confirm a plan. The stay ensures the orderly administration of the estate while that plan process proceeds. This very broad stay cannot be taken lightly. For example, creditors cannot proceed to enforce their liens and cannot take steps to seize assets. Moreover, the stay has the practical effect of stopping the accrual of interest on most unsecured debts. Technically, claims for postpetition (postbankruptcy filing) interest are arguably allowable. As a practical matter, however, such claims rarely are collectible. Unsecured postpetition interest claims are subordinated to even the juniormost creditor claims for principal and prepetition interest. Very few actions are excepted from the scope of the stay. Creditors may request relief from the stay for specified reasons, including situations where the debtor has no equity in the property and the property is not necessary for an effective reorganization.

What does the secured creditor receive in exchange for giving up the ability to look to its collateral for immediate repayment? In recognition of the secured creditor's due-process rights, the creditor must be furnished what is called only adequate protection. This adequate protection is undefined but can take many forms. Additional liens may be given as well as numerous control protections relating to the use of the secured creditor's collateral. The relief may be broad enough to satisfy a secured creditor to the extent that the creditor may not care if the bankruptcy case ever ends.

Indeed, secured creditors are the one category that may be able to continue to receive current interest payments during a bankruptcy proceeding. If their collateral is central to a business's operation (e.g., rolling stock for a railroad), the debtor may have little choice but to pay interest on the collateralized obligations (e.g., equipment trust certificates). The collateral trust bonds of Penn Central railroad, for example, continued to pay their interest as due throughout the bankruptcy/reorganization process.

The restrictions on operation do not prevent the Chapter 11 debtor from using or selling the property of the estate that has been created. However, notice and an opportunity for a hearing are required before the property of the estate can be used or sold outside of the ordinary course of business. The court must evaluate a request to use or sell the property of the estate outside of the ordinary course of business. When performing this evaluation, the court considers the concept of adequate protection, as well as whether the proposal constitutes a scheme to bypass the safeguards afforded to creditors under the provisions of the process for obtaining approval of plans of reorganization. In addition, the proposal by the debtor must prove to be within the sound exercise of good business judgment. After considering these factors, the court may even order the sale of a secured creditor's collateral free and clear of the creditor's lien, with the lien then attaching to the proceeds of the sale. A debtor is not obligated to administer all the assets in the estate. It may simply turn the ownership of the pledged assets over to the secured creditor.

A Chapter 11 debtor may be in the midst of unperformed obligations (requirements contracts, employment contracts, etc.) with other parties. At some point, the debtor must decide whether to accept (assume) or reject these legal obligations. These incomplete transactions are called executory contracts. Leases make up a separate and special category of executory transactions. Usually, those executory contracts that are beneficial to the estate are assumed by the debtor and those that are not beneficial (e.g., burdensome union contracts, requirements contracts) are rejected. A Chapter 11 debtor has no definite time deadline to make its decision to assume or reject many of its executory contracts. The other party to the obligation may seek a court order giving the debtor a definite time period to make a decision, however. The rejection of the executory contract constitutes a breach. Generally, the party whose contract was rejected will have a claim against the debtor for the party's damages.

If a debtor wishes to assume a contract in default, it must cure the default, pay the damages and give adequate assurance for future performance of the debtor's ongoing obligation under that contract. Clauses in contracts saying that they cannot be assumed in bankruptcy are unenforceable. Court approval is necessary for acceptance or rejection; however, the standard is the debtor's business judgment. This rather subjective standard is quite an easy one to meet. Most of the controversy in this area deals with whether a contract is executory or performed to the extent that it cannot be assumed or rejected.

When a trustee is appointed in a Chapter 11 case, the trustee takes over possession of the estate. In a Chapter 7 case, a trustee always takes possession of the estate.

The Avoiding Powers

The Bankruptcy Code seeks to ensure equality in the distribution of the debtor's estate. One of the ways that it accomplishes this objective is by discouraging prebankruptcy attacks from creditors seeking an advantage vis-à-vis the debtor's other creditors. Congress also sought to discourage debtors from favoring selected creditors over others through the prebankruptcy transfer of assets and other prepetition actions. These discouragements are codified in prohibitions of preferential transfers, invalid liens and fraudulent transfers.

Preferential transfers are transfers that enable a creditor to receive payment of a greater percentage of its claim against the debtor than the creditor would have received if the transfer had not been made and instead the creditor had participated ratably in the bankruptcy estate distribution. The key time period for this "look back" generally is the 90 days prior to filing while the debtor was insolvent. The look-back period is one year for creditors who are insiders. One may be classified as an insider by being either a high-level executive of the company or a major investor with substantial influence over the direction of the company. Usually, a 10% or greater ownership of the common stock will classify one as an insider. This very general precept relating to preferences and the look-back period has many exceptions and is subject to a number of complex rules of interpretation.

The Bankruptcy Code also invalidates liens that are not properly recorded under federal or state laws as applicable. In addition, tardily perfected liens are disallowed. In general, the concept of the bankruptcy estate places the debtor in the position of a hypothetical bona fide purchaser without notice of the actual facts. Accordingly, technical imperfections in the creditor's liens may be avoided without regard to the actual state of the relationship under the understandings between the debtor and the creditor.

Prepetition transfers made by an insolvent debtor or for the benefit of the debtor with the actual intent to hinder, delay or defraud creditors are subject to avoidance as fraudulent conveyances. More controversial is the ability to avoid transfers in which the debtor received less than a reasonably equivalent value and was or became insolvent as a result of the transfer, or believed this to be the case. This theory is the cornerstone of the attacks on LBOs in which bankruptcy creditors contend that highly leveraged transactions (with the debtor's assets) defraud the existing creditors who are thereby left unpaid.

How Cases Finally Settle Up:
Paying Claims and Distributing Assets

Claims must be allowed prior to receiving any payment. A claim, however, is deemed allowed once filed unless a party with standing in the instant case objects. In general, postfiling interest on unsecured claims is effectively disallowed. Technically, these claims are subordinated to all other creditor claims. Claims for future rent are severely limited as are claims arising from terminated employment contracts.

The Bankruptcy Code sets out several very exact priorities of distribution. In general, the expenses of administering the estate are paid first (the lawyers receive payment first). Certain employee claims and taxes are paid prior to the general unsecured creditors who are paid in turn prior to holders who filed late claims and claims for fines and penalties. These priorities reflect deliberate decisions by Congress to favor certain groups who might withhold their goods and services if their claims were not given special treatment.

The concept of subordination is expressly recognized in bankruptcy. The Bankruptcy Code states that contractual subordination arrangements (consideration otherwise payable to one class [subordinated] is thereby required to be paid over to its senior class until that class's full claim is satisfied) are to be honored in bankruptcy cases. In light of the numerous other contractual rights that are subject to avoidance in the bankruptcy court, this recognition is notable. This type of treatment also is essential for subordination to be meaningful. If subordination provisions were avoidable in bankruptcies, they would not accomplish the task for which they were devised: Allow a debtor to access additional capital while affording superior protection to those existing creditors who demand it. The treatment of those arrangements also is quite important for the potential bankruptcy investor. Most of the publicly traded investment opportunities in debtors with high-yield obligations have outstanding multiple "layers" of publicly held indebtedness. These obligations frequently contain provisions subordinating certain of those obligations to certain others under a variety of circumstances. Thus, one is likely to encounter terms such as senior-subordinated and junior-subordinated debentures.

The Bankruptcy Code also recognizes, but does not spell out, the ability of the bankruptcy judge to subordinate claims based on equitable considerations. Equitable subordination generally is applied to a creditor who has committed fraud or other inequitable conduct that has given that creditor an unfair advantage over other creditors.

How Cases Are Restructured:
The Chapter 11 Plan and the Disclosure Statement

In the early stages of a Chapter 11 case, the preparation and approval of the reorganization plan is under the absolute control of the debtor. The Bankruptcy Code gives the debtor an initial period of 120 days during which it and it alone can propose a plan of reorganization. Usually, courts will extend this period in major cases. At the end of the exclusivity period, or the period as it is extended, any party in interest can file and seek to obtain approval of its plan.

The plan as proposed will classify claims that are substantially similar in the same class. Usually, a plan proponent will try to create classes in such a way as to ensure a favorable vote on the plan. Secured and unsecured creditors generally will be classified separately, for example.

Parties whose legal, equitable and contractual rights are unaltered will not be required to vote in favor of a plan for it to be approved. Each class of impaired parties, i.e., those whose legal rights are altered, must vote two-thirds in an amount of their claims and more than one-half in the number of claims voting in favor of the plan.

The court requires the preparation of a document called a disclosure statement to provide creditors with adequate information to enable them to cast their votes. Its contents must be approved by the court prior to its being sent to the creditors voting on the plan. Adequate information means information both accurate and sufficient in detail to enable a reasonably able hypothetical investor to make an informed judgment about the plan's acceptability.

After the creditors consider the disclosure statement, their votes are solicited, and after the votes are finally in, the court holds what is called a confirmation hearing. At this hearing, the court considers the tally of votes and hears evidence on a variety of issues:

1. That the plan has been proposed in good faith;
2. That the claims have been classified properly;
3. That the plan is feasible;
4. That the acceptance of the plan has not been procured by any means prohibited by law; and
5. That certain other technical requirements have been met as specified in the Bankruptcy Code.

The prime area of concern frequently is whether or not the plan is in the best interests of creditors. This best-interest test requires that each impaired creditor receive more under the plan than the creditor would receive in a Chapter 7 liquidation.

Even if a class of claims does not accept the plan, the law permits the plan to be approved over the vote of the dissenting class through what is commonly referred to as the "cramdown." To accomplish this overruling of the dissenting class, the plan must not discriminate unfairly and must be fair and equitable with respect to impaired nonaccepting classes. By not discriminating, the law generally means only that the holders of claims or interests with similar legal rights cannot be treated differently. To be fair and equitable to a class of dissenting secured creditors, the secured creditors must receive the indubitable value equivalent of their claims or retain their liens and receive deferred cash payments of a value equal to their interest in the estate's interest in the property.

For a plan to be fair and equitable to a class of dissenting unsecured creditors, the plan must provide either that the unsecured creditors receive property of a value equal to the allowed amount of the claim, or that the holder of any claim or interest junior to the dissenting class will not receive or retain any property on account of the junior claim. In other words, the classes below the dissenting unsecured class generally must receive nothing if the dissenting class is to be crammed down. This requirement is referred to as the absolute priority rule.

An exception to the absolute priority rule has been created under some precedents. This exception often is referred to as the new value exception. This theory has been used by equity holders seeking to retain all or a portion of their equity interest by contributing what amounts to a capital contribution. In exchange for this contribution, in courts recognizing the exception, they retain their interest even in the face of a dissenting vote by a senior class of creditors.

After approval of a plan in a confirmation hearing, the plan is consummated by the parties who exchange the documents and cash required to effectuate the reorganization described in the plan. After a report is given to the judge that the plan is consummated and the pending legal issues are wrapped up, the case is closed.

How Bankruptcies Are Expedited: Prepackaged Chapter 11s

The Bankruptcy Code permits distressed potential candidates for Chapter 11 reorganization to solicit creditor approval of a reorganization plan prior to filing Chapter 11. These prepackaged bankruptcies have gained some current measure of popularity. Their use facilitates obtaining advance approval of what would amount to an exchange offer of public debt with only the two-thirds in amount and one-half in number requirement of creditor approval. Much more stringent requirements usually are found in the public indenture, which outside of bankruptcy must be followed by the indenture trustee. Indeed, customary forms under the Trust Indenture Act prohibit changes in coupon rates, principal or maturity outside of bankruptcy without the unanimous consent of the creditors.

The first advantage in the prebankruptcy solicitation vehicle is that a court-approved disclosure statement is not required at that stage. However, the solicitation must comply with applicable nonbankruptcy laws. In particular, the securities laws must be complied with, or, if none are applicable, then the disclosure statement will be reviewed when the plan is submitted for approval.

The second and primary advantage of a prepackaged plan is the ability to squeeze the holdout bondholder or minority creditor who demands to be paid off at a higher rate than those who are attempting to cooperate with the debtor. Individual bondholders do not have to accept an out-of-court exchange offer, but the results of a court-approved reorganization plan do apply to dissenting bondholders as well as those who voted in favor of the offer.

The third advantage to this approach is the speed with which a debtor can go in and out of Chapter 11 reorganization. The fast action tends to save substantial sums of money in administrative costs and lessen the adverse impact on the debtor's business. While the debtor still must comply with the remaining technical requirements of Chapter 11 reorganization, the advance approval process shortcuts much debate and acrimony because of the realistic advance communication that tends to take place prior to the filing.

Buying and Selling Claims and Investing in Newly Reorganized Debtors

Several specialist investment firms have sprung up that deal specifically with the claims of bankrupt companies. More than $5 billion in bankruptcy claims have been traded according to Fanning, "A Stacked Deck?," *Forbes* 146, no. 6 (June 12, 1989), 126. Additionally, Crain's *Pension and Investment Age* (March 6, 1989) forecast that an additional $1.5 billion in claims will likely be traded during the next two years. One caution should be noted when purchasing a claim, however. When the purchaser buys a claim, the claim still has the same legal rights and disabilities that it had in the hands of the original seller. In other words, if the claim is based on fraud, or on an invalid document, the purchasing of the claim will not change the defense that the debtor would have to the claim.

More often than you might believe, creditors would rather sell claims for immediate cash at a discount as opposed to waiting for the recovery in bankruptcy. Many creditors experience the "domino effect," which occurs when a debt owed to them by a customer filing bankruptcy extends to imperil their own companies as well. Additionally, accountants often will, for tax reasons, advise the creditor to sell a claim rather than keep it on the books. Various tax-planning strategies also lead to the sale of claims.

Also, certain financial institutions place restrictions on the ownership of distressed securities. These institutions would prefer to sell their claims to avoid the regulatory hassles that might result in their owning stock in a particular debtor company, in the event of a plan that proposes a stock-for-debt swap.

Purchasing claims also has been accelerated by using purchased claims to obtain control of the debtor company. For example, gaining control was the motivation for purchasing a number of claims in the case of Apex Oil Company. Once Apex emerged from bankruptcy, the investors who purchased the claims were able to exercise control. Several problems exist with the purchase of unsecured claims for takeovers because purchases may need to comply with tender-offer requirements or comply with securities laws despite being a general "safe harbor" from the securities laws.

An additional area for caution in connection with purchasing claims is to make sure that the purchased claim is not subject to attack on the basis that the seller received a preferential transfer or a fraudulent conveyance. Either of these objections can be used to disallow a claim. However, the transferee of the claim would not be liable for the preferential payment, but rather the preferential payment or fraudulent conveyance would be used only to disallow the claim until the preference was returned.

The role of the bankruptcy court in connection with the purchase and sale of claims in bankruptcy is extremely limited. The rules are not intended in any way to encourage or discourage the transfer of claims. If an objection is filed, the court's role is to determine whether the transfer is effective under nonbankruptcy laws.

The laws recognize the recent emergence of what amounts to an auction market for claims after a bankruptcy case has been filed. The intention of the laws is to restrict any inclination by particular judges to discourage such transfers.

The primary area of concern is the problem created by insiders and members of creditors' committees trading in the securities when they possess confidential information. Customarily, members of creditors' committees are required to sign confidentiality agreements before a debtor reveals sensitive information that would bear on the value and recoverability of claims in the particular case. Trading of the company's securities by those in possession of material nonpublic information is severely restricted. In general, one possessing such information is restricted to trades with other restricted investors and possibly with nonrestricted investors who are properly informed of the restricted person's possession of nonpublic information. This informing process usually is accomplished through documentation suitable to both parties prior to trade execution. Many securities firms will inform parties that they are executing transactions on an agency basis only, not as a principal, when they are in possession of material nonpublic information.

The Bankruptcy Code requires that all votes on a plan must be made in good faith. Accordingly, claims acquired for the purpose of voting against a plan for reasons that amount to pure malice, strikes or blackmail or for the purpose of destroying an enterprise to advance a competitor will be disallowed. However, the mere purchase of claims for the purpose of gaining negative votes against a plan is not per se disallowable. On the other hand, purchasing claims to acquire control without filing a disclosure statement that reveals that interest may be restricted by some courts.

In a recent decision issued in connection with the LTV Energy Products bankruptcy proceeding, a corporation was formed offering to purchase unsecured claims for 33 cents on the dollar. More than 400 creditors accepted the offer. The corporation filed notices of transfer with the bankruptcy court. The debtor challenged the transfer as, in essence, a hostile takeover of LTV Energy. The bankruptcy judge refused to approve the transfer, finding that the corporation had not disclosed that it was a front for another entity (Regal, Inc.) that was attempting to obtain control of LTV through the unsecured-claim purchase mechanism. The judge contended that Regal intended to propose a full 100-cents-on-the-dollar recovery plan after acquiring all the claims. He held that the selling creditors had a right to an "informed judgment" before such a purchase could take place. He further required the claims purchaser to supply the selling creditor with a disclosure document. (See Beard, ed., "Trade Debt Buyers: Players Still Active Despite Variable Market and Judicial Objections," *Turnarounds and Workouts* 4, no. 5 [May 1, 1990]: 2.) A similar order had been made, and rescinded, in the Allegheny International case, as well as in the Revere Copper and Brass case. These situations are the exceptions rather than the rule in claims-purchasing cases and are obviously attempts to impose a judge-made rule of law in an area where no statutory authority is readily apparent for holdings of this nature.

Purchasers of claims and interests after a bankruptcy has been filed may find their activity viewed with favor by the relevant governmental agencies (bankruptcy court, Securities and Exchange Commission [SEC], other regulators, etc.) because by so doing they broaden the debtor's source of future capital through an enhancement of the public market for Chapter 11 debt. In addition, the purchasing creditor is much more likely to be an active participant in the Chapter 11 reorganization case and to provide creditors (who are willing to take a steep discount) a cash market for their claims.

Experience has shown that selective purchases of nonequity securities of companies as the reorganized debtor emerges from Chapter 11 can be profitable. Nonetheless, an aversion to a company emerging from Chapter 11 still exists in the securities market. This aversion frequently causes the securities market to underestimate the potential of the reorganized company.

For example, Itel Corporation confirmed its plan of reorganization in 1983, and its stock started trading late that year at ⅛ bid—1⅜ asked. Six months later, the stock was trading at 3. In late 1991, the stock traded at 13 after adjustments. Itel's preferred stock traded at 22 after emerging from bankruptcy and six months later traded at 26. In late 1991, it traded close to 34, having traded in the 64 range several years earlier.

These are not, however, buy-and-hold securities in many cases. For example, when Braniff Airways emerged from its first bankruptcy in September of 1983, its new common stock traded at 2. A year later, it traded at 4. By early 1991, it was totally worthless. By late 1991, Braniff began operations a third time, but prior equity was extinguished in its second bankruptcy.

Other favorable examples of this postemergence upward swing include Allied Supermarkets Corporation. When Allied emerged from bankruptcy in October of 1981, its common stock traded at ⁷⁄₁₆ bid. Three years later, the stock sold for 2¾. Food Fair emerged in July of 1981 and changed its name to Pantry Pride, Inc. Its Class B preferred stock traded at 2 bid and 2⅝ asked at that time. Three years later, it sold for 4. The common stock that was 2¾ bid at confirmation sold for 3¾ three years later. Mego International confirmed its plan in late 1983 with its common stock at 20 cents. Six months later, the same shares traded at 2⅛. HRT Industries confirmed its plan in February of 1984. The new common stock traded at 1¾. Six months later, the stock was selling at 5⅛.

Some postbankruptcy shares have been losers, however. For example, while Wilson Foods Corporation has been up and down since it confirmed its plan on February 28, 1984, its stock has had more negative trends than other emerging companies, probably because of the relatively high per-share price of its reorganized common stock at 9⅞ at confirmation. The company was acquired by Doskocil, Inc., which filed its own Chapter 11 in 1990. By late 1991, Doskocil common shares were traded at close to $1 per share of stock. When Doskocil came out of Chapter 11 on October 31, 1991, its new common shares traded at $10 a share. By February 1992, the same new postbankruptcy shares of Doskocil were up 40% to $14 a share! Unfortunately, the holders of the prebankruptcy common stock were virtually wiped out.

This scorekeeping was inspired by a statement made in a law review article in 1983:

At present, a substantial evidence as to the nature of the bankruptcy bargain does not exist. The lack of good empirical work is notable and lamentable. Even for reorganization of public companies, plans are often unreported.[1]

Usually, the official disclosure statement does not contain an estimate of the per-share valuation that is easily understood. Of the previously mentioned examples, only one disclosure statement gave an estimate of a per-share valuation. The Itel disclosure statement estimated a preferred share value of 22½ to 26½ and a common-share value of 1½ to 2½.

The Purchase of Assets of an Insolvent Company Immediately Prior to Bankruptcy

Often, virtually everyone who follows a particular company knows that it is headed for protection under Chapter 11 of the bankruptcy laws. Frequently, opportunities will arise for an attractively priced purchase of stock or "hard" assets from the insolvent company.

Two basic methods of purchase are available. You can consider a stock purchase, in which the purchaser becomes liable for all of the debts and obligations of the seller (in the event of the purchase of all of the stock) or an asset purchase in which the buyer purchases some of the assets of the insolvent company and, hopefully, limits its liability by virtue of the purchase. Of course, when a purchase occurs after Chapter 11, many of the successor problems are eliminated. In addition to environmental concerns (asbestos problems, toxic waste, etc.), the purchaser of assets from a debtor still can become liable. Exceptions to the general rule of no successor liability are as follows:

- Where the true circumstances in the background of the transaction warrant a finding that in fact a consolidation or merger of the purchasing and selling corporation occurred;

---

1. Roe, "Bankruptcy and Debt: A New Model for Corporate Reorganization," 83 *Columbia Law Review* 527, 537, n. 32 (1983). Copyright © 1983 by the Directors of the Columbia Law Review Association, Inc. All Rights Reserved. Reprinted by permission.

- Where an expressed or implied agreement between the buyer and the debtor assumes the outside debts;
- Where the purchaser is a mere de facto continuation of the seller; and/or
- Where the transaction was in truth fraudulent.

Primary areas of concern in the purchase of the assets of an insolvent corporation outside of bankruptcy exist in the product-liability area and in the emerging area of environmental-liability exposure. Both of these areas require study. An environmental audit is necessary, as well as a check with respect to possible product-liability claims.

An asset purchaser outside of bankruptcy also can become liable under the bulk transfer laws of the various states. Bulk sales laws require purchasers of substantially all of the amounts of a business to give actual notice of the sale to creditors of the selling corporation who might be relying on the seller's assets for payment of the debt before the transaction is completed. Complying with this law, which is regulated by Article 6 of the Uniform Commercial Code (the Bulk Sales Act) usually is considered impossible. Attorneys always should be consulted before the purchase of substantially all of the assets of a company is considered. Article 6 of the Uniform Commercial Code is not, however, applicable to purchases that occur during a bankruptcy. Assignments for the benefit of creditors also are frequently exempt under state laws. Transfers in settlement of a security interest or lien also are generally exempt, as are sales made by executors, administrators or receivers in the course of judicial or administrative proceedings. Not surprisingly, this exemption frequently causes an insolvent seller to file for relief under the Bankruptcy Code to avoid complying with the Bulk Sales Act.

Fraudulent Conveyance Problems

Purchasing either assets or stock at a bargain is a worthy and desirable goal. However, a current trend among aggressive lawyers is to attack such purchases as being made for inadequate consideration. The general legal basis to attack such sales prior to bankruptcy is contained in the fraudulent conveyance statutes of both the state and federal Bankruptcy Code. As a result of those statutes, under appropriate laws, a purchaser can be held personally liable for the value of the assets acquired. The Uniform Fraudulent Transfer Act and the Uniform Fraudulent Conveyance Act, as well as

Section 544(b) of the Bankruptcy Code, exist to protect the creditors of an insolvent seller, just as the bulk sales laws exist to protect this group. Actual fraud on the part of the purchaser is not required to find the transaction a fraudulent conveyance. Indeed, all that may be necessary to find a fraudulent conveyance is for the negotiated price for the assets to be unreasonably low and certain other conditions to exist. For example, the sale can be attacked if:

1. Insolvency of the seller follows the transfer for inadequate consideration;
2. The seller is left with inadequate capital to engage in business; or
3. The seller is unable to pay its debts when they are due after the transaction.

Questions such as adequacy of consideration and insolvency require serious legal help of a specialized nature. Obviously, caution is advisable with prebankruptcy purchases when these factors appear to be present.

Methods of Purchase

Assuming and Paying the Seller's Debts. When purchasing assets from a seller about to go into bankruptcy, frequently part of the transaction will contain a provision under which the purchaser agrees contractually to assume or directly pay off certain creditors of the selling party. This type of transaction requires considerable caution because paying certain creditors outside of bankruptcy and not paying others can result in an attack under the fraudulent transfer laws referred to previously.

Additional issues exist concerning paying a debt that is not the seller's obligation, but is, in fact, the indebtedness of an affiliate or an insider of the selling company. Consideration or payment to a creditor that holds an obligation from both the seller and the third party can be attacked after the transaction as not benefiting the seller directly. Thus, transactions of this nature require an inquiry regarding whether any accommodation makers or guarantors are involved in the deal and whether or not the value being received is sufficient in terms of *just* the seller.

Purchases at Foreclosure Sales. Recently, some courts have construed the Bankruptcy Code to require a certain percentage payment of the fair value of property sold at a foreclosure sale. Failure to make an adequate payment at a foreclosure sale has caused the sale to be set aside later as a fraudulent conveyance. The general benchmark figure followed in many jurisdictions, although certainly not universally adopted, is known as the "70% rule." This rule, while widely criticized, on occasion has been stated to apply to foreclosure sales of all types of property. In other words, if the price bid at a foreclosure sale does not equal at least 70% of the fair market value of the foreclosed property, the sale may subsequently be attacked. Obviously, this creates a need for a reliable appraisal or an estimate of the value of the property to be purchased prior to the purchase at a foreclosure sale. In short, a foreclosure purchaser must be prepared to justify his or her purchase in a subsequent attack if the seller ultimately goes into bankruptcy court.

Leveraged Buyouts (LBOs).   While a discussion of the intricacies of this issue is well beyond the scope of this material, leveraged buyout (LBO) purchasers currently are providing one of the fertile fields for litigation. In very simple terms, an LBO consists of a purchaser using the company's assets as collateral to finance the acquisition of the company. The proceeds of the sale go to the seller's shareholders, leaving in place the unsecured creditors of the selling company. The usual result of this type of transaction is a company heavily burdened with debt and/or undercapitalized. Frequently, the resulting company is a likely candidate for bankruptcy; often, the transaction is attacked in bankruptcy after the fact as a fraudulent conveyance. While the purchaser's liability is a matter for discussion in the future, this type of transaction requires careful legal structuring and caution.

In any asset purchase prior to bankruptcy, as well as in a purchase of substantial amounts of stock prior to bankruptcy, caution must be exercised. Several devices should be utilized to protect the purchaser from subsequent attack when the selling company eventually slides into Chapter 11. The best avenue for protection is to request that a portion of any purchase price be held in an interest-bearing escrow account. While this precaution does not provide an ironclad assurance of protection, sufficient funds can be held to fund the legal expenses in a subsequent attack on the transaction. Another method of protection is simply to structure the purchase as an installment sale. Such a sale would provide for the buyer's payments to the seller after the greatest risk of bankruptcy of the seller had passed.

Yet another method to protect the purchaser would be to request and obtain a lien on the unsold assets of the seller or on the assets of an affiliate of the seller. This lien would secure an indemnity from the sellers, officers or affiliates in the event of a subsequent attack or breach of the agreement by the selling company. Any contingent payment or lien arrangement with respect to structuring such a sale is advisable to minimize the risk of doing business with an insolvent company outside of bankruptcy. As you can see, the myriad problems of purchasing assets from a shaky seller outside of bankruptcy lead to many bankruptcy filings to protect transactions from subsequent attack.

Bondmail. The junk-bond explosion of the 1980s has led to a curious industry consisting of investors buying bonds already in default, or certain to default, and then as legal holders requesting special treatment or payment. If the defaulting issuer fails to pay or accede to the request, the bondholder puts the company into involuntary bankruptcy. Because this event usually results in a substantial dilution of equity, it is not surprising that many companies feel threatened by "bondmail." Several of the companies that have had the experience of refusing to pay bondmail and suffering the consequences are: General Homes Corporation, MGF Oil Corporation, MCorp, Zale Corporation, Bally's Grand, SCI Television, Inc., and AP Industries, Inc.

A correlate to this activity is the purchase of defaulted bonds that are subject to an exchange offer and an attendant strategy of holding out no matter how attractive the offer, to receive payment at par (or restore the coupon). The risk in bondmail is that the defaulting company will simply file for Chapter 11 and the holdouts and involuntary bankruptcy threats will become meaningless because two-thirds of the creditors' class can vote down one-third of the class. However, holding more than one-third of the amount of outstanding bonds in a class frequently constitutes a block against any plan of reorganization, absent a classification scheme that dilutes the vote, or a cramdown on the class that also extinguishes the junior classes absent a new investment by the junior classes. Accordingly, bondmail is likely to see substantial use in the future. (See "Pay Up . . . Or Else," *Forbes* 147, no. 8 [August 6, 1990]: 74.)

Tax Issues

While tax issues play a major role in the overall estate valuation, they are much more critical to the value of the equity in the debtor. They will be of primary interest if you are contemplating an investment at that level.

Generally speaking, the plan or reorganization seldom will create a tax liability, alternative minimum tax considerations aside. Enough grief already exists in sifting through the ashes of the illustrious defunct. In contrast with out-of-court restructurings where cancellation of debt can create current ordinary income (COD income), the debtor corporation is granted some form of relief, as will be discussed. When working with tax problems, remember that you are merely dealing with the logical manipulation of a self-contained system of artificial propositions and that propositions are only principles that are not always true. So don't expect conventional logic and mores to prevail.

The primary concern in most Chapter 11 tax planning is a preservation of the debtor corporation's net operating loss (NOL) carryforwards. Through the years, preserving the NOLs has become increasingly difficult. The debtor corporation must focus not only on minimizing COD income, which will, as will be discussed, reduce the size of the NOL, but the debtor corporation must also try to maximize the availability of whatever amount of NOL it has coming out of Chapter 11. As a result of the Tax Reform Act of 1986, Section 382(a) of the Internal Revenue Code (the "Code") can limit the amount of its NOL a corporation can use annually if an ownership change (as defined) occurs.

Section 269 provides that tax-motivated acquisitions of control can cause the loss of NOLs. Discussing the detailed nuances involved in determining whether an ownership change has occurred is far beyond the scope of this work because among other things, the rules themselves change frequently. In fact, they are so subject to change that they are published in loose-leaf binders and updated monthly.

Cancellation of Debt Income Section 108(a) of the Internal Revenue Code, while excepting the forgiveness of debt in Chapter 11 from income, does reduce certain beneficial tax attributes, such as tax credit and NOL carryforwards to the extent of the forgiveness. However, the exchange of equity for debt in a Chapter 11 plan can avoid this attribute reduction under certain specific circumstances.

In general, when a company discharges indebtedness, income will be realized (COD income) to the extent of the forgiveness of the debt. Potential income of this nature generally receives the following treatment:

- For a company in Chapter 11, any cancellation of debt will be excluded from income and will be applied to reduce certain tax advantages and particularly any NOLs.

- If a company is solvent and not in any bankruptcy or similar proceeding, debt cancellation simply produces immediate taxable income and cancellation of debt income simply reduces net operating losses.

- If a company is operating outside of Chapter 11 but is still insolvent, cancellation of debt income will be excluded from income only to the extent of the insolvency of the debtor, but also the tax attributes such as the NOLs will be reduced by the cancellation of the excluded debts.

- For the insolvent debtor in Chapter 11, the regulations relating to a discharge in Chapter 11 are fully applicable, thus meaning that cancellation of debt income should be excluded from taxable gross income although the extent to which beneficial tax attributes at a reduced rate will apply will depend on how much, if any, of the discharge qualifies for the stock-for-debt exception.

In short, Chapter 11 companies have a tax advantage by virtue of the fact that they are allowed to exclude from income any debt forgiveness that makes the debtor solvent. A company that is in Chapter 11 does not need to prove its insolvency to the Internal Revenue Service (IRS).

If the debtor's stock is issued in exchange for the debt discharged, the general debt discharge rules may not apply to the Chapter 11 debtor. This exception applies only to insolvent companies during the period that they are insolvent and not after the time that they become solvent. The stock-for-debt exception applies to Chapter 11 debtors as well as out-of-court workouts. The key factual issue for the IRS is the fair market value of the stock issued in consideration of debt satisfaction. Under certain circumstances, income can be created that might be used to offset existing NOLs.

Many plans attempt to capitalize on the substantial tax losses the companies have built up in their bankruptcy years. Often, payouts to creditors in plans will take into account the annual limitation on the use of NOLs that frequently is imposed by Section 382(a). The particular trade-off that frequently occurs pits the desire for cash payouts postreorganization against a tax plan that seeks to preserve tax benefits through reinvestment in the reorganization debtor.

Trafficking in Net Operating Losses

In general, Congress and the Treasury Department do not favor trafficking in NOLs, nor do they encourage Chapter 11s with no other goal than the preservation of NOLs. However, with proper and careful consideration, a reorganized Chapter 11 debtor still may be able to preserve the value of NOLs, which would allow profits generated from the newly reorganized debtor to be sheltered from taxation.

The acquisition of control through purchasing claims in a Chapter 11 case can cause problems under Section 382 of the Code to such an extent that the "Ownership Change Rules" promulgated under Section 382 can cause the loss of certain NOL attributes.

The Effect of an Ownership Change

The change of ownership issue may come into play for a debtor that seeks to utilize its tax loss. A more than 50% increase in the holdings of the stock of the debtor owned by 5% of the shareholders creates an ownership change under the IRS rules. A severe annual limitation on the amount of taxable income of such a debtor that can be offset by NOLs is imposed pursuant to Section 382 of the Internal Revenue Code. This annual limitation is equal to an amount calculated using the value of the debtor's equity just before the ownership change. The number of complexities regarding non-voting stock, convertible debt and other similar interests are set forth. These complexities are far beyond our treatment of this subject.

A general limitation applies under which the amount of income that can be offset in each postchange year by a preownership change NOL is the fair market value of the debtor's stock prior to the ownership change multiplied by the long-term tax exempt rate in effect. Because the value of a debtor's equity in bankruptcy normally will be at or close to zero, the general rule normally will eliminate the NOLs. Accordingly, in Chapter 11 cases, certain exemptions are created for the Chapter 11 debtor. If just before the ownership change the debtor is in bankruptcy court and the pre-reorganization shareholders have at least 50% of the voting power and 50%

all the total value of the stock of the debtor after reorganization and the court approves the transaction, the general rule does not pertain. Instead, the NOLs of the debtor are reduced by:

1. The interest paid or accrued by the debtor during the current taxable year prior to the change of ownership;
2. The interest paid or acquired during the three preceding taxable years on that portion of the indebtedness in respect of which the securities are issued under the plan of reorganization; and
3. One-half of the amount of debt discharged for stock in the reorganization that would not otherwise reduce the NOLs because of the stock-for-debt exception.

Did you get all of that?

Unfortunately for the investor, the bankruptcy exception says that if a second ownership change occurs within two years after the first ownership change, NOLs are lost for all time periods after the second change of ownership. Additional restrictions relating to the "old and cold" shareholders exist that also provide a number of uncertainties for publicly traded claim-holders.

In summary, the operative feature of the bankruptcy exceptions to the extinguishment of NOLs appears to relate to a continuation of preexisting ownership. Obviously, substantial shifts in ownership of a debtor because of a trading of claims or equity interests can impair the retention of NOLs.

Strategies from a Legal Standpoint

The first strategic consideration for a bankruptcy investor is to decide whether to be an active or a passive investor. The answer depends on the type and amount of investment. For instance, investing in equity, which is advisable primarily as a postplan confirmation strategy, normally will be a passive investment that is reviewed periodically through available financial and market data. The more interesting situation is the debt investment. The most advantageous timing for this investment often will occur after a company is in default and Chapter 11 relief has been sought. The price tends to be severely depressed by the event of a bankruptcy filing. The market for the company's bonds often is in total disarray. Some institutional investors are desperate to get out and avoid the stigma of being associated with this example of their poor investment judgment. Others will be assessing their options. They could cut their losses with a quick exit. Alternatively, they could ride out their investment and assign a workout specialist to the situation. This latter approach is likely to be time consuming and relatively costly to the investor. Such a strategy makes more sense for a larger investment (e.g., $10 million) than for a smaller one (e.g., $1 million). Not only are the bonds likely to be depressed, they often are mispriced vis-à-vis each other (secured, senior unsecured, senior subordinated, junior subordinated, parent verses subsidiary debt, guaranteed versus unguaranteed debt, etc.). At this point, no one really knows what the bonds are likely to bring in a reorganization. Uncertainty often brings out pessimism. All of these factors tend to create buying opportunities. In this situation, not merely active but aggressive involvement is likely to be rewarded.

Taking an active posture in the debt investment should be expected and can prove to be one of the most profitable and interesting investments one can make. In early investments, however, the novice should be an active spectator as opposed to an active participant until he or she "learns the ropes." As in most areas, novices should be seen and not heard. Soon you can become more actively involved.

In your first investment, patience will be the key. This is the common trait shared by many successful investors in distressed situations. Plenty of investment opportunities usually are available for those interested in taking a flier in the securities of a troubled company. The investor's first inquiry should seek to determine the reason for the trouble. Is the trouble industry specific or company specific or related to a general economic downturn? In the case of distressed investment opportunities in an economy that is falling away from you, a longer holding period may be required. Financial difficulties attributed to the typical cyclical industry downturn situation may allow for a quicker profit. Company-specific difficulties are less well defined because the duration of their holding periods is determined by many factors external to both industry and economic conditions.

A good beginner's strategy, until you have the experience to become an active player, would be to spread your risk by purchasing into several situations. Such diversification should give you the opportunity to become more familiar with the risks and rewards involved. To lower the risk further during this stage, senior debt obligations should be the primary type of investment. These could be either publicly or privately held securities. In fact, general outright unsecured trade claims also might be considered for purchase. Initially, the amount purchased is not so important as it will be later. If you become a major player, you generally will want to purchase at least one-third of the amount outstanding where possible.

To lessen the risk further, start-up companies and small undercapitalized companies should be avoided because these long shots usually will require more attention than a novice can be expected to give. In the smaller company situation, as in the large company situation, you must be prepared to fight for your recovery. In the large company bankruptcy, however, you usually can rely on someone else also to fight for your class, although not always, especially in the Eurodollar situations. Moreover, only you can fight most effectively for your specific interests (e.g., earlier versus a higher and later payout, more debt or equity in your reorganization package).

The importance of patience cannot be overstated because of the poor liquidity of these investments. You will learn to think of your investment as a buy, hold and negotiate security with rewards coming to those who display the most discipline. In general, equity tends to be a poor investment while a company is in Chapter 11 reorganization, but not necessarily immediately after emergence. Even at this later stage, the equity tends not to be a long-term investment. Debt investments tend to be preferable while a company languishes in Chapter 11.

As important as preferring debt over equity is the decision of which debt security or securities to purchase. Each type of bond initially will trade for a particular price or in a specific price range. The seniormost securities will have the highest absolute price. The lower the priority, the lower the price will be. Which is the best buy will depend on a number of factors. Assessing the relative risk-to-reward ratios is a very important aspect of bankruptcy investing.

CHAPTER 2

Investing in Bankruptcies

Large sums of money have a certain poetry and rhapsody. Judging from the number of investors stumbling into the world of investing in distressed companies, the romance of holding paper with face amounts in the millions of dollars is luring many novices to the bottom fishing arena. Many of them make unprofitable investments, while other more experienced investors have been making and are continuing to make substantial fortunes investing in insolvent situations and bankrupt companies.

How did they do it? By knowing what they were doing. For many years, an investor in the securities of large publicly held companies emerging from bankruptcy could hardly lose.

Any observer of the comings and goings of major companies in and out of the bankruptcy courts has noticed a remarkable trend over the past decade—specifically, an initial precipitous drop in the price of all of the securities held by the public and issued by the new debtor in possession. Frequently, this move turns out to be an overreaction to the company's Chapter 11 filing. When all is said and done, many bankruptcies yield a much higher recovery for investors than the firm's securities were selling for just after or even just before the filing. Not infrequently, the holding period returns turn out to be extremely high. And yet, the results differ greatly from case to case and even from security to security within the same case. Which securities are the ones to buy? This is the key question for bankruptcy investors.

The Rules and Players of the Game

The distinction between successful investors and unsuccessful investors in insolvency situations comes largely from knowing the rules of the game as well as how they are applied. Incredibly, many novices are willing to risk substantial sums of money without adequately understanding the natural process in which they are participating, much less understanding how to evaluate the available data specific to the particular situation in which they are investing. Both types of knowledge are needed to assess the relevant risks and rewards.

Who Is the Judge?

One important variable when purchasing the debt or equity in a company enjoying the magnificent protections of Chapter 11 of the Bankruptcy Code is the bankruptcy judge to whose court the case is assigned. To the Chapter 11 debtor, this person is God. From the moment the case is filed, no decision is made in the corporate offices or in the boardroom without the question being asked: "How is the judge going to like this?" Some judges are notoriously lenient on the debtors. Several reasons may account for this lenience. These judges may believe that they will be viewed favorably by their peers (and those who might review their work in the process of selecting future United States District Judges with lifetime tenure) if they show a measure of compassion to a debtor who is down on its luck. Other judges have suffered the trauma that occurs when a debtor and its counsel "throw the keys on the table" and the bankruptcy judge is faced with the chaos that he or she must resolve by appointing a trustee and praying that the lives of too many innocent employees and creditors are not destroyed in the process.

Most experienced bankruptcy lawyers agree that, unlike wine, bankruptcies do not improve with age. If a bankruptcy judge allows his or her court to be used as a parking lot for a favorite debtor's counsel, you should beware. The biggest enemy you have in this arena is time and its relation to the value of your investment. Asset values tend to deteriorate during bankruptcy. In addition, administrative (mainly legal) costs mount up as time passes.

For a major bankruptcy, the press will report the name of the judge, as well as critique his or her past performance in previous bankruptcy cases. What if the judge's name is not reported? To get information on the judge, first call the company and ask the beleaguered switchboard where its bankruptcy is filed. This is one thing that the company will know. Second, call directory assistance for the city in which the case is filed and get the number of the United States Bankruptcy Clerk. Give him or her a call. Eventually, the clerk will answer the telephone and he or she can tell you the name of the judge to whom the case is assigned.

Various publications give you an ad hoc rundown on every sitting bankruptcy judge, but you don't need to do that much research. Call a bankruptcy lawyer and ask about the judge. If your lawyer does not know much about this particular judge, ask for the name of someone who does. Is this judge a take-charge jurist who will move the case swiftly through the process? Or is he or she an incompetent or, worse yet, a simple good-hearted soul who will give the debtor every extension of every deadline and grant every motion the debtor files and, in particular, every application for attorney's fees (no matter how unnecessary or outrageous) without challenge? If you don't know a bankruptcy attorney, or those you do know draw blanks, look in the *Martindale Hubbel Directory* for the particular city where the case is pending. Every large library has this directory and almost every large or small law firm has a copy. The directory contains a list of the law firms and their specialties for each major U.S. city, including the one where the bankruptcy will be pending. Contact a bankruptcy specialist and ask him or her about the judge. Most will charge little or nothing for this information. If the judge assigned to the case is like most, you'll feel that he or she is a neutral factor in your investment. If the assigned judge has a reputation as an unsophisticated debtor-oriented do-nothing, think twice before committing capital.

Who Are the Creditors?

The next area of concern is the identity of the creditor group. Who are the big losers who bought their bonds at much higher prices? Have any large investors recently entered the picture? Who is accumulating and who is selling out? At what prices? Are the large creditors mainly insiders or affiliates of the debtor or is only one large institutional creditor involved?

The two principal categories of major creditors are institutional investors (banks, insurance companies, mutual funds, college endowments, etc.) and the large individual investors (arbitragers, vulture investors). Trade creditors constitute a third category that is important in some cases. The institutional investors generally purchased their bonds (earlier) at or near par, while the large individual investors are more likely to have acquired their holdings (recently) at a steep discount. As a general rule, the large individual holders will tend to be more aggressive and more interested in a quick resolution and payout. They would like to turn their money over and then go on to something else. The institutional investors, in contrast, are likely to be more patient and more inclined to work the situation for a higher ultimate payout even if it takes a bit longer to achieve.

The major difference between the arbitragers and the institutional investors is their risk-return orientation. The arbitrager sought out the risk and seeks a quiet commensurate return to go along with that risk. The institutional investor, in contrast, is trying to salvage what is possible to save from an investment that didn't work out. Thus, arbitragers will be happy to buy at 10 and receive 30 in a year: that's a 200% return (annualized). The institutional investor might look at the same situation and say let's work the situation for another six months when we think we can get 36. To the institutional investor, that extra six points clearly is worth the wait. It amounts to a 20% greater recovery in six months. That amounts to 40% annualized. Moreover, for one who bought at par, this represents a 36% recovery as opposed to a 30% recovery. The arbitrager will not disagree with the arithmetic, but he or she will be less impressed. Will the wait really be rewarded? More important for the arbitrager, he or she probably has other investments to pursue and wants the money out of this deal now. The institution-arbitrager conflict does not always arise, and if it does, it does not always focus on the same issue. And yet, the two types of investors do enter the bankruptcy investing arena from different directions with different expectations. The beginning investor should take these differences into account.

A debt widely spread over many creditors is preferable to a more concentrated set of holdings for all but the major players in the bankruptcy investing arena. The real "Big Players" like to see one large holder of most of the debt when an inexpensive cheap acquisition is their goal. Even those very large traders prefer a diverse group of holders when their goal is simply to earn a fast and modest profit. All too often, creditors are each owed too little to care. This type of situation presents both an opportunity and a dilemma. Disinterested creditors usually will sell their claims for a song. When they don't, however, they invariably become deadweight later in the case when aggressive action becomes necessary to move a case out of Chapter 11 through the confirmation process.

How do you find out who the creditors are and how much they are owed? From your (soon-to-be) old friends at the bankruptcy clerk's office. When the clerk finally answers the telephone, he or she will tell you how to order a copy of either a list of the debtor's 20 largest creditors (filed with the original petition for relief) or a complete set of the debtor's schedules and statement of financial affairs (extremely complete, detailed and lengthy— filed early in the case). Various services will supply you with this information in most large cases, but it's just as easy to gather it yourself. Better yet, if you can, go to the clerk's office and have a ball reading a wealth of data about your investment target. Would that your local stockbroker knew half as much about the stocks he or she was touting with regularity. Most clerks will let you photocopy the pages that you need. You can expect to find the complete name and address of each creditor and the amount owed each creditor and often the name of the contact person at the creditor's office.

How Much Are the Assets Worth?

To put it another way, how in the world is this debtor going to be able to make its paper worth anything? If the schedules are on file, everything you can expect to know about the identity of the assets will be spelled out fairly well. The values given are another matter. The reported values are generated by accountants from historical data. These numbers may have very little relation to what actually can be derived in a sale of those assets even in an orderly disposition. Moreover, the actual selling prices of the assets are likely to be quite sensitive to whether the sales take place in a strong or weak market environment; whether or not the bankruptcy filing has caused a deterioration of values; and whether the seller can be patient or must sell quickly, even if only distress level prices are likely to be available. Uncertainty over asset values is one of the biggest risk factors early in the case.

As a case proceeds, more and more accurate data on the values of the various assets becomes available. For one thing, the marketplace is exposed to the salable assets and, even for assets that are not advertised, buyers usually will appear. As time passes in a bankruptcy case, the spread between the price of securities of a debtor in Chapter 11 and the actual recovery to be had on those securities normally will narrow. For this reason, most of the gains and most of the risks for investors in the securities of bankrupt debtors result from purchases early in the case.

Because most investors want to achieve as high a return as possible, those not put off by gaps in the asset side of the equation frequently are rewarded for making their investments early in the case. That is, the best time to buy often is before reliable data on assets generally is available and before market forces decide the outcome of a risk you never took. What? You mean buy a pig in a poke? No, of course not. Some information on the value of a company is available from other sources. One should immediately obtain the most recent (prebankruptcy filing) documents issued by the company itself. Specifically, one should obtain a 10-K report, a 10-Q proxy statement and the registration statements on the securities of interest.

The Creditors' Committee

By moving quickly, you can make your purchase decision early enough in the case so you can be on hand for the organizational meeting of the official statutory creditors' committee. This event usually is held within the first two weeks after a company files. The major players in the credit are selected by the U.S. trustee to become members of the official committee. Frequently, an equity securities committee is formed as well. As of this writing, the U.S. trustee in most districts around the country now is appointing only one official creditors' committee. The extra expense of operating multiple committees usually is given as the reason for forming only one committee. The bankrupt estate is responsible for the allowable expenses of the committee or committees. Each committee almost always will retain a law firm to represent its interest. It may or may not hire other professionals (accountants, investment bankers, economists, appraisers, etc.) as the need arises. The members of the committee receive no pay for their work. They are, however, reimbursed for their out-of-pocket expenses (travel, hotels, meals) when attending meetings and performing the work of the committee. Thus, the cost of two committees is likely to be approximately twice that of one committee, perhaps more.

Note, however, that having creditors of different classes serve together on a single committee raises conflict-of-interest problems. For example, a creditor holding a debenture subordinated to senior bank debt has an interest different from the banks. Placing both categories of creditors on the same committee means that these natural economic enemies will have great difficulty agreeing on a common approach as to who gets what. The shifting alliances created by these inherent differences lead to Balkan states alliances and Byzantine plots between the various creditor groups. You may find these intrigues entertaining if you are fond of complicated economic interrelationships.

Separate committees for different categories of creditors greatly reduce the likelihood of internal deadlocks on economic issues. Otherwise, these deadlocks can paralyze and thus delay the "deal making" that is central to the process of reaching a consensual reorganization plan. Therefore, having different economic interests represented on the same committee usually is resisted by most experienced lawyers for the creditors. On the other side of the issue are the U.S. trustee, keeping an eye on expenses, and the debtor's counsel, wanting to achieve the benefits that will flow from the delays that frequently result from stalemates among the creditors.

Divisions among the creditors often have been exploited by the debtor. The committee relationship is an economic one and usually, after awhile, a personal one as well. If different classes of creditors are placed on the same committee, personal relationships will sour and the committee is all too likely to dissolve into bickering deadlocked factions. The attendant delays frequently will cost the estate more than the superficial savings of having one committee and set of professionals. With separate committees, in contrast, each committee resolves internal differences between investors holding similar types of securities within that committee. Then the separate committees resolve their differences through negotiation or, if that fails, through litigation.

If you have enough money and time invested, attending this organizational meeting of the committee(s) is a must. As previously explained, major decisions are being made in an information vacuum, and the die often is cast for the remainder of the case. At this meeting or later, take a look at the members of the committee. Are they owed enough money to give them an adequate incentive to do an effective job of riding herd on the debtor? Is the committee made up of what appears to be contentious lawyers who seem more interested in purely proving a legal point than of businesspeople who simply want to get their money back? What do you think of the professionals that the committee has retained? When you call the law firm that serves as committee counsel, does it return your calls? Have you or anyone else ever heard of the firm? Does the committee seem to have delegated all responsibility to the committee professionals? The U.S. trustee is supposed to oversee all these matters, of course, but in practice you generally should not expect much from that quarter. The U.S. trustee has no economic recovery at stake in the case.

You should plan on calling the members of the committee. Most of them will be happy to talk to you at least once. Remember, however, that these individuals assume a terrific responsibility and perform this public trust without pay. They want to get their money back, but often they just could have sat back and let some other similarly situated person do the job for them. They have stepped forward for all creditors. They will receive no more for their claims than those who do not serve. You should expect to make about one call (or perhaps one call per six months) per member at the most. What questions should you ask? What questions would you ask a stockbroker about a stock? Clearly, what you want to learn is how much is in the estate and what the likely recovery is for each category of creditors. You also would like to find out the probable timing of any distributions.

Committee members are not necessarily going to know the answers and usually are limited in what they can say by confidentiality rules. You want to learn as much as you can without learning too much. If you should be told material nonpublic information, you yourself will become subject to the same restrictive rules for trading as insiders. Thus, you want to ask questions that are on the edge of the issues. Use existing public documents to fashion questions that help you understand what lies behind the numbers and statements. You want to utilize the public documents to sort out the true worth and standings of the assets and liabilities.

The First Creditors' Meeting

Within the first two months after the case has been filed, a first meeting of creditors will be held. If you still are undecided about whether or not to make a purchase, here is your chance to ask the debtor anything your heart desires—within reason. Imagine that you are a large shareholder at a rather small annual meeting of stockholders and you will get some idea of what the first meeting of creditors is like. Note one exception, however: These shareholders are mad as hell. The debtor's officers who have to stand and deliver often are to be pitied, but they always provide more information than at any previous time in their careers. What they say now is being recorded by an employee of the Department of Justice. Because a great deal is at stake, prudent debtor's counsel usually will make sure that someone is present who really knows the answers to the often hostile questions about the debtor's future finances.

Aside from the chance to hear the straight story from the horse's mouth, the first meeting of creditors is a fantastic opportunity to chat with the other creditors. Often, only a few will turn up, even in major cases. All too often the creditors fail to take advantage of their chance to ask direct questions and turn this meeting into a nonevent. Whether or not any questions are asked, those who do attend get a chance to exchange rumors and tell each other who wants out of their investment in the debtor and who is buying the paper and for how much. Note that attending this meeting is not necessary, and many experienced investors do not do so. Adequate information on any major debtor is readily available in public records. The treat of seeing this event is nice, but not absolutely necessary.

In the days after the first meeting of creditors, the price of the investment paper of a debtor may well move dramatically, either up or down. These fluctuations are neither trendsetting nor anything other than reactions to the debtor's performance at the first meeting. Such fluctuations also may provide attractive opportunities to buy on a downward swing or to realize a modest profit if the price runs up and then to move on to something else.

The Action Slows Down

By now you probably are thinking that this sounds like a lot of work. Because these cases go on for a year or two or more, you may conclude that you don't have time to mess around with lawyers and committees and judges. Actually, at about this point in the case, the investor will have little to do until nearly the very end of the case. We have just taken you through the first few weeks of a typical case. Now someone else can do the work: the debtor in possession, creditors' committee and lawyers (unless, of course, you want to be on the committee yourself).

After the short initial period subsequent to the filing, the usual case settles in for a period of stabilization. You probably won't hear much about the debtor for some months. To the casual observer, mention a particular debtor five months or so into a case and you'll get a response like: "Didn't they go bankrupt or something?" Between the second and twelfth month of the usual major reorganization, the people who now are running the debtor are getting into their business plan. Their plan may include divestment, slimming down the business, selling unprofitable lines or just liquidating. During this period, the value of your investment, whether already made or just being contemplated, is being established. For the four months following the filing, the debtor enjoys its basic exclusivity period. During this 120-day period, only the debtor can file a plan of reorganization. Thus, a breathing space is afforded for sorting out the problems that caused the Chapter 11 to be filed.

The lawyers continue to fight and the accountants continue to run manifold hypothetical projections and the costs continue to mount. If nothing is done to move the case toward the plan confirmation stage, these expenses can totally deplete the estate. The major creditors usually start to exercise their muscles behind the scenes. Clearly, they want to try to maximize the value of the estate. You get a free ride. You do not need to hire your own lawyer unless you want someone to talk to.

Exclusivity

You may hear that the debtor has only four months when it alone can propose a plan of reorganization. This time frame is superficially correct. Usually in large cases, the bankruptcy judge will extend this period for many months. Not until the judge starts to express some reluctance about extending the time period will the case enter its most crucial phase—plan formulation. Having the exclusive right to propose a plan gives the debtor considerable leverage. Eventually, the judge may feel that the case has stabilized and that the interests of the creditors are being prejudiced by the continuation of the debtor's exclusivity period. Now things start to get serious. This point usually occurs about a year into the case. In most major cases, judges believe that more than 120 days is needed to give the debtor the opportunity to come up with a first cut at a plan. At this writing, LTV Corporation has received 19 extensions of the exclusivity period. Terminating the debtor's exclusivity period allows any party in interest also to file a plan. Multiple filings give the judge the job of sorting out these competing plans, which is likely to entail a lot of work. Nonetheless, the time always comes when the creditors come to the forefront, whether in completing a plan or in negotiations under the threat of lifting of the exclusivity period, and negotiations begin over who gets what.

The Plan Phase

Most investors who have seen the interplay between various factions at the stage when the gloves come off become frustrated. The problem lies chiefly in the fact that the value in the estate is insufficient to satisfy the claims of the various constituencies except in the rare case of a solvent debtor. And why would a solvent debtor be put into bankruptcy?

Actually, a company may derive enough from asset sales to pay off all of the creditors fully and still have something left over for shareholders (as was the case for the Chicago-Milwaukee bankruptcy where all of the investor classes came out very well), but this is a rare event indeed. Most of the time, liabilities far exceed assets. The tension never is greater than during the fight between the junior and senior bondholders. Their intercreditor struggle provides a typical example. When these players first encountered each other, their goals were much simpler and clear-cut. When the subordinated debt was created, the negotiating parties were seeking technical covenants that, while important at the time, are only slightly pertinent at the stage of the case where the spoils are to be divided. At the loan documentation stage, the senior lenders sought to control the ability of subordinated debt holders to receive payments on account of their indebtedness. These provisions were written when the borrower was at an early stage of financial difficulty. At the same early phase of the lending process, the negotiators for the subordinated lenders expended great efforts to limit the term of the cessation of payments to their group when the borrower (now the debtor) ran into problems. The early debates are largely irrelevant in a negotiation that focuses on liquidation values. The true strength of the junior creditors arises from the fact that their efforts can cause costly litigation and delay proceedings, thereby delaying distributions to creditors. The economic loss arising from the delay and from the additional administrative and other costs of bankruptcy may exceed the amount that the junior subordinated debt holders are seeking as a recovery.

One commentator observed:

The United Merchants and Manufacturers bankruptcy has been offered as an example of an institutional rule of thumb that the seniors will give up 20% of their claim to avoid a 30% loss from litigation in the reorganization court (20% from receiving poor value, 10% from legal and other costs of a challenge). The Equity Funding case has been

offered as an example of compromise to avoid complex litigation that
would depress firm value and the value of the seniors' layer.[1]

When and where is this plan written? Largely out of the public eye. This
stage is where committee membership becomes important for those who
wish to participate in the negotiating process. Note that an investor need not
perform this function in the vast majority of cases. The "major players" in
each class of creditors normally will do the actual negotiating, with the
assistance of their bankruptcy counsel. On your initial foray into this arena,
you probably will prefer to be a spectator to this frustrating spectacle. Term
sheets and epithets fly back and forth between the various groups. These
proposals usually are generated in the offices of the debtor, creditors'
committees and secured creditors. Only the representatives for these various
key players see the early drafts and play a role in their formulation. Of
course, anyone can witness the show—he or she only has to purchase enough
of the claim of any of the players. When does this process occur? Remember
the all-important discussion of the debtor's exclusive period for filing a plan.
The bankruptcy judge and the creditors determine when either of them feels
the case should come to an end. The draconian possibility of a failure of the
Chapter 11 reorganization, a conversion to Chapter 7 liquidation and the
appointment of a trustee drives the parties to draw up an agreed-on plan to
present to the public.

The Disclosure Statement

Frequently, the plan will be presented with less than total unanimity.
Just as often, the combatants will iron out their differences on the eve of the
hearing on the disclosure statement. This is the hearing on the document that
will describe who gets what in the plan. It resembles a prospectus and the
typical investor is just about as likely to read it. But as with most proceedings
before the court, the judicial process subjects this document to careful
scrutiny.

---

1. Roe, "Bankruptcy and Debt: A New Model for Corporate Reorganization,"
83 *Columbia Law Review* 527, 543 n. 49 (1983). (Citations omitted). Copyright
© 1983 by the Directors of the Columbia Law Review Association, Inc. All Rights
Reserved. Reprinted by permission.

A great deal of money usually is spent assuring the court that indeed the rights of the public creditors will be protected when they are given the opportunity to vote on the plan of reorganization. The main issue the court will determine at the disclosure statement hearing is merely the adequacy of disclosure in the proposed document (or documents in the case of competing plans of reorganization). After the court is satisfied with the adequacy of the information disclosed, the plan proponents send out the disclosure statement and the plan to the various creditors and other parties who have requested copies. The main document in the mailing will begin with a summary, followed by a detailed exposition of the plan and its implications for the various categories of creditors. Usually, it also will contain a number of exhibits including historical financial statements. Additionally, the mailing will include your ballot to enable you to vote for or against the plan.

When you receive the disclosure statement and the plan, handle it carefully. If you are a creditor, it costs you a lot of money. Lawyers and accountants and investment bankers frequently are paid very high fees to undertake the congressionally mandated process that places a complicated convoluted document in the hands of someone who asks only that his or her debt be repaid. How do you analyze this tome?

To answer this question, we must determine what kind of an investor you are. Are you primarily concerned with the return you get on your investment? In other words, as long as you get what you feel is a satisfactory return on capital, are you satisfied? If so, you need only read the part of the disclosure statement that deals with what you get. Find out what class you are in. This will be right up front. Then read the section that describes the treatment that your class receives (what you get). Next, read the description of the assets in terms of what is on hand and what is expected to be received. Is your treatment (payout) enough for you?

Frequently, the distribution will be a package of different securities (cash, new debt, preferred stock, common stock, warrants of various categories). What is the package likely to be worth? The cash is easy to value, but all the paper will have uncertain market values. Each must be looked at separately in the context of the reorganized firm. The debt securities will have a face value and terms (coupon, maturity date). The investor must assess the risk and the corresponding discount rate to apply. Almost always this paper will be worth less than its face value. Preferred stock also may be evaluated as an income instrument. It also will start trading at a substantial discount from its par value. The common stock is the most difficult to value.

In theory, one values the reorganized company, backs out the senior claims (debt and preferred) and divides the value attributable to the common equity by the number of outstanding shares. Warrants are even more difficult to assess. Their value depends on the chances of the common price rising high enough before the warrants expire to make exercising them attractive. Warrants issued as part of a bankruptcy package generally are far out of the money (striking price much above the initial market price of the new stock). Normally, one should not place too high a value on the warrant part of the package.

Note that the package is not necessarily so complex as previously described. A typical package may contain only two or three separate instruments (e.g., cash, bonds and common stock). In some cases, it will contain only one element (e.g., cash or common stock). Other cases, however, have offered even more complexity. For example, Crystal Oil (a relatively small bankruptcy case) exchanged a package of securities that included zero coupon bonds, senior preferred stock, junior preferred stock, common stock and five different classes of warrants for its prebankruptcy securities. Adding further to the complexity, the zeros and preferreds were convertible into common stock and the warrants could be exercised with either cash or with the zeros (at 110% of their face value) or the senior preferred stock (at its liquidation value). The large array of convertibles and warrants made the potential common stock dilution exceedingly difficult to assess. Because no meaningful preissue market existed for these securities, placing a value on the package was no easy task.

What are the surrounding circumstances? Would the later payout be greater if the current plan is defeated? Is the window of opportunity so narrow that it will prevent your class from holding out for the last dollar? In true democratic fashion, you and your class generally will get to vote based on what is in your own economic best interests. As is the American way, the majority rules.

If you are the kind of person who is not so much concerned with your own absolute return but rather measures your results against the results others receive, you will want to read the entire plan and disclosure statement. You will want to analyze the treatment of each and every class to see who, if anyone, is getting a better deal than your class. If you are this type of individual, you probably won't be very happy investing in this area for small hard-nosed creditors in particular situations often will be found lurking in a plan with a disproportional recovery because they often possess some unique leverage (e.g., the particular creditor may be an indispensable business partner or customer). Another possible reason for reading the entire document is to decide whether you want to make additional investments. Perhaps one or more of the other instruments are slated to be treated significantly better than the current market price recognizes. If so, perhaps you should try to buy one of these instruments rather than more of what you currently own. You want to buy the instrument that has the highest expected payoff relative to its risk. Which instrument holds this characteristic will vary over time as information emerges and market prices change.

How Is the Pie To Be Divided?

The most crucial negotiation usually takes place over how much is left for equity. The inherent conflict that exists for management is apparent. Usually, management has the shareholders' interests paramount in its mind. Under normal (i.e., nonbankruptcy) circumstances, managers are likely to see themselves as working for the shareholders. After all, the shareholders are technically the company's owners. The creditors merely are suppliers of the debt capital not unlike some other supplier of the company (e.g., the electric or telephone company). Moreover, the managers frequently are shareholders themselves. Finally, the board of directors is elected by the shareholders and, at least in theory, directs management in the shareholders' behalf. On the other hand, when a company is severely troubled, management is supposed to shift more and more of its attention to protecting the interests of the creditors. Indeed, once a company becomes insolvent (whether or not it has filed for bankruptcy), the creditors are in effect the owners. At that point, managers should see themselves as owing virtually their complete allegiance to the creditors (as opposed to the shareholders).

Certainly, once a troubled firm files for bankruptcy, management should act as a fiduciary for the unsecured creditors. As a part of the reorganization process, these competing interests of shareholders and creditors are on a collision course. Equity, by law, is supposed to get paid only after the secured and unsecured debt. And yet, management would like to preserve some value for the shareholders. How can this conflict be resolved? This is the subject of the basic negotiation in the plan. How much goes to the creditors and what, if anything, is left for the shareholders? The lawyers and accountants argue and threaten with notions of a litigated plan confirmation and "cramdown" and thousands of dollars are spent in posturing. The issue must be resolved either in or out of court.

If we assume that the issue of how much is to be divided among the creditors and other claimants is resolved, and it will be, then the only matter to be considered is the most important one—how do the creditors divide the assets of the estate among themselves? The problem also could be approached from the other direction. The creditors can decide to divide the assets of the estate between themselves first and then decide what will be left over for equity. No matter what approach is taken, the negotiations that take place between the secured and unsecured groups will be intense and frequently acrimonious. In this era of junk bonds, most large businesses in Chapter 11 reorganizations have various levels of unsecured indebtedness outstanding. In practice, a simultaneous solution will be achieved in iterative steps. Each party will be seeking the most advantageous treatment for its class. Alliances will form and dissipate and re-form among different groups. The process can be tedious and tortuous, but eventually it may reach a successful conclusion that no one really likes.

The significance of "subordinated debt" is critical. The Bankruptcy Code requires a plan to divide creditors' claims and equity holders' interests into separate classes; the economic rights of these classes then are dealt with under the plan. Each class only can contain claims that are "substantially similar." The claims within a particular class cannot be treated differently (absent agreements of a particular class member being treated less favorably). For example, all unsecured trade creditors should receive the same pro rata payments. However, different classes of claims may receive disparate treatment, providing that the protections built into the Bankruptcy Code for nonconsenting claims and interests are satisfied.

The Vote on the Plan

Holders of valid claims against and interests in a debtor are allowed to vote for the acceptance or rejection of a proposed plan. A class is deemed to have accepted a proposed plan if more than one-half in number and more than two-thirds in dollar amount of the members actually casting votes accept the plan.

A plan still can be confirmed over the objections of a nonconsenting member of a class that votes for the plan if that class member receives or retains under the plan property of a value that is equal to or greater than what that member would receive or retain if the debtor were liquidated under Chapter 7 of the Bankruptcy Code.

If a class as a whole rejects the plan, a plan proponent still may have the court confirm that plan if the plan "does not discriminate unfairly" and is "fair and equitable" with respect to the dissenting class. This is the so-called "cramdown" of the Bankruptcy Code. With respect to unsecured creditors, the condition that a plan be fair and equitable includes the "absolute priority rule": i.e., no class junior to the dissenting class may receive any property until the higher dissenting class is paid in full.

A plan proponent facing a dissenting class and a contested confirmation hearing is placed in a difficult position. An enormous expense and delay is inherent in a judicial determination of whether the cramdown safeguards for dissenters are satisfied. A protracted delay can and usually will prove fatal to a company attempting to continue operations in Chapter 11 reorganization as a going concern. A dissenting class of creditors (such as subordinated debt) may be able to veto a plan provision providing for a continuing participation of existing equity when the dissenters are not satisfied. This ability enables such a class effectively to block confirmation of the entire plan. In cases requiring certain tax treatments or the participation of key debtor personnel, retention of a small equity position by management is often a quid pro quo for continued operations or for cooperation with an outside investor. In almost every case, creditors (whose rights are superior to equity interests) are receiving less than a 100% payout on their claims. Therefore, absent the agreement of each more senior creditor class, a plan providing that equity holders receive some distribution is not confirmable. For these reasons, most successful Chapter 11 reorganizations involve consensual plans.

A variety of factors combine to give subordinated debt holders considerable leverage (vis-à-vis senior creditors) in the bankruptcy negotiation process. In most instances, the classification scheme, voting requirements and class protections built into the Bankruptcy Code; the considerable court bias toward obtaining consensual plans and the frequent desirability of including existing equity in the distribution scheme all work to the subordinated debt holders' advantage. Junior debt holders will tell the seniors that they have relatively little to lose by blocking or delaying confirmation of a plan that provides them little or no recovery. Senior creditors, in contrast, will have much more at stake. The seniors can, however, get a recovery in a Chapter 7 liquidation that provides nothing for the juniors. Both sides may play a game of chicken, hoping that the other one will blink.

Many otherwise viable companies are forced to file bankruptcy to reduce an overbearing debt burden. In effect, they would like to shave off or at least shave down and convert to equity existing contractually subordinated debt.

Usually, this subordinated debt arises from unsecured junk bonds issued by the company. The leveraged buyout (LBO) boom of the 1980s created many such situations.

The Subordination Issue

Most indentures (the stated contract between issuer and borrower) involving publicly issued subordinated debentures provide for "inchoate forbearance": The subordinated debt may be paid according to the terms thereof unless a default exists with respect to senior creditors. "Senior creditors" typically include borrowed money or particularly designated categories of debt owed by the borrower. In the real world, senior creditors typically do not include trade debt; i.e., trade debt is neither senior nor junior to the debenture issue, but rather is characterized as "neutral" even though its proper place usually is more with the senior than the junior unsecured debt holders.

Just who is senior to whom and who is not is often in dispute. For example, the trade creditors will want to claim seniority to the subordinated debt, while the juniors will want to claim the contrary. The indenture may not be totally clear as to just what other debt the subordinated debt is subordinated to. If, for example, the trade debt is clearly pari passu with the senior unsecured bank debt, but the junior debt is only subordinated to senior bank debt, a complicated payout formula is called for. First, the available proceeds are allocated to the three categories of debt holders as if they were of equal standing. Then the money allocated to the subordinated debt generally will be reallocated to the senior bank debt holders up to the amount of their shortfall. Any remaining monies are retained for distribution to the juniors. Other formulas are applicable for other classifications. An example will help clarify this scheme. First, consider the result if the subordinated debt is only subordinated to the bank debt:

Claims

Bank debt	$ 50 million
Trade debt	50 million
Subordinated debt	50 million
Total	$150 million
Available for distribution	$ 99 million

Initial Allocation		*% of Recovery*
Bank	$33 million	66
Trade	33 million	66
Subordinated	33 million	66
Total	$99 million	

The bank debt's shortfall is $17 million, which is taken from the subordinate holders' initial allocations. The final allocation would become:

		% of Recovery
Bank	$50 million	100
Trade	33 million	66
Subordinated	16 million	32
Total	$99 million	

Now contrast this result with other possibilities. Suppose, for example, that both trade and bank debts were classified as senior with the debenture debt subordinated to both. For that situation, the initial allocation of the subordinated holders would be allocated pro rata to both trade and bank debts. The result:

		% of Recovery
Bank	$49.5 million	99
Trade	49.5 million	99
Subordinated	0	0
Total	$99 million	

Now suppose that both trade and debenture debts are subordinated to bank debt, but the trade and bank debts are pari passu. The bank's initial $17 million shortfall would be taken pro rata from both the trade and subordinated debt holders. The result for this (unlikely) situation would be:

		% of Recovery
Bank	$50.0 million	100
Trade	24.5 million	49
Subordinated	24.5 million	49
Total	$99 million	

Finally, suppose the bank debt is senior to both and the trade debt is senior to the subordinated debentures. The result of this situation would be:

		% of Recovery
Bank	$50 million	100
Trade	49 million	98
Subordinated	0	0
Total	$99 million	

Clearly, the way a subordination clause applies can have a major impact on the payout for the various classes of creditors.

These results represent possible outcomes from what might be called for by the subordination provisions in the indentures. A consensual plan may tend toward one of these kinds of distributions (the one fitting the specific legal circumstances of the subordination clause), but in the give-and-take of negotiations, the plan is likely to depart from it at least somewhat. Generally, the juniors will fare a bit better and the seniors a bit worse than the subordination provisions imply. On the other hand, if the case is converted to Chapter 7, the subordination provisions become fully enforceable. This threat is a potent weapon for the senior creditors.

Senior Strategy for Dealing with Subordinated Debt

Plan proponents may utilize any of several strategies in an attempt to limit the bargaining position of subordinated debt. First, even though seemingly technically improper, plans have been structured so that subordinated debt is treated for voting purposes as in the same class as senior and other debt. The subordination provisions of the two creditor classes are, however, left intact. If the amount and number of holders of senior and other debts in the same class are sufficiently high, the subordinated debt vote can be sufficiently diluted so that it cannot by its own vote carry a class and cause the class to reject the plan. This result, in turn, takes the potent weapon of the absolute priority rule out of the hands of the subordinated debt. This option may be useful in plans where distribution to existing equity is desired.

Advocates for this combined classification approach usually argue that the subordination agreement in question contained in the indenture is strictly between the senior and subordinated debt holders and does *not* involve the debtor. In other words, the senior debt holders and subordinated debt holders are similarly situated with respect to the debtor; they are just debts that happen to have a private (subordination) contract with each other. On a consensual basis, senior debt holders, able to enforce their subordination agreement against the subordinated debt holders, may be willing to accept a payout below that which will assure a return to the subordinated debt holders to speed confirmation of a consensual plan. These senior creditors then can claim all of the money allocated to themselves plus all of the money initially allocated to those creditors who are subordinated to their position. Similarly, neutral creditors (typically trade creditors) might be willing to accept a lower payout to ensure the continued existence of a current customer.

Discussions often become heated over the classification issue for subordinated debt in workout scenarios both prebankruptcy and postbankruptcy. Clear answers to the powers of the absolute priority rule often are absent. Of course, classification issues sometimes become moot if equity is not retaining an interest under a plan and the subordinated debt holders are "out of the money" (i.e., under a liquidation scenario, no distributions would be available for the benefit of junior unsecured creditors in any event). When determining the position of unsecured debt under a liquidation analysis, investment bankers sometimes will allocate "relative values" to subordinated debt, particularly where multiple layers of subordinated debt exist. This analysis may assign value to subordinated debt issues even though all subordinated debt is out of the money (presumably, based on an analysis incorporating the results of the workout/bankruptcy "dynamics"). So, despite accounting results to the contrary, the "dynamics" of bankruptcy often yield returns to deeply subordinated and deeply out-of-the-money paper.

A plan proponent also may attempt to reduce the subordinated debt holders' leverage by enforcing indenture provisions assigning the right to vote subordinated claims to the senior debt holders. This technique has been attempted only where the underlying subordination agreement provides for the assignment of the subordinated claim to the senior creditor when senior debt is in default.

In yet a third approach plan, proponents are increasingly utilizing what might be called the "alternative plan" or "either/or" plan to limit the leverage of subordinated debt. Under this scenario, proponents file a plan setting forth some modest payout for subordinated debt. However, the plan also will provide that in the event the subordinated debt class rejects the plan, the class will receive a starkly different treatment:

1. The subordination provisions of the subordination agreement, otherwise released under the plan, will remain in effect on rejection by the subordinated class. Senior debt holders then would be able to enforce their subordination agreements against the subordinated debt holders (outside the bankruptcy court if necessary) and
2. The subordinated debt holders and all junior claims and interest holders receive *no distributions* under the plan on rejection by the class.

Faced with this choice, consensual agreements often follow. Subordinated creditors thus are faced with a Hobson's choice: Vote for the plan and if it carries and is confirmed, receive a very modest payout. Vote against the plan and if the plan is confirmed over the subordinated class's objection, receive nothing.

Subordinated creditors can, of course, try to defeat not only the vote for their class but also the plan itself and then hope that a new plan emerges that is more to their satisfaction. Usually, however, the lawyers who drafted the plan on behalf of the debtor and senior creditors have been careful to produce a confirmable plan. If the judge has approved the disclosure statement and allowed the plan to go out with the either/or provision as part, the plan probably is confirmable even over the subordinated creditors' objections. Moreover, even if the plan is defeated, the next plan may not treat them any better and conversion to Chapter 7 is almost certain to treat them worse. Faced with this choice, the subordinated creditors frequently will vote for the plan even though they are dissatisfied with their share of the pie.

In appropriate situations, the plan proponent (such as a third-party investor) also may eliminate existing equity interests, thus removing the threat of invoking the absolute priority rule by the subordinated debt holders.

The single most important goal for subordinated debt holders in plans providing for distributions to junior claims is to be able to control the voting of a class. As you can see, considerable advantage exists in controlling 34%

of the class for the holder can block a consensual plan in many instances. Buying 34% of the bonds is the most straightforward approach to acquiring such veto power. Alternatively, one can form alliances with other holders to get to the 34% level. Even more desirable is an alliance controlling two-thirds of the vote. Such a group usually can deliver the class affirmatively (assuming that it also can obtain a majority in number).

The general rule under bankruptcy law is that an unsecured claim against the debtor will not receive interest accruing after the petition date except in the (unlikely) event of a solvent creditor. An unresolved question is whether "senior indebtedness" under a subordination agreement such as an indenture for a debenture issue includes claims by the senior creditor for postpetition interest. The resolution is likely to turn on the specific wording in the subordination provisions of the relevant indentures. The senior creditor's ability to include postpetition interest in his or her senior debt vis-à-vis subordinated debt holders can become a significant factor in the leverage equation in bankruptcy cases lingering on for two or three years.

Investing in Bankruptcies: Summary and Conclusions

Successful investing in bankruptcy situations involves a number of dimensions. Two important considerations are the players and the rules of the game: Who is the Judge? Who are the creditors? What are the assets worth? What is the creditors' committee like? What happens at the first meeting of creditors? What are the roles of exclusivity? The plan? The disclosure statement? How is the firm's value to be divided? How are the subordination provisions to be applied? These are the issues treated in this chapter.

CHAPTER 3

Bankruptcy/Reorganization Examples

What do real-life bankruptcy plans look like that play out all of these various factors that we have been discussing? Let's look at a few examples that come from our actual experience.

Storage Technology Corporation

Storage Technology Corporation (Storage Tech), Storage Technology Leasing Corporation (Storage Leasing) and 16 of their affiliates filed voluntary Chapter 11 petitions in the United States Bankruptcy Court for the Southern District of Colorado in 1984. Storage Tech and its subsidiaries confirmed a consensual plan of reorganization in 1986.

Storage Tech designed, manufactured, marketed and serviced computer peripheral and retrieval subsystems used in information storage and retrieval. Its principal products were high-performance tape and disk storage subsystems and impact and nonimpact printers. Storage Tech and its subsidiaries had approximately $800 million in prepetition debt. Of that total, senior unsecured debt held $570 million, subordinated debt held $131 million and the balance ($99 million) was held by various secured lenders and the Internal Revenue Service.

The subordinated debt of Storage Tech and one of its subsidiaries, Documation Incorporated ("Documation"), consisted of three issues of debentures: the 9% Subordinated Debentures due May 15, 2001 ("Storage Tech Debentures"); the Documation 12% Senior Subordinated Debentures due May 1, 1999 ("Documation Senior Debentures") and the Documation 11½% Subordinated Debentures due May 1, 1988 ("Documation Junior Debentures"). At one time or another, all of these could be purchased at well below their ultimate recovery.

Under the joint plan confirmed by Storage Tech and its subsidiaries, creditors secured by assets of the debtors other than lease or installment sale agreements were unimpaired under the plan, while creditors secured with leases or installment sales contracts as collateral were issued five-year promissory notes.

OK, how was the pie divided? When Storage Tech is characterized, as it often is, as a success for the creditors who bought into the problem, what did they see when the plan was presented to them?

Unsecured creditors with superior rights to the Storage Tech Subordinated Debentures (i.e., claims for funds due on borrowed money) received a pro rata distribution of approximately $83 million in cash, $245.5 million in new debentures and 138,637,726 shares (approximately 60%) of common stock in the reorganized Storage Tech. This distribution equated to a 14.4% cash payout, a 42.1% payout in new debentures and a distribution of 228 shares of common stock per $1,000 claim. The distribution totaled 100 cents on the dollar shortly after receipt.

Unsecured trade creditors received a 12.4% cash payout, a 39.1% payout in new debentures and a distribution of 254 shares of common stock per $1,000 claim. Within a matter of weeks, this also proved to be a complete payout.

Under the joint plan, the three series of debentures were classified as separate subclasses within one class. The holders of claims pursuant to the Documation Senior Debentures received a pro rata distribution of $17.4 million in cash (of which $300,000 would be withheld by the indenture trustee pursuant to the indenture to satisfy the trustee's compensation and expenses claims), $12.76 million in new debentures and 6,471,047 shares (approximately 2.8%) of common stock. This distribution equated to a 5.4% cash payout, a 48.1% payout in new debentures and a distribution of 244 shares of common stock per $1,000 claim.

The holders of claims pursuant to the Storage Tech Debentures received a pro rata distribution of $500,000 in cash, $22 million in new debentures and 34,459,643 shares (approximately 14.9%) of the outstanding common stock. The debtors noted in the plan that substantially all of the cash portion of the distributions received by the indenture would be allocated to satisfy the trustee's claims for compensation and expenses. This distribution

TABLE 3.1   Storage Tech Distributions to Unsecured Creditors per $1,000
of Claims

	Cash	*Debentures*	*Shares*
Senior unsecured creditors	144	421	228
Unsecured trade creditors	124	391	254
Documation senior debentures	54	481	244
Storage Tech debentures		251	394
Documation junior debentures		299	369

equates to a 25.1% payout in new debentures and a distribution of 394 shares
of common stock per $1,000 claim. While no cash was received, these
holders also received a handsome return relative to the postfiling prices of
their debentures.

The holders of claims pursuant to the Documation Junior Debentures
received a pro rata distribution of $260,000 in cash (all of which would be
retained by the trustee), $4.74 million in new debentures and 5,852,197
shares (approximately 5%) of common stock. This distribution equates to a
29.9% payout in new debentures and a distribution of 369 shares of common
stock per $1,000 claim. Table 3.1 summarizes three various distributions.

The point is that the interplay between the junior and senior creditors
over what appeared to be not enough to go around was bridged by new paper
that included realizable returns from the future of a reorganizable debtor.
The securities issued proved to have a significant value after the plan was
approved. In other words, you should not expect to be cashed out on
confirmation of the reorganization plan. That is the exception rather than
the rule.

Suppose you were a holder of subordinated debt from Storage Tech.
What would the disclosure statement you received from the bankruptcy
courts have looked like?

The disclosure statement stated:

4.   Subordinated Unsecured Claims

a.   *Class 4A (Storage Tech Subordinated Debentures).* Class 4A consists of all claims based upon or which have been or could be asserted
under the indenture or otherwise on behalf of the holders of the Storage
Tech Subordinated Debentures, other than claims, if any, in Class 6D

(securities litigation claims). The aggregate amount of such claims is approximately $88 million. This amount includes the principal amount of such debentures, interest accrued prior to the filing date and the fees and expenses of the indenture trustee.

The Plan provides that on the Effective Date, the holders of Class 4A Allowed Claims will receive a pro rata distribution of $500,000 of Cash, New Debentures having a principal amount of $22 million and 34,459,643 shares of Common Stock representing approximately 14.9% of outstanding Common Stock on the Effective Date. Debtors are informed that all or substantially all of the Cash portion of the distributions received by the indenture trustee will be retained, pursuant to its indenture, by the indenture trustee to satisfy its claims for compensation and expenses, including compensation of any counsel or other consultants which may have been retained by the indenture trustee.

b.   *Class 4B (Documation Senior Subordinated Debentures).* Class 4B consists of all Allowed Claims against Documation and/or Storage Tech based upon or which have been or could be asserted under the indenture, the supplemental indenture or otherwise on behalf of the holders of the Documation Senior Subordinated Debentures, other than claims in Class 6E (securities litigation claims). The aggregate amount of such claims, which include the principal amount of the Documation Senior Subordinated Debentures, interest accrued thereon prior to the Filing Date, and the fees and expenses of the indenture trustee for the Documation Senior Subordinated Debentures, is approximately $26.8 million.

The Plan provides that on the Effective Date, holders of Class 4B Allowed Claims will receive a pro rata distribution of $1.74 million Cash, New Debentures having a principal amount of $12.6 million, and 6,471,047 shares of Common Stock representing approximately 2.8% of the outstanding Common Stock on the Effective Date.

The amount of cash that will actually be received by the holders of Documation Senior Subordinated Debentures will be reduced by the amount of Cash withheld by the indenture trustee for such debentures pursuant to the indenture to satisfy claims for indenture trustee compensation and expenses, including compensation of any counsel or other consultant which may have been retained by the indenture trustee.

c. *Class 4C (Documation Subordinated Debentures).* Class 4C consists of all Allowed Claims against Documation and/or Storage Tech based upon or which have been or could be asserted under the indenture, the supplemental indenture or otherwise on behalf of the holders of the Documation Subordinated Debentures, other than claims in Class 6F (securities litigation claims). The aggregate amounts of such claims which include the principal amount of the Documation Subordinated Debentures, interest accrued thereon prior to the Filing Date, and the fees and expenses of the indenture trustee for the Documation Subordinated Debentures is approximately $16.1 million.

The Plan provides that on the Effective Date, the holders of Class 4C Allowed Claims will receive a pro rata distribution of $260,000 in Cash, New Debentures having a principal amount of $4.74 million and 4,852,197 shares of Common Stock representing approximately 2.5% of the outstanding Common Stock on the Effective Date.

Debtors are informed that all or substantially all of the Cash portion of the foregoing distribution shall be retained by the indenture trustee for such debentures pursuant to the indenture to satisfy claims for indenture trustee compensation and expenses, including compensation of any counsel or other consultant which may have been retained by the indenture trustee.

In summary, the nonsubordinated unsecured creditors received a cash payout of 12.5 to 14.5%, a 39 to 42% "new debenture payout" and a 22.8 to 25.4% "share dividend." The subordinated debt holders (except for the Documation Senior Debenture holders) received a 0% cash dividend, a 25 to 29% new debenture payout and a 37 to 39% share payout. The Documation Senior Debenture holders received a 5.4% cash dividend, a 48% new debenture payout and a 24.4% share dividend. Under the joint plan, equity retained about a 13% ownership interest.

The disclosure statement and joint plan each contain a detailed provision regarding the effect of confirmation on the release and satisfaction of claims, including the waiver of rights attendant to contractual subordination.

Do all cases involving several layers of debt work out as well as Storage Tech? Of course not. What does a failure look like? Here's one of our favorites.

MGF Oil Corporation

MGF Oil Corporation ("MGF") filed a voluntary Chapter 11 petition in the United States Bankruptcy Court for the Western District of Texas, Midland-Odessa Division, in 1984. MGF confirmed a plan of reorganization on December 2, 1987.

MGF was an oil and gas exploration and production company. MGF and its subsidiaries had approximately $287 million in prepetition debt, allocated as follows: bank lenders (including deficiency claims)—$145 million, general unsecured claims—$32 million and subordinated debt— $110 million. The subordinated debt consisted of the following series of debentures:

1. 6% Senior Subordinated Debentures due 1988 ("6% Debentures") issued by MGF

2. 14½% Senior Subordinated Debentures due 1995 ("14½% Debentures") issued by MGF

3. Class A and Class B Noninterest-Bearing Convertible Senior Subordinated Debentures due 1989 ("0% Debentures") issued by MGF International Finance N.V. ("International") and guaranteed by MGF

4. 8¼% Convertible Subordinated Guaranteed Debentures due 1995 ("8¼% Debentures") issued by International and guaranteed by MGF

The First Amended Plan filed by MGF classified the debtor's subordinated debt and senior unsecured debt in a single class. The trustee for the 14.5% debentures objected to confirmation of this plan on that basis. Additionally, one of the banks filed a motion to enforce the subordination agreements contained in the indentures. The plan provided for a handsome (noncash) return for the subordinated debt holders:

As a measure to permit distributions to holders of Public Subordinated Debt, it is a condition to Confirmation of the Plan that the Lenders and other holders of Senior Debt enter into the Subordination Enforcement Agreement. Under this agreement with respect to each holder of Public Subordinated Debt who does not seek to enforce any rights as a Senior

Creditor against any other holder of Public Subordinated Debt, the holders of Senior Debt will limit the exercise of their rights as Senior Creditors to allow distributions to holders of Public Subordinated Debt as follows:

a. to holders of Class 4 Claims based upon 6% Debentures and 14½% Debentures, 1.36 shares of Preferred Stock and 27.88 shares of New Common Stock per $1,000 face amount of such Debentures; and

b. with respect to Class 4 Claims based upon MGF's guarantee of the 0% Debentures and 8¼% Debentures, 0.88 shares of Preferred Stock and 19.72 shares of New Common Stock per $1,000 face amount of such Debentures. The remainder of the shares distributable with respect to such Class 4 Claims based upon subordinated debentures will be distributed to the Lenders. (From the First Disclosure Statement)

This Plan Failed

A sufficient number of the subordinated holders determined that they would hold out for more to block the plan. They voted accordingly. Many of the key players were more concerned with what the other person was getting than with what they were getting. After further intensive negotiations, MGF filed its Second Amended Plan of Reorganization in December of 1985.

In the Second Amended Plan, each debenture series was properly and separately classified in a subclass of its own. Under the Second Amended Plan, MGF's bank lenders would have received a controlling interest in the preferred stock of the reorganized debtor to be issued pursuant to the plan. Senior unsecured debt claimants would have received 1.83 shares of preferred stock for $1,000 of the allowed claim, i.e., .00183 times the allowed amount of their claim. A paltry recovery it would seem.

The distribution to subordinated debt holders increased under the Second Amended Plan. The interests of existing equity holders were extinguished under the Second Amended Plan, with distributions of stock previously going to equity accruing to the benefit of the subordinated debt holders. The Class A and Class B 6% debentures and the 14½% debenture claimants (debentures issued by MGF) received 1.36 shares of preferred stock for each $1,000 of allowed claim—i.e., .00136 times the amount of stock for each $1,000 of allowed claim—i.e., .00136 times the amount of its allowed claim. The holders of claims pursuant to the 0% debentures (issued by International) received 0.88 shares of preferred stock for each $1,000 of allowed claim—i.e., .00088 times the amount of their allowed claim. The senior unsecured and subordinated debt also received common stock under the Second Amended Plan in the following ratios: senior unsecured debt—37.41 shares per $1,000 in allowed claims, Class A 6% debentures—33.83 shares, Class B 6% debentures—37.41 shares, 14½% debentures—35.86, 0% debentures—21.52 and 8¼% debentures—21.82.

The Second Amended Plan also contained a provision stating that the plan gave effect and enforcement to subordination provisions and that no class would retain any right to any consideration received by another class:

9.0 The Plan shall be deemed to give effect and enforcement to all claims for consensual, contractual or equitable subordination pursuant to Bankruptcy Code §510. No class of creditors shall have or retain any right or claim to any consideration distributed under the Plan to any other class of creditors.

The Second Plan Unconfirmed

MGF did not seek confirmation of the Second Amended Plan because of a precipitous drop in oil prices. In other words, its core business fell apart because of market conditions while it languished in Chapter 11. The case dragged on. MGF subsequently submitted a Third Amended Plan. Additionally, other parties in interest submitted plans for reorganization. Among the plans filed was a plan by Parker & Parsley Petroleum Company ("Parker & Parsley"). A modified version of this plan was confirmed on December 2, 1987.

The Confirmed Plan

Under the confirmed plan, the bank lenders sold their secured debt position to Parker & Parsley for approximately $40 million, received certain MGF oil and gas interests and certain MGF accounts receivable. With respect to the bank lenders' unsecured claims, the bank lenders received 5,250,000 shares (10.5%) of common stock in the new, much smaller reorganized debtor, or 70 shares of common stock for every $1,000 in claims.

Other secured creditors were paid in full or had the collateral securing their claim abandoned to them. Priority and small unsecured (less than $100) claimants were paid in full. General unsecured creditors received 4,550,000 shares (9.1%) of common stock, or 140 shares for every $1,000 in claims. The various debenture holders were classified into separate subclasses in a single class with no other members. Debenture holders collectively received 7,700,000 shares (10.5%) of common stock, or approximately 70 shares for every $1,000 in claims. Existing equity received no distributions under the Parker & Parsley plan.

The plan contained a provision that it should be deemed to enforce subordination in favor of general unsecured debt as against the subordinated debt holders and in favor of the 6% debenture holders and 14½% debenture holders as against the 0% debenture holders and 8¼% debenture holders. The disclosure statement stated:

Enforcement of Subordination. The Plan is to be deemed to enforce subordination of subordinated debt to senior debt, and no holder of senior debt, as such, shall have any claim against or right to obtain any property to be distributed to a holder of subordinated debt, as such, under the Plan. The Plan does not make adjustments to take into account seniority and subordination between the various issues of Subordinated Debt and does not purport to enforce subordination within Class 3, except in all cases as between holders of MGF Debentures and holders of Guaranteed Debentures. Holders of senior issues of subordinated debt may be able to enforce subordination against holders of junior issues of subordinated debt upon application to the Bankruptcy Court pursuant to the provisions of Bankruptcy Code §510.

The lesson was clear. After insisting on their "rights," the subordinated parties managed to preserve their "rights" to get less because of the diminished return available two years later. The case was a failure for all but the secured creditors.

Wait a minute, you say. You mean that I can invest in this area only to find that any one irate group can destroy or for whatever reason delay a case while the bankruptcy process consumes the debtor and any hope of a recovery for anything other than the senior and secured creditors? The MGF experience created among many of the same players a solution when the problem next arose. Enter the "either/or" plan.

Global Marine, Inc.

Global Marine, Inc. ("GMI") and 11 of its subsidiaries filed voluntary Chapter 11 petitions in the United States Bankruptcy Court for the Southern District of Texas, Houston Division, on January 27, 1986. (Two other subsidiaries subsequently filed for Chapter 11 relief.) GMI and its subsidiaries ("Global") confirmed a consensual plan of reorganization on February 2, 1989.

GMI was a publicly traded company whose subsidiaries engaged in offshore oil and gas drilling, exploration and extraction. Global had approximately $1.2 billion in prepetition debt allocated as follows: secured drilling rig-related debt—$660 million, unsecured debt—$156 million and subordinated debt—$400 million.

The subordinated debt consisted of four issues of subordinated debentures issued by GMI: the $16\frac{1}{8}\%$ Senior Subordinated Debentures due 2002; the 16% Senior Subordinated Debentures due 2001; the 13% Convertible Senior Subordinated Debentures due 2003 and the $12\frac{3}{8}\%$ Senior Subordinated Debentures due 1998.

Under the plan confirmed by Global, the claims of all debenture holders were treated in the same class. Under the plan, *all* holders of debenture claims were allocated a pro rata share of common stock of the reorganized debtor and receipts from any recovery of successful avoidance actions against affiliates of Global; however, this distribution remained in the possession of GMI for distribution to the holders of unsecured claims that constituted senior indebtedness under the various debentures.

Nevertheless, under an "either/or" structure designed to promote a unanimous acceptance of the plan, the plan provided that if the classes containing the claims of the debenture holders and equity interests of GMI accepted the plan, then each holder of an allowed claim arising out of the debentures would receive its pro rata share out of a pool of 7.5 million shares of common stock, with warrants to purchase its pro rata share of an additional 7.5 million shares. The disclosure statement provided:

(i) GMI Class 9—Debenture Claims. GMI's subordinated bonds are in the aggregate face amount of $453,481,456 (including accrued prepetition interest), resulting in Debenture Claims, net of any unamortized discount amount, totaling approximately $399,133,920. On the Effective Date, all bonds and other instruments evidencing a Debenture Claim will be canceled, annulled and extinguished. Although the holders of Debenture Claims are allocated a pro rata share of Majority Common Stock and Affiliate Receipts, along with the holders of Unsecured Claims and Affiliate Claims, they do not actually receive any of such property. Instead, such amounts of the Majority Common Stock and Affiliate Receipts remain in the possession of GMI for distribution to the holders of Unsecured Claims that constitute Senior Indebtedness.

Nevertheless, but only if the Plan is accepted by holders of Debenture Claims and Equity Interests at GMI, and is thus a Consensual Plan, each holder of Allowed Debenture Claims will receive, upon tender to the indenture trustee of the bonds and other instruments evidencing each holder's Claim, a pro rata share of 7,500,000 shares of New GMI Common Stock ("Minority Common Stock") and GMI Warrants representing a right to purchase 7,500,000 shares of New GMI Common Stock ("Minority Warrants"). GMI estimates that each holder of a $1000 bond will receive the following amount of New GMI Common Stock and GMI warrants.

| | Issue | | | |
	12⅜%	16%	16⅛%	13%
% of Allowed debenture claims	7.004%	24.509%	38.062%	30.385%
New shares	528,300	1,838,175	2,854,650	2,278,875
New warrants	528,300	1,838,175	2,854,650	2,278,875
Number of bonds	25,000	100,000	149,600	122,500
Per bond:				
New shares	21.13	18.38	19.08	18.60
New warrants	21.13	18.38	19.08	18.60

As described in section G.2(d) herein, GMI may elect to cash-out New GMI Common Stock holdings of 100 shares or less.

11. Equity Interests

The Equity Interests that are treated under the Plan include the publicly held Common Stock and Preferred Stock interests at the GMI level and the Debtor-held stock interests at all other levels.

(a) Equity Interests in GMI. All Equity Interests in GMI, which include Common Stock and Preferred Stock holdings, will be canceled on the Effective Date of the Plan. Under the absolute priority rule, the holders of Equity Interests at GMI are not entitled to retain or receive any property on account of their interests; however, the absolute priority rule will be invoked only if the classes containing Debenture Claims, Old Common Stock Equity Interests and Old Preferred Stock Equity Interests vote against the Plan. On the condition that such holders vote in favor of the Plan, the Plan provides for a distribution to the holders of GMI's Equity Interests. As described in more detail in sections E.1(1) and E.1(m), that distribution consists of 2,500,000 shares of New GMI Common Stock and 5,200,000 GMI Warrants.

With common stock of the reorganized debtor assigned a value of $1.50 per share in the disclosure statement, this distribution amounted to a 2.8% return on the debenture holders' claims. By contrast, the secured rig lenders received distributions equal to 77.5% of their claims; senior unsecured debt received distributions equal to 39.3% of their claims.

The leaders of the subordinated debt holders had been able to muster the votes of a sufficient number of debenture holders to accept the plan but failed to obtain the requisite dollar amounts voting in favor of the plan. The subordinated debt holders, at great cost, managed to reopen the voting and get one major holder with a sufficiently large amount of debt to change his vote. The equity class then found a large interest holder who had not voted and voting approval was obtained. Clearly, *a fine recovery for the subordinated debt holders was achieved.*

But wait. You must understand how ideas and trends grow in this area. The "either/or" plan having come on the scene, the bankruptcy bar next took the concept one step further. You guessed it, the multiple "either/or" plan. To wit:

In Re Buttes Gas & Oil Co., Inc.

The concept of a multiple either/or plan also was utilized by the debtors in the bankruptcy case of Buttes Gas & Oil Co., Inc. ("BGO"), and several of its subsidiaries. The first of these bankruptcy cases was filed on November 15, 1985. A consensual plan was confirmed on December 23, 1988.

BGO was a stock holding company whose subsidiaries engaged in exploration, development and production of oil and gas both in the United States and abroad. In addition, BGO subsidiaries provided offshore contract drilling services, operated a California vineyard, held interests in mineral properties and engaged in the acquisition, operation, development and resale of agricultural lands.

The subordinated debt in the BGO case consisted of two issues of subordinated debt issued by BGO: the 16½% Senior Subordinated Debentures due August 15, 1994, and the 10¼% Subordinated Debentures due August 15, 1997. Additionally, Buttes Resources Company ("BRC"), a subsidiary of BGO, had issued the 10% Subordinated Convertible Debentures due January 1, 1991. These debentures were guaranteed by BGO. The 16½% senior debentures were senior to the 10¼% Debentures.

The debtors first filed separate plans of reorganization for BGO, BRC and BGO's other subsidiaries in September of 1987. Under the first BGO plan, each series of debentures was classified separately. Additionally, the 10% debentures, although issued by BRC, were classified and treated under the BGO plan. Under this plan, holders of all three classes of subordinated claims were to share pro rata in a distribution of 33⅓% of the common stock of the reorganized BGO.

Additionally, the first BGO plan utilized an "alternative plan" mechanism. The cornerstones of the debtors' plans were an agreement by a potential purchaser (the "Investor") to purchase a controlling interest in BGO and an agreement with the debtors' secured bank lenders ("Bank Group") regarding satisfaction of the debtors' obligations. Under the alternative choice, if the Investor or the Bank Group terminated the Investor agreement and the Bank Group agreement remained in effect, confirmation of the "alternative plan" would be pursued. Under the "alternative plan," no class of creditors with priority below general unsecured creditors received any distributions. The disclosure statement's liquidation analysis demonstrated that no class below general unsecured creditors would receive any distribution in a Chapter 7 liquidation:

2. *Liquidation Summary.*

Set forth below is BGO's best estimate of the distribution of its assets in a liquidation, assuming an Effective Date of liquidation of January 1, 1989:

Buttes Gas & Oil Co.
Estimated Liquidation Analysis
January 1, 1989
(In Thousands)

Current assets	$ 5,226
Property and equipment	200
Accounts receivable—long term	1,029
Total assets	$ 6,455
Liabilities:	
Class 1—Administration Claims	$ 1,162
(Chapter 11 and Chapter 7)	
Class 2—Priority nontax claims	25
Class 3—Priority tax claims	545
Class 4—Bank Group	
Secured	189
Unsecured	3,344
Class 5—Fushion Holdings[1]	
Class 6—Unsecured	1,190
Class 7—Subordinated 16½% debentures	0
Class 8—Subordinated 10¼% debentures	0
Class 9—Subordinated 10% debentures	0
Class 10—Intercompany claims	0
Total Liabilities	$ 6,455
Class 11—Claims of preferred equity interests	0
Class 12—Claims of equity interests	0
Total liabilities and stockholder interest	$ 6,455

1. Class 5 would receive the common stock of BRCL.

The 16½% senior debentures and the 10¼% debenture holders objected to inclusion of the 10% debenture holders in distributions under the BGO plan, and the debtors amended their plans in May of 1988.

The amended BGO plan now provided for "contingency plans." Under the "primary plan," the 16½% senior debenture holders and the 10¼% debenture holders, although classified separately, would share pro rata in a distribution of 32% of the reorganized BGO common stock. The 10% debenture holders, although still classified under the BGO amended primary plan, received no distribution thereunder (these debenture holders were treated under the BRC plan). This treatment, however, now was predicated on a unanimous acceptance by all classes of the plan; if one or more impaired classes voted to reject the primary plan, then no class below general unsecured creditors would receive any distributions. This amended plan also contained the same "alternative plan" contained in the original plan.

The 16½% senior debenture holders objected to their pari passu treatment with the 10¼% debenture holders irrespective of their contractually subordinated status, and further negotiations ensued. On September 3, 1988, the debtors amended their plans again. The BGO primary plan now provided that in allocating the 32% pool of reorganized common stock between the 16½% senior debenture holders and the 10¼% debenture holders, each dollar of claim of the 16½% senior debenture holders would be worth 1.67, while each dollar of claim held by the 10¼% debenture holders would be worth 1.0 in calculating the relative distributions. This treatment of the subordinated claims eventually was submitted to creditors and confirmed on a consensual basis.

By contrast, general unsecured creditors received a distribution equal to 21% of allowed claims (capped at $6.3 million) with the lesser of 2.833% or $850,000 to be distributed in cash on the distribution date and the remainder to be paid over eight years with repayment commencing in the third year.

We have discussed the possibility of a small nuisance-value recovery as a minimum baseline even in cases where the subordinated debt is clearly going to finish "way out of the money." A well-known case in the early 1980s provides a classic example of a situation where several million dollars in value was given to achieve the cost savings of a consensual plan.

In Re Braniff Airways, Inc. (Braniff I)

Braniff International Corporation ("International") filed for bankruptcy on May 13, 1982, in the United States District Court for the Northern District of Texas, Fort Worth Division. Braniff and International confirmed a consensual plan of reorganization on September 1, 1983.

Braniff was a certified air carrier engaged in the domestic and international air transportation of persons, property and mail. International was the holding company parent of Braniff and also was the parent for certain other wholly owned operating subsidiaries.

Under the plan confirmed by the bankruptcy court, Braniff was reorganized and was to engage in fixed base operations at Love Field in Dallas, Texas, and, through a subsidiary to be formed, resume operation of a scheduled domestic airline route system with its hub at Dallas–Fort Worth Airport using 30 Boeing 727-200 aircraft, leased to the subsidiary by a liquidating trust established for the benefit of the holders of Braniff's senior debt. The reorganized operations would be funded principally by Hyatt Air, Inc., which would control the reorganized companies as a result of its investments (anticipated to total in excess of $10 million).

All of the debtor's aircraft, related engines and rotatable spare parts, as well as certain other assets of Braniff, would be transferred to or for the benefit of the senior creditors. Additionally, the senior creditors, the general unsecured creditors and the holders of certain debtor's preferred stock received an aggregate of approximately 12.3% of the common stock of Braniff plus preferred stock convertible into 7% of the common stock of the reorganized Braniff. Furthermore, the senior creditors received warrants to purchase 526,000 shares of common stock of the airline subsidiary formed under the plan, cash and undivided interests in the liquidating trust.

In contrast, subordinated claims of Braniff (approximately $25 million) received 52,000 shares of common stock in reorganized Braniff, and subordinated claims of International received, along with certain other claims and interests that together aggregated approximately $145 million, 180,000 shares of common stock. By comparison, Hyatt received, among other things, 8,000,000 shares of common stock, and 1,402,000 shares were issued to other claimants under the plan.

The plan also provided that in the event the subordinated debt holders of Braniff did not accept the plan, the debtors would seek confirmation under 1129(b) ("cramdown"), and any recoveries by subordinated debt holders under the plan would remain subordinated to the rights of the senior creditors. The plan operated to release any and all claims from other creditors if accepted by the requisite majorities.

The disclosure statement provided:

Class VII creditors are those holding subordinated claims against Airways, including publicly held 5¾% subordinated debentures, pursuant to a certain indenture dated as a December 1, 1966, and a certain subordinated credit agreement dated as of March 15, 1973, with Boeing. The Debtors estimate that the total amount of claims which will qualify for participation in Class VII will be approximately $25,000,000.

Under the terms of the 1966 indenture and the 1973 subordinated credit agreement, any recoveries that such creditors make are subordinated to the rights of the Senior Creditors. Therefore, the Senior Creditors would have a right to any recoveries by such subordinated creditors. For this reason, the Class VII claimants would receive nothing in a liquidation of the debtors. The allegations made by OUCC, SBOCC and U.S. Trust in their lawsuits (described above under "Litigation Regarding the Indenture" and "Inter-Secured Creditor Litigation"), if established, might result in the elimination of subordination rights of certain Senior Creditors. If those rights were to be eliminated, the Debtors believe that Class VII claimants nevertheless would remain subordinated to the claims of the public secured bondholders and the Class VII claimants would only be entitled to receive payments as Class VII claimants from the amounts remaining after the satisfaction in full of the claims of the public secured bondholders.

In recognition, on the one hand, of the Senior Creditors' subordination rights, and, on the other hand, in settlement of claims asserted by SBOCC, U.S. Trust, and the OUCC against the Senior Creditors, the Plan provides that the Class VII claimants will receive their respective pro rata shares of 52,000 shares of BA Common Stock free from any subordination rights of the Senior Creditors, but the Class VII claimants will not receive other distributions to which they would be entitled as Class VIA claimants. Class VII claimants and Senior Creditors will release any claims either have against the other including but not limited to Senior Creditors' subordination rights if and only if Classes V, VIA and VII vote to accept the Plan and the Plan is confirmed.

If the requisite majorities of Class VII creditors do not vote to support the Plan, the Debtors intend nonetheless to seek confirmation of the Plan over their rejection pursuant to § 1129(b) of the Bankruptcy Code. In that event, any consideration otherwise distributable to junior claimants against Airways would remain subject to the subordination rights of the Senior Creditors against the Class VII claimants as well as such defenses to those claims and their own claims as the Class VII claimants may have against the Senior Creditors. The result of the foregoing to the Class VII claimants is that they would not, in all likelihood, receive any distribution under the Plan if it is confirmed over their objection.

This means, on the one hand, that if the Class VII creditors vote in favor of the Plan, they will receive relatively prompt distributions of their pro rata shares of 52,000 shares of BA Common Stock, but no more. On the other hand, if the Class VII claimants do not vote in support of the Plan, they may receive distributions of approximately the same number of shares of BA Common Stock (assuming the Debtors' estimate as to the amount of Class VIA claims is correct) plus shares of Series AA Stock and possibly certain other distributions to which Class VIA claimants may be entitled, but (a) such distributions may be delayed for as long as two years and, as to the shares of BA Common Stock, may be less than would be distributed under Class VII because of the uncertainties with respect to the total amount of Class VIA claims, and (b) such distributions would be subject to the subordination rights, if any, of the Senior Creditors.

The economic realities of the Chapter 11 reorganization process provide a backdrop that generally leads to the payment of some tribute to deeply subordinated debt holders to achieve a maximum return to the senior debt holders. The economic time-delay costs in bankruptcy usually lead senior debt holders to conclude that paying a modest return to the junior classes is preferable to exposing their recovery to the risks involved in allowing the debtor to remain in Chapter 11 for the many months necessary to "cram-down" the subordinated debt holders.

When one considers that the subordinated paper of Braniff could be purchased early on in the bankruptcy for a few cents on the dollar, the returns, while small in absolute terms, represented large returns to those who had the courage to buy.

It's time to talk about the last act. The first scene in the final act of the bankruptcy process is the confirmation hearing. After the announcement of the vote by the voting classes, the court goes through the technical requirements to make sure that the plan has met the requisite technical requirements of the Bankruptcy Code. A fantastic amount of logrolling occurs at this hearing with bluffing dissenters and holdouts clamoring to get on board the plan before the train leaves the station. Adamant dissenters who don't like the plan stage their last battle against the plan. In major cases, lone holdouts face long odds in front of a court that faces the prospect of a major social and public achievement if the judge follows the wishes of the great body of creditors and rules against a small number of dissenters.

The final scene of the bankruptcy process occurs, some say appropriately, behind closed doors. The consummation of the plan is quite similar to a closing of any other financial transaction. In some lawyer's office after the documents that implement the terms of the plan or reorganization have been approved by the various parties, the various groups exchange their old paper for new paper or cash and the debtor gets its fresh start.

What type of securities will the creditors likely receive at the closing of the bankruptcy case? A leading bankruptcy treatise gives insight into the reasoning usually utilized in that decision:

> Consideration should be given in cases involving holders of public debt instruments to providing such holders under the plan with debt securities of a similar nature (except generally speaking, with respect to the principal amount or interest rate thereof). . . .[1]

A. Herzog & L. King earmarked the following checklist of terms to scrutinize if you are to receive debt securities:

1. Principal amount
2. Interest rate
3. Maturity
4. Subordination provisions
5. Security
6. Sinking-fund requirements
7. Mandatory and/or optional redemptions
8. Conversion rights
9. Variations in any of the foregoing characteristics based on various types of contingencies

---

1. Herzog & King, eds., 5 *Collier Bankruptcy Practice Guide* 90.06[5][b] (1984). (Footnote omitted.)

For equity, the same authors give the following checklist:

1. Dividend rate
2. Cumulative dividend provisions
3. Liquidation preference
4. Mandatory and/or optional redemption provisions
5. Conversion rights
6. Preemptive rights
7. Voting rights
8. Registration rights
9. Restrictions on transfers

Because of the inefficiency of the bankruptcy process, which our discussion thus far has highlighted, you should not expect the culmination of the reorganization process to provide any permanent cures for the companies that confirm plans of reorganization. Recidivist debtors are common, e.g., Braniff, Continental Airlines, Wilson Foods. Your goal is to profit from the process, take your profit and go on to the next opportunity. The reason for the inability of the bankruptcy courts to provide permanent cures is fundamental:

If a plan is particularly complex, bankruptcy courts might be unable to determine whether the level of debt in the plan is excessive. Except at the extremes, that question is highly speculative and would usually be grappled with by judging the relative credibility of expert witnesses and investment bankers. Thus, because of a lack of judicial expertise, a potential need to rely on the parties, and the ease with which bankruptcy litigation problems can be resolved by using complex structures, there is a substantial basis for concluding that action in the reorganization court seems unlikely to lead to a capital structure as sound as those ordinarily derived from marketplace bargains. More important, the reorganization court seems unlikely to lead to quick resolution of the problem of recapitalization.[2]

2. Roe, *"Bankruptcy and Debt: A New Model for Corporate Reorganization,"* 83 *Columbia Law Review* 548. (Footnotes omitted.) Copyright © 1983 by the Directors of the Columbia Law Review Association, Inc. All Rights Reserved. Reprinted by permission.

C H A P T E R   4

Estimating Bankruptcy Values

The key to successful bankruptcy investing is assessing the likely outcome (value of the estate and relative distributions to claimants) and then identifying those securities (or other claims in interest) that are most underpriced relative to that prospective outcome. One can perform this type of analysis at any point in the case: prefiling, immediately after the filing, while the plan is being formulated, while the plan is out for a vote, at the confirmation hearing stage, just before or just after the effective date or even just before or just after distributions are made. Significant profit opportunities may be available at any of these points. Frequently, however, the biggest profits are earned by those who make early commitments. Moreover, once you are involved, you can adjust your position as circumstances warrant. Accordingly, let's start the analysis just before a bankruptcy filing. What is happening?

Steps in the Bankruptcy Process

Companies do not move immediately from healthy to bankrupt. They begin by becoming less healthy and then troubled. They may move on to try to deal with their problems outside of the court's protection. If this effort fails, they will find themselves in a full-fledged bankruptcy proceeding. Let's start the analysis just before bankruptcy filing.

A Company Gets into Trouble

If the company is large (e.g., Pan Am, Bank of New England or TWA, for example) the press is full of stories of its problems. Each earnings (sic) report is anticipated with foreboding. First common and then preferred dividends are suspended to conserve cash. Will the company be able to avoid or put off a bankruptcy filing once the next installment of bad news is out? As losses mount, the company's net worth account is eroded. Various plans are discussed—mergers, employee givebacks, asset sales, informal work-outs with creditors, equity infusions from abroad or elsewhere or even federal assistance (Chrysler and Lockheed). As solutions to the problems, these ideas are mostly pipe dreams. Occasionally, one of them will be tried and very occasionally such an approach will work. On other occasions, although a little time is bought, it only puts off the inevitable. The decline continues relentlessly.

As the trouble worsens, the securities markets react. All of the company's securities suffer, but they do not suffer proportionately. The more junior the security, the greater the decline. Warrants become virtually worthless. The common stock falls ever lower. A year earlier, the stock may have sold for a double-digit price. Now it qualifies as a penny stock (priced under a dollar). The preferred stock also suffers but perhaps not quite so much, particularly if it is cumulative. The dividend is, or soon will be, suspended, but an accrual may be being built up. If the situation turns around short of bankruptcy, the preferred holders will have a shot at a major recovery before the common holders see any cash. On the other hand, a bankruptcy filing is just about as likely to wipe out the preferred as the common equity. All equity's priority, particularly in a bankruptcy, is behind that of all of the debt.

The Bonds

The debt securities also will experience a decline. Under normal conditions (a healthy and profitable company), the different categories of debt securities will tend to sell for similar prices. That is, most or all of the securities will sell for a relatively high percentage of their par or face value. Different coupon rates, of course, will apply to the different securities, thus causing some price differentials. The most secure investments with adequate collateral backing them will be able to be issued for the lowest interest cost to the issuer, perhaps within one percentage point of the yield on equivalent Treasuries. If 20-year Treasuries are yielding 8.5%, well-collateralized 20-year corporate bonds would be priced to yield perhaps 9.5%. Senior debentures of a financially secure company would be priced similarly. If the company has plenty of unpledged assets to cover the senior indebtedness, coupled with more than sufficient cash flow to cover all of its debt service, the bonds also should sell at a price that would result in a yield within about one percentage point of Treasuries. If the collateralized bonds are priced to yield 9.5%, perhaps the senior debentures would be priced to yield 9.75%.

The senior debentures are slightly less secure and in a liquidation would tend to receive a lower recovery. If, however, the senior debentures have no collateralized bonds to compete with in this company's capital structure, they should be almost as well protected as they would have been if they themselves had been collateralized.

Subordinated debentures, in contrast, are much more at risk than either the collateralized or the senior debentures. Their subordination clause calls for them to pay over to the seniors any consideration allocated to them up to the point where the senior creditors recover their full prepetition claim. Depending on the relevant indenture, the subordination may be also applied to postpetition interest. Only after the seniors have been made whole do the subordinated creditors get to keep any of their initial allocation. While a Chapter 11 reorganization plan usually treats them less harshly than absolute priority would imply, the juniors do withstand a much bigger hit than more senior creditors. Accordingly, even under healthy conditions, the subordinated debt will be priced to yield appreciably more (a larger risk premium) than senior debt. If the company is relatively healthy and the senior debt yields 9.75%, the subordinated debt might be priced to yield 11%. If both senior and junior subordinated debts are outstanding, the junior subordinated debt would require a still higher yield to be marketable. If, for example, the senior subordinated debt yields 11%, the junior subordinated debt might need to yield 12% to be salable, even for a relatively healthy company.

The less healthy the company, the greater is the penalty for subordination and the greater the differential penalty for deep subordination. Each lower level of priority would tend to cost the issue about one rating grade. Thus, we might see the collateralized bonds rated AA, the senior debentures A, senior subordinated debentures BBB and the junior subordinated debentures BB. Income bonds and still lower levels of subordination would have even lower ratings and require still higher yields.

These differentials are likely to be accounted for in the coupon and original issue price. Thus, as the firm issues more debt of lower priority, it will set the coupons higher and higher so that the issue price still will be near par. If market conditions remain similar and the company's financial condition remains healthy, all of its different priority bonds will sell for prices near par. Only the coupons will differ with ever higher coupons set for the lower priority issues.

In a more realistic situation, the bonds will have been issued at different times under different market (interest-rate) conditions requiring different coupons at issue. They also will have different maturities. Thus, their market prices will reflect these differences. Nonetheless, most of the bonds probably will sell within a range of about 20 points of each other. Some bonds might sell near par and others in the 80s, but all are selling into a market that expects them to continue paying interest and to repay principal at maturity. Special features such as a conversion option, call feature, sinking-fund provision or different maturity date may impact the pricing on specific issues. This situation is typical before the firm starts getting into trouble. All of its bonds are selling for relatively high prices (close to par) but with different coupons and yields to maturity that reflect their different priorities.

Problems Begin To Surface

Now the company starts encountering some financial difficulties. Initially, perhaps, all that is observable from the outside is that reported earnings are declining. As long as earnings remain positive, things may seem satisfactory. Under the surface, however, cash is getting scarce. Maybe accounting tricks can hide the problem from the investment community for a while. Inventories probably are building up, but no markdown is taken on the older (out-of-style, technologically obsolete) items. Perhaps depreciation rates are reduced (the useful life estimate is extended, straight line is used rather than accelerated). Other assets may not have been written down to their true economic value. Some operations are discontinued, but the reserves established for the shutdown facilities are inadequate or nonexistent. Other money-losing operations are kept going to avoid calling attention to the company's festering problems. Payments to creditors are slowed and payables start to accumulate. Research and development (R&D), marketing and product-development spending is cut back. Support staffs are cut. Service and quality deteriorates.

Consequently, a very short-term focus emerges. The company is robbing Peter to pay Paul. Paul is a squeaky wheel, while Peter can be put off. But even Peter eventually comes home to roost. Sooner or later, the firm has to acknowledge two major related problems. First, it is suffering substantial losses and the consequent erosion of its net worth. Second, and of more immediate concern, the company is running short on liquidity and, consequently, is having trouble paying its bills. Credit sources are drying up and the bills keep mounting. Large interest payments get more and more difficult to make. Any scheduled principal payments become more and more of a challenge to refinance or roll over. Trade creditors get nervous and may start demanding cash on delivery or increases in letters of credit.

As all of this bad news is coming out, what happens to the bonds? Clearly, they react negatively to the news that their issuer is getting into deeper and deeper financial difficulty. They do not decline proportionately, however: the lower the priority, the greater the decline. Prior to a bankruptcy filing, the typical decline for a troubled company might be as follows: Collateralized bonds are down 30%, senior debentures are down 50%, senior subordinated debentures are down 80% and junior subordinated debentures are down 90%. Obviously, reactions can be varied, but these figures are representative.

Chapter 11 Filing

Next, the company files for Chapter 11 protection. While the market probably anticipated the filing, the confirmation of the need to file is a further negative for the company and its creditors. Prior to the filing, some chance remained for an out-of-court workout. Now the expenses of a bankruptcy are unavoidable. Thus, the market prices for the firm's bonds are likely to decline further. Moreover, in Chapter 11 or 7, all creditors' interest effectively stops accruing.

Consistent with our previous discussion, just prior to filing, we may have seen the following price structure: collateralized bonds, 70; senior bonds, 50; senior subordinated, 20 and junior subordinated, 10. To complete the picture, the preferred stock was trading at 2 (par of 50) and the common stock at ½ (down from 40).

Immediately following the filing, price reaction to filing Chapter 11 is as follows: The collateralized bonds fall to 65, senior bonds to 40, senior subordinated to 10, junior subordinated to 3, the preferred stock to 1¼ and the common stock to $\frac{3}{8}$. Even at these low prices, the stock probably is overpriced relative to the debt securities. Any scenario that provides much upside for the stock will make the bonds worth a lot more than these prices. On the other hand, many other scenarios wipe out the shareholders entirely while leaving something (often a handsome profit) for the bondholders (who may buy at these knockdown prices). On a risk-return basis, the bonds are almost certainly a better buy than the stock. But at this point, are they a good buy? This is the key question.

Assessing the Initial Situation

Suppose you have been following the situation and now you are ready to act. What do you do? You will need to try to assess the worst-case scenario and what it means for each security. Does the situation offer promise and if so, which security is most attractive? This is where some real detective work is called for. Reliable information is scarce. However, you have to make do the best you can.

You should quickly collect all of the publicly available information. Call the company and ask it to send you each of the following: the most recent 10-K, 10-Q, proxy statement and any 8-Ks and press releases that it may have issued during the past six months. You also may want to see the registration statements on any recently issued securities. Expect to find some holes and some dated materials. Still, this may be the best you can obtain initially. Later, you can start accessing the court filings. At the outset, prefiling documents will be all you have to work with. This is OK, for this is pretty much all that is available at this stage. You want to understand the publicly available information as well as you can. Remember that in the land of the blind, the one-eyed man is king.

Evaluate the Assets

Once you have these documents, what do you do? You probably will have three to six inches of material, perhaps more. Do not become over-whelmed. Most likely, much of it is out of date anyway. What you really want is a realistic balance sheet for your potential investment. Start with the company's last report (probably the 10-Q filed the quarter before it failed). Now you want to make some quick adjustments. First, focus on the asset side. If you see an entry for goodwill or deferred organization cost, mark through it. A company that has to file for bankruptcy has no goodwill (but perhaps some ill will). Similarly, mark through any capitalized expenses or other intangibles. Most intangibles have little or no value in a bankruptcy, particularly in a liquidation.

Now examine the other asset categories one by one. Take a hard-nosed view of each one. What are they really worth in a liquidation? Granted, cash is cash, but the real value of everything else is suspect. Even the cash number is suspect if the balance sheet is relatively old. Much of that money may have gone out the door (paying the most immediately pressing bills) as the bankruptcy filing approached. Accounts receivables probably are worth close to their stated value but only if the obligator itself is solvent. Look for any problems. Trouble often breeds more trouble.

In 1991, for example, Tonka was having problems and one of its biggest customers, Child World, had filed for bankruptcy. If retailers are in trouble, those who supply them also will be affected. Thus, Tonka's receivable from Child World was a very questionable asset. Look for these special situations and make appropriate adjustments.

Next, examine marketable securities. If this information is not contained in the body of the report, check the footnotes for cost and market. By the way, the footnotes are a key part of a financial statement. They should be read carefully for the information that they contain. Always use market values. If a breakdown is given regarding what specifically is owned, check current prices. Total these up and compare this figure with the end-of-quarter report. Use the most recent value. Mark that number down by some percentage for the cost of liquidating the position. If the holdings are Treasuries or some other easy-to-sell portfolio of securities, the selling costs will be modest. On the other hand, if company X owns 10% of the outstanding shares of company Y, realize that such a large block of Company Y's stock may not be easy to sell. To be conservative, mark down the current price by some substantial discount. Circumstances differ, but perhaps a 10 to 20% haircut would be appropriate in typical situations, with deeper discounts appropriate for real estate and partnership interests, which will be discussed shortly. In other situations, however, the position may be salable at a premium, particularly if the position is controlling. Sometimes the company itself or another large shareholder will be interested in the block. Find out what you can about this other company.

Now move on to notes and mortgages receivable and the like. These are valued on the balance sheet on a going-concern basis. They probably were executed to facilitate an earlier transaction. What would their value be in a forced sale? Again, a discount usually is called for. Are the note and mortgage originators sound? How good is the collateral if any? Are the interest rates at market levels? Are the instruments in economic units that are sufficiently large to be attractive to a buyer? Does a meaningful secondary market exist for such assets? If so, how liquid is it? A discount of 5% might be appropriate in some situations, while 30% or more is needed in other circumstances.

Inventories are another tricky area. Make separate analyses of raw materials, work in process and finished goods. Raw-materials inventory may well be worth close to its cost if the market is active, well defined and easy to buy and sell in. The more commoditylike the raw material is, the more salable it is (i.e., steel, copper, etc.). The raw materials may even be worth a premium if the last in, first out (LIFO) method is used and materials prices have gone up. On the other hand, every case is different. Evaluate the market itself. Raw materials always are easier to buy than to sell. Finished-goods inventories usually are much more difficult to evaluate. If inventory levels have been growing, that is a sign of a problem. Liquidating them is sure to require a markdown. Perhaps fire-sale prices will be required to move them. For example, you could be dealing with a farm-implements manufacturer in the midst of an agricultural depression. On the other hand, some highly sought-after finished-goods inventories may be worth close to their cost values. Again, check the market. What does the trade think? Is technological or stylistic obsolescence a problem? If so, big markdowns are in order.

Work-in-process inventories and incomplete projects (for example, a half-built shopping mall) are among the toughest assets to value. A bankruptcy filing is likely to cause all types of problems for such incomplete projects or production runs. These assets are likely to have relatively little value in an intermediate stage, but many barriers stand in the way of their completion. To value them, you have to assess the value if incomplete, the cost of completing them, their value if complete and the likelihood of completion. If completion is unlikely, their value is minimal. If turning them into a finished product or project offers the greatest chance of recovery, you must make three estimates: the value of the finished items, the cost of completing them and the time required. Be conservative with each estimate. Every job tends to be more difficult to perform when operating in bankruptcy.

Next, assess real estate holdings. First, check for prior or senior mortgages. These can be troublesome. A building could be carried on the books for $10 million. You might wonder to yourself how bad could things get? Maybe it is worth $7 or $8 million or at least $5 million. But suppose the book value on the building is $50 million with a $40-million mortgage against it. That $10 million in equity is at a much greater risk with a lot of debt in front of it. In bankruptcy, the owners may not be able to service the mortgage. The same circumstances that put the owner into bankruptcy may have caused the building's value to deteriorate. The company's equity in the building could quickly evaporate. The same principle applies to any other assets with prior liens, such as airplanes or railroad rolling stock with equipment trust certificate liens. Undeveloped land is another tough area to evaluate. In a distress sale, such property has very little value. With time and money to develop it, the value could be substantial. Bankrupt companies, however, rarely have the resources to develop risky ventures.

Now look at the plant and equipment. Most plant and equipment usually has rather specialized uses. It may be essential to the (now-bankrupt) company's operations, but in a distress sale, it has little value to anyone else. Again, the same problems that brought the company down could be hurting the market for its specialized assets. For example, when the oil market collapsed, so did the market for drilling rigs. When crude oil fell to $10 to $12 a barrel, rigs weren't even worth scrap metal.

Raw undeveloped land, mineral rights, closed-up mine shafts, discontinued facilities and any other unproductive assets are likely to be a drag on the market. In fact, they may be worthless. Facilities associated with toxic-waste dumps and buildings with asbestos problems are likely to have negative values. If you have any hint of such problems, check into it. These exposures can constitute a major liability.

Investments in subsidiaries and affiliates must be evaluated on a case-by-case basis. Sometimes the parent experiences financial difficulty and the subsidiaries continue to prosper. At other times, the parent's problems are reflected in the subsidiaries as well. What does the profit-and-loss (P&L) statement for the subsidiary look like? Does the subsidiary depend on the parent for capital or as a customer or supplier? Can the enterprise stand on its own? Each case is different. You must realize, however, that a bankrupt estate seldom gets top dollar even for its crown jewels.

Did we miss any odds and ends? Patents and trademarks are intangibles with usually little value in liquidation. But let's not go too fast. Some assets' values are hidden or understated. Some things are worth far more than their book values. Airlines, for example, may have airport gate rights or landing slots that are quite valuable. TV and radio stations have allocated public broadcast frequencies that may be worth far more than the values carried on the books. Similarly, cable TV and cellular telephone franchises have considerable value based on their rights to operate. Note, however, that if these types of rights and franchises were recently acquired, they may conversely be carried on the books at inflated values. Railroads may own land (from 19th-century land grants or downtown terminal sites) worth far more than their book valuations. Oil and gas companies may be carrying their proven reserves at $3 or $5 a barrel when the market is several times that level. Some very old historical real estate values may be only a small fraction of the actual market value. Long-term leaseholds may be at rental rates well below the market. If so, they may have considerable value if they are transferrable. Pension funds may be overfunded and therefore contain a substantial surplus. Some troubled companies may have large tax refunds in process. Net operating loss (NOL) carryforwards may have some value if they can be preserved and eventually utilized to offset subsequent income. Franchises (e.g., a Coca Cola bottling company or a McDonald's hamburger franchise) are other potential sources of value. But each case is different.

First, take a hard-nosed view of assets and then look for the upside. Come up with a valuation range. Under a fire-sale liquidation, the assets would bring in X. With a better market environment and viewed as a going concern, the company would be worth Y.

Evaluate the Liabilities

Now let's evaluate the liability side. Be careful. Don't let any contingent liabilities go unnoticed. Unfunded pension obligations could be a big over-hang. The Employee Retirement Income Security Act (ERISA) puts these claims ahead of all other creditor claims. Also expect legal and other administrative fees and taxes to take a big chunk off the top. Check for guarantees as well as damage and other claims arising from unresolved lawsuits. Next, list all the ordinary creditor claims: pension claims, bank debt, senior bond debt, trade credits, employee claims, subordinated debt, debt to subsidiaries, tax claims, lease obligations. Put each debt in its proper order of priority.

Now compare the asset range with the liability range. Under absolute priority, who would get paid what? If the going-concern value is used, what percentage of total liabilities is covered?

Estimate the Payout

Now the really tough call must be made. What is the probable outcome of the case? If the company is likely to be liquidated, the analysis is relatively straightforward. How much would the seniormost debt be slated to receive in a simple liquidation? Suppose this debt is 90% of the senior creditors' claim. This means that the rest of the creditors are out of the money. They may negotiate some consideration, but don't count on much.

Take a hard look at the senior and subordinated obligations. What is the ratio of the market price to the expected outcome? Suppose the seniors trade for 65 and your analyses predict they should get 90 in a liquidation. Is that a buy? Probably not, at least not early in the case. Remember that you will receive no interest on your investment while you wait. The junior debt holders may make enough noise to get something (thereby reducing the senior recovery) and markets for the company's assets could deteriorate. Paying 65 cents on the dollar to get a possible 25-cent appreciation probably is not worth the risk and wait (unless the risk is minimal and only a short wait is expected.) Moreover, a costly administration of the estate could erode values substantially. On the other hand, if bonds sell for 30 or 40 cents on the dollar, the price may be right. Investing 30 or 40 cents on the dollar to get possibly double or triple the amount back in perhaps a year is an attractive return given the risks. Assess the likely wait and risks and then act accordingly.

The case gets much more complicated when you consider the going-concern scenario. Suppose the company as a going concern is worth 80% of its outstanding (prebankruptcy) debt obligations. How you might come up with this assessment is a story in itself. Suppose, however, that the reorganized firm can produce operating income of some amount of Z dollars, and otherwise similar firms sell for a multiple of five times their operating income. Then this firm might have a valuation of perhaps four Z dollars. The lower multiple (four rather than five) is appropriate because of the higher risks associated with projections for a firm coming out of bankruptcy. In fact, a multiple of three times the operating earnings might be even more appropriate.

Now look at the classification of creditors. Suppose the total creditor claims break down as follows: seniors are 30%, trade creditors 10%, senior subordinated 30% and junior subordinated 30%. How is the pie likely to be divided? If this were a liquidation accomplished within Chapter 7 with absolute priority applying, the results would be obvious. First, administrative and tax claims would be paid. These are the claims arising out of administrating and liquidating the estate. Lawyers, accountants, appraisers, trustees and the like will each reduce their fees. Moreover, in a liquidation, the sale will not bring in so much as the firm might be worth as a going concern.

Assume that the firm sells for 75% of its going-concern value. This works out to 60% of creditor claims ($.75 \times .80 = .60$). Depending on market conditions and the effectiveness of the selling effort, the actual discount required to sell the company could be more or less than this assumed 25%. Administrative claims will come off the top. These claims could easily take an amount equal to 10% of the creditor claims. That leaves 50% ($.60 - .10 = .50$) to go to the creditors. The seniors get their 30%, leaving 20% for the trade creditors and senior subordinated creditors. If trade creditors are judged also to be fully senior, they will get their 10%, while senior subordinated will get the remaining sum. Because they had claims equal to 30% of the total of the creditor claims but only 10% of this amount is left for them, their recovery equals one-third of their claims. One also should take into account the likelihood that the liquidation process will be time-consuming. Unsecured creditors usually accrue no postpetition interest while they wait for the last move through the courts. Creditors and equity holders who are junior to the senior subordinated creditors technically would receive nothing under absolute priority.

Negotiating a Consensual Plan

Now, rather than considering a liquidation in Chapter 7, let's see what might happen in a reorganization coming out of Chapter 11. A consensual plan probably will need to provide something for all of the creditors and perhaps even something for the shareholders to succeed in a short time period. If the NOL carryforward is to be preserved, the shareholders will have to be left with more of the common stock of the reorganized firm than their priority often would indicate. The seniors, at the same time, will insist on coming out whole or nearly so and the shareholders also will demand something. The tough question is determining how well the intermediate debt will fare. Those investment categories in the middle probably are where the reward-risk ratio tends to be highest. Let's return to the earlier case immediately following the filing. The senior bonds are at 40, senior subordinated at 10 and junior subordinated at 3. These prices are totally hypothetical, but they are useful for illustrating the analysis.

Again, we assume a valuation of the company equal to 80% of its creditor claims. Rather than a liquidation sale, however, we assume that its debt and equity securities are distributed to the old investors (bondholders and stockholders). We might see a negotiated plan provide something like the following: Administrative expenses, which are less for reorganization than liquidation, take the first 5% (of the 80% that we start with). That leaves 75% for the claims of prepetition creditors. Senior bondholders receive consideration equal to 95% of the amount of their (prepetition) claims (95% of 30%, or 28.5% of the value of their claims). That leaves 75% – 28.5%, or 46.5% for the rest of the investors. Shareholders (who must be left in place to preserve the NOL carryforward) might be able to grab 3%, which now leaves 43.5% for the trade creditors (10%), senior subordinated creditors (30% of total claims) and junior subordinated (30% of total claims). At this point, we have 70% (.10 + .30 + .30 = .70) of total claims to be satisfied out of value equal to 43.5% of the total claims. On the average, these intermediate categories of creditors are slated to receive value equal to 43.5% ÷ 70% = 62% of their claims. The trade creditors have the highest priority after the senior creditors and thus might be able to demand a recovery equal to 90% of their claims. Take this 9% (.90 × .10 = .09) away from the 43.5% and we are down to 34.5% for the senior and junior subordinated debenture holders to divide. Suppose the senior subordinated are able to get 85% of their claims (85% of 30% is 25.5%). Subtracting 25.5% from 34.5% leaves 9% for the junior subordinated. This corresponds to a recovery of 9% ÷ 30% = 30% of their initial claim.

Now you ask, why did the senior subordinated receive 85% of their claims and the junior subordinated 30%? Why not 90-25, 95-15 or 80-35 or even 70-45? All of those outcomes would have been possible. Recall that in a Chapter 7 liquidation, the senior subordinated would have received 33% and the junior subordinated nothing. Clearly, any of these outcomes in a reorganization gives both categories of creditors more than they would get in a liquidation. This unwritten feature is the dynamic that makes successful Chapter 11s. All groups have a strong incentive to agree to a consensual plan. And yet each knows that the other also has a lot to lose if the case is converted to Chapter 7. In the give and take, the senior subordinated group has the better bargaining position. They can say to the junior subordinated creditors that they (the juniors) are getting something in reorganization that surely is better than getting nothing in a liquidation (Chapter 7). The junior subordinated group can threaten to torpedo the entire deal, but everyone knows that doing so hurts them more than the other creditors. At the end of the day, the resulting split will turn on a number of factors: personalities, specific indenture provisions, characteristics of the two groups of creditors, how well their lawyers represent them, etc. The result presented here is one of many possible outcomes. Assuming this assessment is correct, which security is the better buy? Well, let's look at the expected outcome to price (payoff to cost) ratios:

$$\text{Senior} \qquad \frac{95}{40} = 237.5\%$$

$$\text{Senior subordinated} \qquad \frac{85}{10} = 850\%$$

$$\text{Junior subordinated} \qquad \frac{30}{3} = 1{,}000\%$$

Clearly, the junior subordinated has the greater expected payoff as a percentage of current cost. It, however, also has the greatest risk. Our analysis is based on a number of assumptions, any of which could prove to be too optimistic. Many things could go wrong. For example, the senior creditors could demand most or all of the available consideration. If they stand firm, the juniors may be forced to blink. The 80% of creditor claims estimate for the reorganization value could be high. In either case, the junior subordinated creditors could get much less or even be wiped out. If the case is converted to Chapter 7, they are almost certain to be entitled to nothing under the absolute priority that applies in such situations. Thus, the senior subordinated bonds (which would get something in a Chapter 7) could offer the better combination of security and return. If the situation ends up as a liquidation, the seniors still come out about whole (although they would have a longer wait without interest, which is not really so good). Our earlier projections show the senior subordinated would get a 33% recovery in a liquidation (again with a longer wait). This would amount to a ratio of payoff to cost of 330%. Thus, in Chapter 7 and Chapter 11, our projected outcomes become:

	Liquidation (longer wait)	*Reorganization*
Senior	250%	237%
Senior subordinated	330	850
Junior subordinated	0	1,000

Another factor to consider in a reorganization is the form of the payout. The more senior are the claims, the more likely the payout will be in the form of higher quality (more senior) securities. In the previous scenario, therefore, the senior creditors are likely to get a package heavily weighted toward cash and senior debt instruments. The junior creditors, in contrast, are likely to get a package weighted toward more junior paper (warrants, common stock, preferred stock and deeply subordinated debt instruments). Just after the company comes out of bankruptcy as a reorganized firm is usually a difficult time for an investor to liquidate his or her position. After all, other investors have has just received their packages of securities. Most distressed-securities investors do not want to hold these particular securities for a long term. The senior securities are easiest to sell for a price close to their intrinsic (underlying) values. Moreover, a quick sale is likely to have adverse tax consequences for one who bought in at a distress-level price. Thus, even though the junior subordinated debentures appear to offer the greater upside potential, their risk and potential illiquidity may offset that potential.

Clearly, each case is different. At times, the seniormost security offers the best prospects. At other times, the intermediate or juniormost security offers the highest potential reward relative to the risks.

In this analysis, we considered investing early in the case with a projection for the ultimate outcome in hand. Realistically, one is unlikely to have more than a vague idea of that outcome until the case is well under way. By then, however, prices of securities are much more likely to reflect the underlying values. Still, opportunities may well remain.

Evaluation at the Disclosure Statement Stage

Suppose we are now at the stage where a disclosure statement has been sent out and a plan is up for a vote. If the plan is truly consensual, all of the creditor groups will have agreed to support it and a favorable vote is therefore likely. Moreover, a favorable vote, if it does occur, is quite likely to result in confirmation of the plan itself. While such circumstances remove some of the uncertainty, a business (as opposed to legal) risk remains. Specifically, what is the reorganized company's worth and how is this worth to be divided up among its various categories of securities? You can refer to the disclosure statement to see what the company's balance sheet is expected to look like and what kind of package of securities will be issued to you. At this point (before the plan is confirmed and becomes effective), you have a number of options: You can sell your position at current prices, buy more of the security (e.g., senior subordinated) that you already own or switch or diversify into something else (perhaps a combination of senior and junior subordinated debentures). What should you do?

First, find the section of the disclosure statement that reports the firm's anticipated (pro forma) balance sheet coming out of bankruptcy. Mark out any intangible assets such as goodwill and assess the rest of the assets. What does the company really have to work with? Next, determine what is projected for income and cash flow. Do these numbers appear adequate to service debt and other fixed costs going forward? They should, or the reorganization process has not been planned properly. The plan should be feasible. No one is offering any guarantees, but the court should not approve a plan that will put the company right back into trouble once it comes out of bankruptcy.

Suppose that in our example the company has $100 million in debt when it goes into bankruptcy. After reorganizing and paying administrative claims, it emerges with $75 million in properly valued assets. It also has a going-concern value of $75 million. What kind of capital structure makes sense? The creditors will want to be paid, if not in cash, in senior claims, while the debtor will want to limit the company's ongoing exposure to fixed charges, particularly interest. Suppose this $75 million can generate operating income that should average $15 million a year. This money first must be allocated to pay overhead, taxes and debt service. These are contractual or other legal obligations that must be paid. Anything remaining then would be available for reinvestment in the company and eventually something might be available for preferred and common dividends.

Also, the company's capital structure should contemplate that some years will be better than others. Fifteen million dollars may be a reasonable estimate for an average year, but by its very nature, an average is composed of the results from both good and poor years. If the company operates in a volatile industry, operating income might range between $5 and $25 million. With a fixed overhead of $2 million, that kind of range implies that in a poor year, only $3 million remains for debt service and everything else. Reserves (if any) then would have to be tapped to make up any shortfall.

The Securities Packages

With this information as background, we see that the firm should not overburden itself with debt, at least not debt that requires a lot of cash interest to service it. Still, the creditors will push for what they can get. In this give-and-take, the seniors are in the best position. They had $30 million in claims. They will demand and probably get $30 million face amount of the new debt. They will, however, have to give up something. To make the deal work, they agree to accept relatively long-term bonds (ten-year) with a 10% coupon. They insist that it be senior to all other debt. Still under current market conditions, these bonds will trade at less than their face value. To determine what the seniors are getting, one must consider the likely risk and returns and compare this issue to the market. Suppose otherwise similar bonds are trading for prices that yield 11%. This bond would need to be priced at about 95 to offer a similar 11% yield. You can check these figures in a bond book or use a financial calculator.

Next, consider the trade creditors. They did not start out as investors and they have no interest in being long-term investors in the reorganized company. Still, the firm does not have the cash to pay them off. Whatever securities these creditors receive are likely to be quickly sold for whatever they will bring. In this instance, the trade creditors are given $5 million of the same bond as the seniors and another $5 million in senior subordinated debt. The senior subordinated debt also is given a 10% coupon, but it has a 15-year maturity and is subordinated to the senior issue. The company wants to stretch out any need to refinance its debt. The senior debt comes due in ten years, but the senior subordinated debt runs another five years. Again, you have to estimate this (senior subordinated) instrument's value. Because of its longer term and subordinated status (but equivalent coupon), this bond surely will sell for a larger discount from par than the senior bond. Using a similar methodology as with the earlier issue, you estimate it to be valued with a 12% discounted rate and thus worth about 85% of its face value.

At this point, we have $35 million of senior bonds and $5 million of the senior subordinated issued. By themselves, these bonds would require $4 million cash in debt service each year. The reorganized firm has only $75 million in hard assets. Thus, the company must satisfy the remaining claims, without issuing too much more debt.

The senior subordinated creditors are to receive the following: $10 million in senior subordinated debentures, $10 million in junior subordinated [optional 12% payment in kind (PIK)] 20-year debentures (10% coupon), $10 million in preferred stock (10% noncumulative dividend) and common stock equal to 35% of the outstanding shares of the company coming out of bankruptcy. The junior subordinated debenture holders are to receive $5 million of the junior subordinated debentures, $5 million in preferred stock and common stock equal to 14% of the outstanding stock of the reorganized company. The old common shareholders retain 51% of the new stock. To evaluate these packages, we must value each of the parts in the context of the firm's pro forma balance sheet and income statement (see Figure 4.1).

What can we make of all of this? If the senior subordinated 10% debentures are priced at 85, the junior subordinated must be priced even lower. Moreover, the junior subordinated debentures have a feature that allows the firm to pay the interest in more bonds (at a 12% rate) if the company chooses. This PIK feature allows the company to conserve cash when times are bad, but the feature reduces the bond's value to the investor. Cash always beats paper. After some analysis, you conclude that these junior subordinated PIK bonds should be discounted at about a 15% rate and, therefore, are worth about 70% of face value.

The preferred stock's dividend is payable only at management's discretion. It is not cumulative. Management does not expect to pay the dividend for at least the first two years. Again you check around. With luck, the company will be able to start paying its dividend in about three years. As an equity instrument, the security's dividend will qualify for the dividend-received deduction, which adds, modestly, to its value (for corporate holders). Your analysis suggests that the preferred will be worth about 60% of its face value.

Now what about the stock? No hard assets on the balance sheet appear to lie behind this juniormost security. In a liquidation, nothing would be left for the common shareholders. Additionally, no common dividends can be paid until after the preferred dividend is resumed. In all likelihood, the company will conserve cash and pay no common dividend for at least the first five years. And yet, as the residual owners, the common shareholders do have a claim to any upside beyond what is necessary to service the debt and preferred.

FIGURE 4.1 Sample Pro Forma Balance Sheet and Income Statement

Pro Forma Balance Sheet
(in millions)

Assets	Liabilities and Net Worth	
	Liabilities	
$75	Senior debt	$35
	Senior subordinated debt	15
	Junior subordinated debt	15
	Total liability	60
	Net worth	
	Preferred stock	15
	Common stock	0
Total $75	Total	$75

Pro Forma Abbreviated
Income Statement

Operating income	$15.0
Overhead	3.0
	$12.0
Senior debt interest	3.5
	$ 8.5
Senior subordinated interest	1.5
	$ 7.0
Junior subordinated interest	1.5
	$ 5.5
Taxes*	2.0
	$ 3.5
Preferred dividends**	1.5
Retained earnings	$ 2.0

*Taxes may not be due if the NOL is
preserved in the reorganization.
**Preferred dividends may not be paid in
the first several years.

In an average year, the common shareholders should have $2 million of retained earnings accrue to their ultimate benefit. If they could receive that money as a cash distribution, it would make the stock like an annuity with considerable value. They cannot, however, gain access to those retained earnings, at least not initially. The company must build up its equity position if it is ever to be in a position to pay a common dividend. The $2 million is only a projection, and even if it is realized, it will be retained by the firm to accumulate as a cushion against harder times. Thus, at the outset, the common stock is a relatively low-valued high-risk security, with some upside potential. And yet, the common shareholders are the residual owners. If these projections are correct, value will build up over time. Perhaps the stock is worth a multiple of three times its projected retained earnings (and because no common dividends are expected to be paid, retained earnings equals total earnings attributable to common stock) or $6 million. This amount would be divided: approximately $3 million to old common shareholders, $2 million to senior subordinated and $1 million to junior subordinated creditors.

So what do the senior and junior debenture holders receive (see Figure 4.2)?

At this point of the analysis, the seniors, senior subordinated and junior subordinated are slated to receive packages of securities with estimated values equal to 95%, 78% and 25% of their claims. These amounts are close to but not precisely the same as our earlier projections (95, 85 and 30). If we had made these initial projections early in the case, we could consider ourselves very close to the mark with this outcome. Suppose that just after the disclosure statement is released, the bonds themselves are selling for 80, 50 and 15. Again, which is the better buy and are any of them attractive instruments?

First, look in the disclosure statement to see when the plan is expected to become effective. How long must you wait? Time is money. Also look to see what is said about the anticipated markets for the securities. Will they be listed on an exchange or on the National Association of Securities Dealers Automated Quotations (NASDAQ)? Realistically, in the previous example, markets for these new securities are likely to be thin and trading a bit of a problem for a seller. Again, the seniormost securities are likely to be the easiest to sell. All of them, however, will incur selling costs if the investor wants to realize a quick cash recovery.

FIGURE 4.2 Distributions to Debenture Holders

Senior Subordinated		New Senior Subordinated	New Junior Subordinated	Preferred Stock	Common Stock
$30 million in claims	Amount	$10	$10	$10	35%
	value par	85%	70%	60%	
Value in $ millions		8.5	7	6	2

Total $23.5 (8.5 + 7 + 6 + 2)

% Recovery 23.50 + 30 = 78%

Junior Subordinated		New Junior Subordinated	Preferred Stock	Common Stock
$30 million in claims	Amount	$5	$5	14%
	value par	70%	60%	
Value in $ millions		3.5	3	1

Total 7.5 (3.5 + 3 + 1)

% Recovery 7.5 + 30% = 25%

Take Account of Trading Costs

As always, specific circumstances will vary from case to case. Still, bid-ask spreads are likely to increase as the quality and amount outstanding of the instrument decrease. Perhaps the senior bonds will cost 5% to sell (spread plus commissions) in modest-sized quantities. Similarly, the senior subordinated bonds may cost 8%, junior subordinated bonds 9%, preferred stock 10% and common stock 15% to trade. Using these estimated trading costs we would expect the seller to derive 95% of the market price of the senior bonds. Similarly, sellers of the senior subordinated, junior subordinated and preferred and common stock should receive 92%, 91%, 90% and 85% of the market price of their securities. As a result, the realizable value for the seniors would be 95% − (.5 × 95%) = 90%. The senior subordinated bondholders would see their realizable recovery reduced as follows:

Gross Value $ Millions		% Received by Seller		Net Receipts
8.5	×	.92	=	7.82
7.0	×	.91	=	6.37
6.0	×	.90	=	5.40
2.0	×	.85	=	1.70
Total =				21.29

$$\frac{21.29}{30} = 70.97\% \text{ or approximately } 71\%$$

Similarly, the junior subordinated recoverable value (after deducting selling costs) equals:

Gross Value $ Millions		% Received by Seller		Net Receipts
3.5	×	.91	=	3.18
3.0	×	.90	=	2.70
1.0	×	.85	=	.85
Total =				6.73

$$\frac{6.73}{25} = 26.94\% \text{ or approximately } 27\%$$

Thus, taking account of selling costs we have the following:

	Market Price	Realizable Value	Market Price / Realizable Value
Senior	80	90	112.5%
Senior Subordinated	50	71	142%
Junior Subordinated	15	27	180%

Suppose the projected effective date, assuming the plan is confirmed, is four months away. All three securities seem to offer a potentially attractive return. Nothing is ever that simple in investing—particularly investing in distressed securities. First, we must consider the cost of purchasing the securities. This cost could be large or small depending on the nature of the market and the size of the trade. Second, we have to consider the risk that the plan might not be confirmed. That is a much greater problem for the junior than the senior debt. Third, we should note that our value estimates for the securities are only educated guesses. Moreover, the more junior the security, the more uncertain the estimate.

On the other hand, we are at a stage of the case where many of the uncertainties have been narrowed. If our plan is confirmed and if our value estimates are accurate and if the securities can be bought for close to the current market prices, the potential annualized returns are quite attractive. Indeed, the returns for the more junior securities seem particularly attractive.

Assessment:
Summary and Conclusions

We have tracked through a hypothetical troubled company from the stage when it gets into financial difficulty to the point where it comes out of bankruptcy as a reorganized firm. Every real-life case will be different. The example was constructed to illustrate the kinds of issues that tend to arise at various points in the case. One always is trying to evaluate the overall situation and apply that analysis to the specific securities. Thus, one wants to assess the likely returns for each instrument and compare that with its corresponding risk. The process is neither easy nor precise. Many uncertainties are lurking in the weeds. The successful distressed/defaulted securities investor, therefore, will assemble a well-diversified portfolio.

One can diversify within a case by buying securities of various categories (secured, senior subordinated, junior subordinated, preferred, common). This spreading of the money hedges one's bets as to how the pie is split. One can diversify across cases by purchasing distressed/defaulted securities in a variety of cases. To be most effective, such diversification should be across types of cases. For example, the companies should be in different industries (e.g., banking, retail, oil, real estate, etc.) and should be subject to a variety of different environmental influences (government regulations for some and not others, highly interest-rate sensitive for some but not others, high tech versus low tech, hard assets for some and "iffy" contingent assets for others, etc.).

C H A P T E R 5

Quantitative Analysis of High-Yield Securities

Effective high-yield credit analysis involves a number of carefully executed steps. These steps are designed specifically to minimize the risk of invested capital, enhance total portfolio returns and differentiate between actual and perceived value. This type of analysis includes in-depth valuations of assets and their coverage of total indebtedness, market multiples and their relationship to liquidation values, differing interpretations of cash-flow coverage of interest expense and the write-up of assets and increased depreciation expense (or, in rare instances, a write-down of assets and a corresponding decrease in depreciation expense) brought about through purchase accounting adjustments.

Quality research is an elusive commodity. Similarly, the visible differences between an outstanding credit and a terrible one often are extremely small. The margin for error is very thin. Subtle differences in credit quality can be compounded into enormous opportunity and, conversely, enormous capital losses. Indeed, an entire book could be written on the topic of high-yield credit analysis. We shall focus here on those (credit-specific) analytical avenues that we believe warrant particular attention.

This discussion is divided into several parts. The first part covers certain quantitative techniques that are important in the financial analysis of high-yield securities. The second part (in chapter six) deals with those aspects of high-yield securities analysis that are qualitative in nature and thus more subjective and dependent on interpretation. Both types of analysis must be incorporated into the larger context of high-yield security analysis. Sources of investment information are covered in the final part (in chapter six).

101

Financial Analysis

We have divided financial analysis into four primary areas:

1. Asset values,
2. Cash flow (defined as Earnings Before Interest, Taxes, Depreciation and Amortization (EBITDA),
3. Liquidity and balance-sheet analysis and
4. Leverage.

Without sufficient levels of the first three attributes, a high-yield company cannot survive. With burdensome levels of the latter, survival also is questionable.

Asset values, if in excess of the total debt, allow for some cushion in the event of bankruptcy. Moreover, such values represent an excellent appraisal of enterprise value on a private-market basis. Negative cash flows will, however, dilute the protection provided by asset values that may at an earlier time have appeared high. Indeed, sufficient cash flow is needed for the timely payment of interest and principal and for the expansion of the business and to improve the overall levels of credit quality. With the possible exception of certain real estate/asset-intensive businesses, however, most high-yield credits should be evaluated on the basis of their going-concern values, rather than by their estimated liquidation values. Liquidation analysis does, however, afford a certain degree of comfort, particularly if the going-concern assumption turns out to have been substantially in error.

Financial Position

An attractive industry environment, a strong competitive position and effective management are important components of a company's fundamental position. Only companies with adequate financial resources can fully exploit their opportunities, however. Accordingly, much of fundamental analysis involves assessing the company's financial strengths and weaknesses.

Basic Accounting Concepts Used
in Fundamental Analysis

Accounting data is utilized extensively in financial analysis. According-ly, we shall briefly review the principal types of financial statements. First, a balance sheet provides an instantaneous picture of a company's resources and obligations. A classified listing of assets appears on the left side of the sheet. The plant and the equipment are valued at historical cost less accu-mulated depreciation, whereas most other assets are valued at the lower of either cost less accumulated depreciation or current market value. Liabilities (both long-term and short-term debts) and net worth (the residual ownership position) appear on the right side of the balance sheet. Because net worth equals assets minus liabilities, the two sides of the balance sheet always are equal, hence its name.

The income statement begins with total revenues. Various expenses then are subtracted until only the company's earnings remain. The income state-ment helps answer questions such as: How much did the company make or lose in the recent period? How much of its earnings went to its stockholders? How do current earnings compare with past results? Every year (unless the company sells or buys in its stock), the company's net worth will change by that year's retained earnings (profit after taxes less dividends). The income statement and balance sheet thus are connected by changes in net worth.

The statement of cash flows, the third of the principal statements, helps analyze the company's liquidity/cash-flow position. Figure 5.1 summarizes the three types of statements.

Preparing accounting statements necessarily involves many subjective judgments and that subjectivity opens up opportunities for abuse. This temptation may be too great for some managers. Permissible accounting conventions frequently are misused to alter a company's financial appear-

FIGURE 5.1   Types of Accounting Statements

Balance Sheet	*Income Statement*	*Statement of Cash Flows*
Instantaneous picture of resources (assets) and obligations (liabilities)	Revenues less expenses equal earnings	Liquidity/cash-flow position

ance: for example, decreasing depreciation expense by extending the estimated useful life of assets for no apparent economic reason other than to increase current earnings. Nevertheless, the vast majority of accounting statements probably reflect a consistent and meaningful financial picture.

Ratio Analysis

Relative magnitudes of financial data generally are more revealing than absolute levels. A company with a bank balance of a million dollars could be very rich (local retailer) or very poor (Fortune 500 company) depending on its overall size. Accordingly, ratios of financial aggregates have long been used to assess the financial positions of various-sized companies.

Ratios may be grouped into three categories:

1. Liquidity ratios measure the company's ability to meet its short-run obligations.
2. Debt ratios measure the company's long-run strengths and weaknesses.
3. Profitability and efficiency ratios are designed to reflect the firm's productivity.

Liquidity and Liquidity Ratios

High degrees of financial liquidity allow for the advantageous and timely realization of business opportunities. Additionally, financial flexibility provides a cushion during times of economic crises or during a sudden and unexpected downturn in a company's business. Financial liquidity is measured primarily in three ways: balance sheet analysis and working capital projections, available bank lines and cash flow.

Liquidity difficulties usually are encountered in conjunction with one of three problems: slow working-capital turnover, insufficient borrowing capacity and credit availability and insufficient cash-flow generation.

Working capital is obtained either from internally generated funds or, in the case of many high-yield companies, through periodic drawings against available working-capital facilities. Working capital generally is comprised of cash, accounts receivable and inventory, along with smaller components. Projections of peak seasonal borrowing needs must be evaluated against currently available borrowing lines. Bumps against current line limits may be indicative of future sales constraints.

Three ratios are of utmost importance in evaluating working-capital efficiency: accounts receivable turnover, inventory turnover and inventory to sales. They are calculated as follows:

$$\text{Accounts receivable turnover} = \frac{\text{Net sales (1) on credit}}{\text{Average accounts receivable (AR) (2)}}$$

(1) Generally assumed to be on credit unless otherwise reported.
(2) Calculated as beginning plus end of period AR, divided by two.

$$\text{Inventory turnover} = \frac{\text{Cost of goods sold (COGS) (1)}}{\text{Average inventory (2)}}$$

(1) Cost of goods sold normally is used to reduce calculation bias caused by fluctuations in gross margins. If COGS is unavailable, use sales.
(2) Averaged by the same method as accounts receivable, see #2 above.

$$\text{Inventory to sales} = \frac{\text{Ending inventory}}{\text{Yearly sales}}$$

From the company and its investors' standpoints, the higher the level of inventory and accounts receivable turnover, the better. In fact, many supermarkets turn over inventory in excess of 12 times per year. Think of it this way. If they have to pay their suppliers no more frequently than every 30 days and their inventory turns in excess of 12 times, they are financing their entire inventory needs with their suppliers' money, consequently freeing up tremendous amounts of working capital for other purposes.

The lower the inventory to sales ratio, the better, assuming that there are sufficient levels to meet current demand and maintain adequate sales growth. Lower inventory as a percentage of sales equals higher turnovers and consequently lower financing costs.

The inventory turnover ratio equals the cost of goods sold divided by the average yearly inventory. Although monthly inventory figures generally are unavailable to external analysts, yearly averages may be successfully calculated from quarterly, or even yearly, inventory balances. The ideal inventory level differs with the industry and in some cases with the season and business cycle. A high turnover suggests brisk sales and well-managed inventories. A very high ratio might indicate inadequate inventories, however. A low turnover, in contrast, reflects idle resources tied up in excess inventories and/or a large obsolete inventory component.

The average collection period (ACP) is the weighted average life of outstanding accounts receivable. It should be compared with the company's stated credit policy. For example, a manufacturer might have a credit policy based on an expectation of receiving payments within 30 days of billing. An ACP close to or longer than 30 days may indicate that the firm has a problem with credit extensions. Perhaps the firm's credit standards are too lax or its collection policy is too loose. The presence of one or more large, slow-paying customers in financial difficulty also would lengthen the ACP. Although not indicative of a lax collections policy per se, the reliance on one or several large customers can inflict financial stress on a company if the customers themselves experience financial difficulty.

The current ratio is an index of the short-run picture. It is defined as current assets (cash, short-term investments, accounts receivable, prepaid expenses and inventories) divided by current liabilities (accounts payable, notes due in one year and the current portion of long-term debt). According to conventional wisdom, the current ratio should be two or greater. As with all ratios, however, the optimal value varies from company to company and industry to industry and over time. Stable incomes and reliable sources of short-term credit lessen the need for liquid assets and therefore reduce the optimal current ratio level. Indeed, a high current ratio may indicate that resources are being tied up unnecessarily. A ratio below two generally is less worrisome than a sustained major decline in the ratio.

The quick, or acid-test, ratio is defined as liquid assets (current assets less inventories) divided by current liabilities, including interim debt. Therefore, inventories, which may be relatively difficult to liquidate, are part of the current ratio's numerator but are excluded from the quick ratio. Most analysts recommend a quick ratio of one or more. The appropriate level, however, varies from industry to industry, over time and with special characteristics of the company.

Unless substantial losses or a major adjustment (i.e., a large merger) has clouded the picture, short-run financial conditions of most established companies will be found to be satisfactory. Small, less-experienced companies, in contrast, frequently encounter short-run financial difficulty either because of poor capitalization or poor rates of profit and/or cash flow.

Borrowing Capacity

Ideally, one should prefer to invest in companies that have adequate credit availability even during times of peak seasonal borrowings. Additionally, an investor should prefer a company to have either a relatively long-term (three to five years) revolving credit facility or one that can be converted, at the option of the company, into a term loan. Long-term bank agreements allow for a substantial amount of flexibility; they also enable management to focus on the operation of the business as opposed to constantly being interrupted to procure bank lines. The relatively permanent nature of long-term credit facilities helps to prevent banks from pulling a company's credit without warning. Such protection is critically important to issuers of high-yield securities.

Additionally, prospective investors should look for consistency and conservatism in the application of generally accepted accounting principles (GAAP). Extreme and frequent policy changes can indicate an attempt to manipulate earnings. Such changes should be highly scrutinized. Because many GAAP decisions are the ultimate responsibility of management, consistency and conservatism over long periods of time can be viewed as indications of management's attitude toward the operation of its business. Also look for low volatility of earnings and cash flow and a high degree of stability in cash flow itself. The degree of volatility is reflected in the range of historical patterns. The stability of cash flow can be measured by analyzing the percentage of the depreciation component of cash flow in relation to total EBITDA. From the company's standpoint, the higher the percentage the better, for depreciation almost certainly will vary less than earnings, financing costs and tax policy.

Leverage and Debt Ratios

Leverage is analyzed in a number of ways including debt-to-capitalization and debt-to-equity ratios and degrees of operating leverage. One interesting and important measure is cash-flow leverage. Cash-flow leverage is defined as long-term debt (LTD) divided by EBITDA. As with other leverage indicators, the lower the better. In contrast to the "years to pay off debt," this ratio attempts to measure the degree of leverage inflicted on cash flow or, conversely, cash flow's ability to support a given debt level, rather than measuring deleveraging potential.

The actual degree of leverage, in and of itself, is not particularly important, and in many cases should not be of great concern to creditors. In fact, many defensive recapitalizations have high degrees of negative equity because of the accounting treatment for the type of transaction. When book equity is negative, no meaningful leverage ratios may be computed. For perspective, keep in mind that the majority of new-home loans reflect 80 to 95% leverage when initially written. More important than a mechanical ratio such as debt to assets, however, is the intent, and particularly the ability, to service a given level of debt. Consequently, cash-flow analysis and coverage ratios are much more important to the financial health of a company than are the static measures of debt levels.

Debt-equity and times-interest-earned ratios are used to assess the prospects for a company's continued success and stability. The times-interest earned or cash-flow coverage ratio is defined as EBITDA divided by interest expense. It measures how many times the cash flow generated by the company is in excess of required interest payments. Although cash-flow coverage of interest is extremely important, investors should not overlook the importance of meeting principal replacements. Keep in mind that required principal payments either must be paid out of cash flow or refinanced. Large, looming principal payments generally create some degree of concern, particularly during restrictive financing environments.

To assess a company's ability to repay principal, many analysts subtract from EBITDA such items as cash interest, working-capital changes (or add working-capital savings) and capital expenditures. Cash interest is deducted from EBITDA because it must be paid currently. Sustainable growth cannot occur without additions to working capital or increased turnover. Therefore, net increases in working capital (working capital in period two minus working capital in period one) are subtracted from EBITDA. Likewise, working-capital savings (a decline in net working capital), either from increased turnovers or decreases accompanying sales declines, are added to cash flow. Because revenues cannot increase indefinitely without investments in plant and equipment, capital expenditures also are subtracted from EBITDA. The amount remaining after subtracting these items reflects the amount of EBITDA available for principal payments. This amount should be compared to the actual principal payment requirements. Although a company may exhibit excellent EBITDA coverage of interest, large capital expenditures and uneven principal payment requirements may hamper future financial flexibility.

Ideally, a high-yield company's capital structure should be self-amortizing. That is, the projected EBITDA after subtracting cash interest, working-capital changes and capital expenditures should be sufficient to retire debt as it comes due. The ability of a firm's cash flow to exhibit this self-amortizing feature significantly reduces the firm's reliance on external sources of funds and greatly enhances the firm's financial flexibility.

Debt-equity ratios (liabilities divided by net worth) vary considerably from industry to industry and company to company and over time. A public utility with highly predictable earnings, a bank with very liquid assets or a construction company that undertakes very large projects relative to its equity base may have quite a hefty ratio. This ratio could be as high as 2:1 or even 20:1. Companies with volatile earnings (e.g., automobile manufacturers) may choose to have a much lower target ratio, such as 1:10.

Companies generally take on debt in an effort to increase their profit rate relative to their net worth (i.e., return on equity). This is the principle of leverage. A company that can borrow at $x\%$ and earn $(x + y)\%$ on the money gains the difference. Leverage is, however, a two-edged sword. The company that borrows has incurred debts that must be serviced regardless of the returns earned with the borrowed funds. Thus, companies that are planning to be heavy borrowers must be relatively confident that the return they earn will exceed their borrowing costs. Moreover, interest payments, unlike dividends on common and preferred stock, must be made when due whether or not a profit was made in that period. Accordingly, a company with a stable return is in a better position to borrow than one with a similar average but less stable profit rate. During difficult times, burdensome debt obligations may force a company with favorable long-run prospects to liquidate needed assets and, in an extreme case, to file for bankruptcy. Thus, a substantial amount of leverage (high debt-equity ratio) is both potentially profitable and risky. The more secure the company, the greater is the percentage of debt that may be safely accepted.

A company's appropriate debt-equity ratio varies directly with its earnings stability. A comparison of debt-equity ratios over time and within the industry may help assess the adequacy of the current debt burden. A rapid rise in the ratio suggests potential problems. If the increased debt still leaves the firm with a substantial cushion of equity and profitable operations, no immediate concern need be shown. The company simply may be taking advantage of heretofore unused debt capacity. If the firm is experiencing losses or only modest profits, however, its increased reliance on debt suggests possible problems. The company may well be taking on additional debt to finance a risky strategy. Such debt, for example, may be designed to finance a program that the borrowing firm hopes eventually will show profits. Such hopes, however, may not be realized. Even if the firm's greater debt is accompanied by increased profits, the investor must be cautious. The recent profit growth may not be sustainable. At a minimum, further growth would be difficult to finance if it required a still greater proportion of debt.

Debt is not the only type of fixed-payment obligation. In particular, leases may further complicate accounting statement analysis. Purchasing assets with borrowed funds increases the debt-equity ratio, whereas leasing the same assets does not increase debt per se. The long-term obligations are very similar, however, whether the assets are leased or purchased. Thus, debt-equity ratios do not always accurately reflect a company's financial commitments. Investors must look beyond the debt ratios of companies that lease a large fraction of their operating assets. Companies must show their capitalized long-term lease obligation on their balance sheets. Leases that call for payments of less than 80% of the asset's value need not be capitalized. Under current accounting rules, less-than-majority-owned joint ventures need not be consolidated on a company's financial statements. However, these off-balance-sheet obligations must be properly recognized and thus included in a company's overall debt level when they are recurring in nature or excessively large in relation to reported debt.

The absence of an allowance for unfunded pension liabilities also can distort a corporation's reported financial picture. Rising values on pension liabilities also can distort a corporation's reported financial picture. Rising values on pension-fund portfolios are expected to pay a substantial part of the promised benefits. When the funds invested in the portfolio do not produce the expected gains, these resources may be inadequate to cover pension obligations particularly under defined-benefit plans where pension risk is shouldered by the employers. Moreover, many pension plans are underfunded by the corporation. Pension reform legislation now requires that many benefits be paid even if the employee leaves well before retirement age (vested benefits) or the company leaves the industry. These unfunded pension liabilities have a high priority claim in any bankruptcy proceeding. Over the next several decades, companies are required to set up reserves to cover such liabilities.

Some financial analysts prefer to use the debt-asset ratio rather than the debt-equity ratio. Assets equal debt plus equity. Thus, the two ratios are closely related. They have the same numerator. Moreover, both have equity in the denominator. The debt-equity ratio's denominator is equity, whereas the debt-asset ratio's denominator is assets, which is the sum of debt and equity. Therefore, the debt-asset ratio's denominator is increased by the same number that appears in each ratio's numerator. The main difference in the two ratios is in their scales. Equity can be a small or large percentage of assets or something in between. Thus, the debt-equity ratio can vary from a number close to zero (almost no debt) to a very large number (almost no equity). Because the debt-equity ratio varies over a larger range, some analysts prefer it to the debt-asset ratio.

Profitability and Efficiency Ratios

Six important and related profitability-efficiency ratios are: return on equity (ROE); return on assets (ROA), sometimes also called return on investment (ROI); return on sales (ROS), sometimes also called profit margin; asset turnover; debt margin; and gross profit to selling, general and administrative expenses.

Annual averages generally are used to compute profitability and efficiency ratios. Of course, one can use a shorter time frame, but seasonal influences may distort the results.

$$\text{ROE} = \text{After-tax profit} \div \text{Shareholders' equity}$$

$$\text{ROA} = \text{Before-tax before-interest profit} \div \text{Total assets}$$

$$\text{ROS} = \text{After-tax profits} \div \text{Total revenues}$$

$$\text{Asset turnover} = \text{Total revenues} \div \text{Total assets}$$

$$\text{Debt margin} = \text{Total assets} \div \text{Shareholders' equity}$$

Note that ROE is the product of ROS, asset turnover and debt margin:

$$\text{ROE} = \text{ROS} \qquad \times \text{ Asset turnover } \times \text{ Debt margin}$$

$$\frac{\text{After-tax profit}}{\text{Shareholders' equity}} = \frac{\text{After-tax profit}}{\text{Total revenues}} \times \frac{\text{Total revenues}}{\text{Total assets}} \times \frac{\text{Total assets}}{\text{Shareholders' equity}}$$

Thus, one can examine the source of profitability or profit problems by looking at these components of ROE. ROE as a measure of profitability relative to shareholders' equity is a major determinant of share prices. Because its denominator (equity) is smaller and more variable, ROE tends to be more variable than ROA.

ROS also is called the profit margin. ROS tends to vary inversely with inventory turnover. A high-turnover operation such as a supermarket tends to have a low profit margin, whereas a high-profit-margin operation such as a jewelry store tends to have a low turnover.

Profitability and growth prospects are forward-looking concepts. Is the past profit and growth record likely to improve or get worse? An examination of past results helps assess various possible scenarios.

High growth rates resulting primarily from increased debt, higher capacity utilization, accounting changes, cost cutting or price increases eventually must cease. Earnings forecasts should project a more favorable margin, debt-equity ratio, output-asset ratio or depreciation rate only if the projected change seems likely to take place.

One other ratio that is of particular importance is gross profit to selling, general and administrative expenses. This ratio is a measure of management's efficiency in generating gross profit dollars. In other words, how many dollars does management have to spend to generate a dollar of gross profit? Generally, with this ratio, the higher the better. However, too high a ratio might be unattainable and thereby invite other companies to enter the industry and cause competitive pricing unless their entry was blocked by patent protection or high capital costs. A declining ratio would indicate an inflating cost structure relative to the level of sales.

Other Ratios

In addition to liquidity, debt, profitability and efficiency ratios, investors may find several other ratios useful. Earnings per share (EPS) is the company's total earnings (less any preferred dividends) divided by the number of shares outstanding. Several different earnings numbers often are reported.

Fully diluted EPS gives effect to the exercise and conversion of any outstanding warrants and convertibles. Earnings figures may include or exclude extraordinary items and the results from noncontinuing operations.

As previously mentioned, the PE ratio or ratio of the per share market price to EPS is a measure of the relative stock price. The current annual dividend rate (usually four times the quarterly rate) divided by the price per share is the current yield. The total return reflects both capital gains and dividends. The dividend-payout ratio equals dividends per share divided by EPS. A very low payout may indicate a substantial need to finance internal growth, management's desire to expand or abnormally high current earnings. A very high ratio may suggest few attractive investment opportunities.

Cash flow per share is the sum of operating earnings and depreciation divided by the number of shares outstanding. When reported depreciation is overstated (understated profits) or depreciating assets are not replaced (funds available for other uses), the cash flow per share figure reflects an important source of discretionary funds. Because many high-yield companies often report net losses due to high interest and depreciation expenses, the PE ratio often is not meaningful. In this instance, investors should use the ratio for the per-share market price to cash flow per share as the measure of the relative stock price.

Book value per common share equals the company's net worth (after subtracting that attributable to preferred shareholders) divided by the number of its common shares outstanding. One would typically compare the per-share book value with the current stock price. A high book value relative to the stock's price may indicate either unrecognized potential or overvalued assets on a book basis. Railroad book values, for example, often are many times the market price of the stock. Unless the assets can be sold for close to their book values, however, the railroads' modest profit rates justify their low stock prices. Alternatively, the per-share price of the stock may reflect some hidden or undervalued assets such as highly recognizable consumer brand names (patents or real estate valued at historical costs). Because book values that diverge appreciably from stock prices suggest that securities may be misvalued, further analysis could be indicated. Table 5.1 summarizes the various ratios discussed here.

TABLE 5.1 Types of Fundamental Ratios

Liquidity Ratios	
Accounts receivable turnover	$$\frac{\text{Net credit sales}}{\text{Average accounts receivable}}$$
Inventory turnover	$$\frac{\text{Cost of goods sold}}{\text{Average yearly inventory}}$$
Inventory sales	$$\frac{\text{Ending inventory}}{\text{Yearly sales}}$$
Debt Ratios	
Average collection period	$$\frac{\text{Accounts receivable}}{\text{Credit sales (total sales if credit sales not available)} \times 360}$$
Current	$$\frac{\text{Current assets}}{\text{Current liabilities}}$$
Quick, or acid, test	$$\frac{\text{Current assets} - \text{Inventories}}{\text{Current liabilities}}$$
Cash-flow leverage	$$\frac{\text{Long-term debt}}{\text{Earnings before interest, taxes, depreciation and amortization}}$$
Debt-equity	$$\frac{\text{Total debt}}{\text{Shareholders' equity}}$$
Times-interest-earned	$$\frac{\text{Earnings before interest, taxes, depreciation and amortization}}{\text{Current interest payment}}$$
Debt-asset	$$\frac{\text{Total debt}}{\text{Total assets}}$$
Profitability and Efficiency Ratios	
Return on equity (ROE)	$$\frac{\text{After-tax profit}}{\text{Shareholders' equity}}$$
Return on assets (ROA)	$$\frac{\text{Before-tax before-interest profit}}{\text{Total assets}}$$
Return on sales (ROS)	$$\frac{\text{After-tax profit}}{\text{Total revenues}}$$
Asset turnover	$$\frac{\text{Total revenues}}{\text{Total assets}}$$
Debt margin (leverage)	$$\frac{\text{Total assets}}{\text{Shareholders' equity}}$$
Gross profit to selling, general and administrative expenses	$$\frac{\text{Gross profit (Sales} - \text{Cost of goods sold)}}{\text{Selling, general and administrative expenses}}$$

TABLE 5.1 Types of Fundamental Ratios (continued)

	Other Ratios
Earnings per share (EPS)	$\dfrac{\text{Profits after taxes} - \text{Preferred dividends}}{\text{Number of shares}}$
Price-earnings (PE)	$\dfrac{\text{Price per share}}{\text{Earnings per share}}$
Market price/cash flow	$\dfrac{\text{Market price}}{\text{Cash flow per share}}$
Current yield	$\dfrac{\text{Indicated annual dividend}}{\text{Price per share}}$
Dividend payout	$\dfrac{\text{Dividends per share}}{\text{Earnings per share}}$
Cash flow per share	$\dfrac{\text{Earnings before interest, taxes, depreciation and amortization}}{\text{Number of shares}}$
Book value per share	$\dfrac{\text{Net worth attributable to common shareholders}}{\text{Number of shares}}$

Sources of Ratios

A company's ratios are most effectively analyzed by comparing them with ratios of similar companies. Thus, averages of industrywide ratios would be helpful when analyzing a company's ratios. Robert Morris Associates collects data and computes ratios for a large group of industries. Other sources include Dun & Bradstreet and Standard & Poor's. Individual industry ratios may be computed with appropriate data from several similar companies.

Asset Values and Cash Flow: An Example

Estimated asset values may be derived in a number of ways, including multiples of earnings and book value and discounted cash flow (DCF) analysis. We rely herein almost exclusively on DCF analysis, which we believe generally is more reliable than other approaches.

Credit analysis, and particularly high-yield credit analysis, may be effectively illustrated through an example. The following example illus-

TABLE 5.2   Expected Cash Flows for Company A ($ Millions)

	Year 1	Year 2	Year 3	Year 4	Year 5
Net income	$ 27.11	$37.27	$51.23	$70.43	$96.82
Interest expense	100.00	89.17	79.51	70.90	63.22
Taxes	37.41	45.95	56.43	69.31	85.13
Depreciation and amortization	92.94	99.48	106.48	113.98	122.00
EBITDA	$257.46	$271.87	$293.65	$324.62	$367.17
Capital expenses (CAPX)	98.62	105.56	113.00	120.95	129.45
Free cash flow (FCF)	$158.84	$166.31	$180.65	$203.67	$237.72

trates how a company may be valued. Determining the value of, in this case, Company A involves a number of steps: the expected cash flows are valued; the future sales price of the enterprise is estimated; the two expected cash flows then are discounted to a present value (PV); and other factors (net working capital and long-term debt) are factored into the analysis.

A key variable in this analysis is the rate used to discount the expected cash flows. The appropriate rate will depend on a number of circumstances, especially current credit market conditions and the risk associated with the cash-flow estimates. The 15% rate that is used in this example is not unreasonable in a typical market situation. However, any actual valuation is quite sensitive to the rate used in this analysis. Table 5.2 illustrates a number of interesting points relevant to high-yield analysis that will generate the expected Company A cash flow.

Company A also has the following attributes at Year 1 (dollars in millions):

Total debt: $875   Other working capital: $ –66.50
Cash: $4.5   Number of shares: 38 million
Current market price: $23.00

To determine the asset value, calculate the present value of the free cash flows as shown in Table 5.3.

Assume that the business is to be sold in Year 5. How much will it sell for at that time? One approach is to apply the 15% discount rate to Year 5 EBITDA. That corresponds to a 6.667 × multiple of EBITDA, or 6.6667 ×

TABLE 5.3   Present Value of Free Cash Flow for Company A ($ Millions)

	Year 1	Year 2	Year 3	Year 4	Year 5
Free cash flow	$158.84	$166.31	$180.65	$203.67	$237.72
× Present value factor	.8696	.7561	.6575	.5744	.4972

= Present value
of free cash
flow (at 15%) $138.12 + $125.75 + $118.78 + $116.99 + $118.18
Total present value of $617.82
Calculated as 1 + (1 + Discount rate)

$367.17 = $2,447.80. The multiple is derived by dividing Year 5 EBITDA by the discount rate, or $367.17 + 15 = $2,447.80, and dividing this number by $367.17 (2,447.80 + 367.17 = 6.6667). Note that by applying a 15% discount rate to Year 5 EBITDA, we are assuming, very conservatively, that EBITDA remains constant after Year 5. To account for the possibility that EBITDA would continue growing after Year 5, divide Year 5 EBITDA by the discount rate minus the expected growth rate, or $367.17 + (.15 – growth rate). Note the rapid growth in net income (shown in Table 5.2), compared to the relatively slower growth in depreciation expense. This apparently anomalous discrepancy in relative growth rates is a function of the rapid deleveraging that is expected to take place (shown in Table 5.4). The buyer who purchases this company in Year 5 may choose to realize another round of deleveraging in subsequent years, assuming growth continues.

Discount this selling price ($2,447.80) to its present value by multiplying it by Year 5's PV factor of .4972, or $2,447.80 × .4972 = $1,217.05. This result is the residual asset value. Add the PV of FCF ($617.82) to the residual asset value ($1,217.05) to derive a total fixed asset value of $1,834.87.

Enterprise value covers debt by 2.02x ($1,772.87 + $875). Interest coverage as measured by EBITDA + interest expense is 2.57x in Year 1 ($257.46 + $100) and is expected to grow to 5.83x in Year 5 ($367.17 + $63.22). This is an example of the "cash-flow coverage" ratio.

Additionally, cash flow of $58.84, $77.14, $101.14, $132.77 and $174.50 after interest expense and capital expenditures during the next five years will allow for meaningful debt reductions (see Table 5.4).

TABLE 5.4 Expected Deleveraging for Company A

Beginning Debt $875.00

	Year 1	Year 2	Year 3	Year 4	Year 5
Cash flow after interest and CAPX (1)	$ 58.84	$ 77.14	$101.14	$132.77	$174.50
Ending debt (2)	$816.16	$739.02	$637.88	$505.11	$330.61
Years to pay off debt (3)	14.87	10.58	7.30	4.80	2.89

(1)   Termed in this example, "Excess Cash Flow" or ECF.
(2)   Assumes excess cash flow is applied to debt reductions.
(3)   Calculated as beginning debt divided by next year's projected excess cash flow, or total debt + ECF.

A prospective investor should be sure to determine whether or not the company that is being evaluated is reducing capital expenditures below the levels needed to meet maintenance spending on plant and equipment or below the levels necessary to meet expansion and sales projections. Some companies will seek to make their current cash flows appear stronger than they actually are on sustainable bases. In effect, they are robbing Peter to pay Paul. If this is done on a short-term basis in reaction to severe economic distress, such a policy is a simple matter of survival. A short-run focus that is kept up for extended periods of time, however, can be devastating to sales and ultimately fatal to the enterprise.

You, as an investor, would be willing to pay $897.87 ($23.62 per share), the net equity value (private market value)—See Table 5.5—and assume the debt of $875 for Company A, assuming you could control the disposition of its cash flow and further assuming that your required rate of return for similar investments of comparable risk is 15% (discount rate).

DCF analysis is an easily applied concept of valuation. The trick comes not in the math itself, but in the projection of cash-flow statements, the choosing of an appropriate discount rate and the assignment of exit-year cash-flow multiples. Recall that in the example, EBITDA was not projected to continue growing past Year 5. Had we factored in such growth, the valuation would have increased and Company A would appear undervalued.

Company A is a relatively high-quality issue (among high-yield credits). Most of its debt securities are trading above par with yield levels in the 12.60% range. As illustrated previously, the company is expected to have

TABLE 5.5   Calculation of Net Equity Value for Company A

Fixed asset value	$1,834.87
Add: Cash	4.50
Add: Other working capital	−66.50 (1)
Equals: Enterprise value	$1,772.87
Subtract: Total debt	875.00
Equals: Net equity	$ 897.87

(1) Negative because of the cash nature of the company's business. For example, no accounts receivable.

very strong cash flows and is expected to deleverage rapidly. The market is very comfortable with Company A's prospects, as evidenced by the trading levels of the company's debt securities and by the equity market's confirmation of the company's true asset value.

In addition to the ratio of total debt to ECF, the EBITDA margin also is very important, particularly in identifying underlying trends and cash-flow strength. The EBITDA margin is calculated as EBITDA to sales and is an indicator of the percentage of cash flow per dollar of sales. In general, the higher the level of EBITDA margin, the better. Declines over time in this margin generally indicate inefficient levels of cash-flow generation.

Quantitative Analysis:
Summary and Conclusions

We have focused here on four important areas of financial analysis for high-yield securities: asset values, cash flow, liquidity and leverage. Asset values are critical in high-yield research work. Indeed, most high-yield securities can be viewed as coupon instruments in conjunction with short positions in put options on the equity value of the company. In other words, if a company defaults on its interest obligations, many holders of high-yield bonds ultimately end up owning (equity holders exercise their put) a substantial equity stake as the company emerges from bankruptcy. Therefore, assets must be valued properly in advance. Internally generated cash flow is necessary for any measurable degree of credit quality improvement. Additionally, liquidity is important for the simple reason that many companies of less-than-investment-grade status cannot borrow with the ease of most double A–rated firms. Leverage is generally important in all security analysis.

Thorough financial analysis plays an important role in the overall analysis of high-yield securities. Unlike many other types of securities, however, the values of high-yield issues are very sensitive to qualitative characteristics as well. Such characteristics would include covenant provisions, financing structure, type of transactions and the nature (quality) of management. Indeed, such characteristics are distinctly separate from the actual number crunching, but they must be included in the overall context of high-yield credit research work. Granted, the numbers themselves must be acceptable, but the risk goes beyond cash-flow coverage and other financial measures. We now shall discuss these qualitative topics.

CHAPTER 6

Qualitative Aspects of High-Yield Analysis and Investment Information Sources

Compared to the quantitative aspects, qualitative issues are not well defined, and many times they are left to professional judgment and interpretation. In today's high-yield market, acceptable financial figures alone are not adequate to make most issues successful. To be sure, the numbers must be convincing. For high-yield security analysis to be truly successful, however, one must go beyond the numbers. Prospective investors must evaluate management's intent to the degree possible. In particular, investors should analyze the specific issuer's covenant package, taken as a whole. These topics, and many others, make up the unquantified "gray" area of thorough high-yield analysis. We now shall focus on some of the more important subjective qualities of high-yield security analysis.

Covenants

Financial indenture covenants have become increasingly important over the past several years. This increased emphasis results from the propensity of many issuers to releverage their balance sheets and pay out huge dividends to stockholders, or to use their companies as acquisition vehicles, taking on huge amounts of additional debt in the process. Both of these actions tend to work to the detriment of bondholders. These types of activities greatly increase the amount of debt relative to assets. In a few isolated instances, where both the intent and history of management are understood, some covenants can be relaxed or eliminated altogether. Generally, however, the market now is demanding that tighter restrictions be placed on management, particularly financiers.

Many types of covenants have been written, including change-in-control "puts" that enable bonds to be sold back to the issuer if the ownership of the company changes significantly. Additionally, one rating agency has begun to assign certain event risk ratings to a number of issuers. However, much of the actual protection reportedly supplied by these covenants remains untested. Relatively little history of market interaction as yet exists to determine if such covenants actually provide the benefits promised.

Protective covenants are more likely to be found in recently written indentures rather than in indentures of bond issues that have been outstanding for some time. An investor must be particularly careful with older issues. Many of these issues do not contain covenants to prevent such actions as releveraging, large dividend payouts and changes in control. Investors may obtain information about the presence or absence of covenants by reading brokerage house reports. However, in many covenants, the strategic placement of an "and" or an "or" can make a tremendous difference in the actual effectiveness of the covenant. Therefore, successful covenant analysis almost always involves an examination of the registration statement itself. Indentures are much harder and more costly to obtain. The registration statement generally contains the covenant language as written in the indenture. Some of the more important types of covenants include the following:

Net Worth Requirements

This covenant generally requires periodic monitoring of net worth and usually contains provisions that require repurchase of bonds by the company if its net worth falls below stipulated levels. Ideally, the definition of net worth should read "tangible net worth," thus excluding goodwill from the calculation. As noted in the section on leverage, the stated amount of equity, or net worth in this case, is not a particularly reliable indicator of financial health. Therefore, this covenant is not vitally important. Be aware that some companies have intentionally violated this covenant to create a situation whereby they were required to purchase bonds at par value that were previously trading at premiums (above par).

Limitation on Restricted Payments

Restricted payments provisions usually apply to dividends, distributions on, or requirement of, capital stock of the company. This type of covenant is extremely important for it attempts to prevent equity holders from substantially releveraging the company and paying out undue amounts of dividends, while at the same time maintaining voting control. The restricted payment itself is generally limited to 50% of the cumulative net income from some specified date, plus the proceeds realized from the sale of equity in the company. Ideally, this covenant should exclude asset sales and other gains outside of the ordinary course of business from the calculation of net income, thus preventing the company from, in effect, being liquidated through overgenerous dividend payments.

Limitation on Indebtedness

This covenant usually limits indebtedness to the debt existing at the time of the offering, plus a defined amount of additional debt, subject to the maintenance of maximum debt ratios or minimum cash-flow coverage of interest expense. These minimum acceptable financial ratios generally escalate upward over time to provide increasing levels of credit protection. In other words, as long as a company meets its escalating coverage tests, it may incur additional debt. The increasing nature of financial tests is in place to provide for gradual credit improvement while at the same time allowing for continued growth of the business. Thus, this type of covenant is designed to accomplish two goals simultaneously: growing credit protection and business expansion. In a few instances, a fixed-dollar amount is placed on additional debt incurrence.

Typically, certain levels of capital spending and increased borrowings under existing bank facilities are "carved out," or excluded from this test. Rather than cause alarm, this carve-out should be viewed in the context of allowing necessary growth in the business. This covenant is a key determinant of whether a company will be continually used as an acquisition vehicle or whether it will gradually deleverage as its cash flow improves. Again, this covenant ideally should be based on cash-flow coverage tests rather than on static debt measures. These cash-flow tests are more indicative of credit quality. Antilayering clauses also are beneficial for they prevent debt from being inserted (layered) junior to bank debt and senior to existing bondholders. These antilayering clauses also are called the "me-first" rule.

Restrictions on Mergers and Asset Sales

This type of covenant is designed to prevent the company from merging with or selling substantially all of its assets to another company unless the following conditions are met:

1. The surviving company is a U.S. corporation.
2. It expressly assumes the obligations of the company under a supplemental indenture.
3. No event of default would occur as a result of the merger.

To be of any economic worth to the bondholders, this covenant must include some type of financial test, such as an "offer to repurchase" bonds or the maintenance of net worth.

Change in Control

This covenant generally provides for a "put" back to the company at a predetermined level (usually par plus accrued interest) in the event that the ownership of the company changes significantly. Most covenants of this type exempt a "friendly" (with the approval of the board of directors) change in control from the definition of a significant ownership change. Virtually every significant transaction that has occurred during the past several years ultimately has been approved by the board of directors and consequently been deemed "friendly." Thus, unless some financial test is attached, this covenant essentially is worthless.

Financing Structure

The advent of increasing financial creativity in the capital markets led to a dramatic increase in the types of high-yield securities. In addition to straight coupon bonds, many issues were zero-coupon bonds, payment-in-kind (PIK) bonds that pay interest in like securities, increasing rate notes, floating rate notes and a myriad of others. An investor generally should prefer to invest in the straight coupon debt obligations because of their ease of analysis and relative market stability. The overall demand for these bonds tends to be greater and they provide a significantly higher level of actual cash income than do the other types of bonds.

In addition to the actual type of security that is issued, the "use of proceeds" is very important. The company should have stated a reasonable use for the money, rather than simply issuing bonds for future acquisition possibilities or for general corporate purposes. Investors should rarely, if ever, participate in any kind of blind pool offering. Additionally, many companies issue high-yield bonds in amounts that exceed the company's actual need for funds. The company's cost of carry almost always is negative and many times management chooses to invest excess proceeds in (risky) high-yielding securities to minimize this adverse spread. This need for the company to cover its interest spread can be a tremendous distraction, particularly in times of tight cash-flow generation in the early stages following a high-yield financing. Management must be entirely focused on the operation of its business rather than on the pressing need to cover carrying costs.

Type of Transaction

Five different situations give rise to high-yield financing needs and/or high-yield securities:

1. Strategic acquisitions or financings
2. Financial leveraged buyouts (LBOs)
3. Defensive recapitalizations
4. Broker-based buyouts
5. Fallen angels

Strategic acquisitions or financings involve the acquisition of a similar or complementary company by a strategic purchaser. A strategic purchaser generally has in mind such objectives as expanding its market share in a given product, expanding into complementary businesses that have similar distribution channels to the company or some type of vertical or horizontal integration. The ultimate goal is to expand the business and capitalize on real or imagined economies of scale.

Financial LBOs are those that are associated with corporate or other strictly financially motivated buyers. They involve a tremendous amount of leverage, usually are hostile in nature and generate huge amounts of press coverage as the debate rages about the net economic benefit of such transactions. Compared to strategic acquisitions, creditors need significantly tighter covenants in most of these deals.

Defensive recapitalizations typically involve a company that is initially approached on a hostile basis and subsequently releverages and pays a special, one-time dividend. Historical owners thereby maintain their equity interest in the company. Provided management was competent in the first place, a defensive recapitalization actually can be a positive for the company and its high-yield investors. Such a recapitalization provides enormous incentives for efficient operation and refocuses management on the maximization of cash flow rather than on increases in short-term earnings that otherwise would be needed to satisfy a demanding investment community.

Broker-based buyouts are much like financial LBOs for they are typically initiated by investors who are largely motivated by the financial returns. Many of these entities trade portfolios of entire companies instead of portfolios of stocks. In most cases, a large brokerage firm will own nearly all of the equity of the company in question. Again, covenants must be relatively strict for this type of transaction to be attractive.

Fallen angels are those companies that once were rated investment grade and subsequently have been downgraded to high-yield status. Chrysler Corporation is a recent example of a fallen angel. Most often, this fall from grace is caused by ineffective management and poor operating performance over long periods of time. Such fallen angels may or may not come to the market with new high-yield securities (to refinance existing debt as it comes due or for other purposes). In any case, existing issues of a fallen angel will be priced as high-yield securities.

Competitive Position

While somewhat more difficult to evaluate than its financial strengths and weaknesses, the company's competitive position is an important performance determinant. How able is the firm to withstand competitive pressures? How vigorous are its rivals? What is the government's attitude? Clearly, these are interesting questions.

A company's ability to compete within its industry depends on how its resources compare to those of its rivals. Scale economies in production, distribution and advertising generally give larger companies an advantage. On the other hand, difficulties in exercising effective control increase with size. For example, U.S. Steel (now USX) since its inception has been described as a lumbering dinosaur too large for effective control. Antitrust vulnerability is yet another disadvantage of size. Every competitive move of high market share companies such as Kodak, IBM, Xerox, General Motors and AT&T risks antitrust action. Mere size does not constitute an offense, but a company whose own sales represent a very large percentage of its market has difficulty competing aggressively while simultaneously avoiding illegal actions. Kodak, for example, has sought to avoid antitrust suits by sharing new product technology with its competitors. Similarly, IBM's chairman ordered his salespeople not to solicit RCA customers after Sperry Rand bought out RCA's customer base. Antitrust pressure led AT&T to agree to spin off its operating companies.

Even when within-market expansion is legal, a dominant firm has little opportunity to grow other than in line with its industry or by diversifying. For the giants, even diversification-inspired mergers may provoke an antitrust suit. Procter & Gamble's acquisition of Clorox and General Foods' acquisition of S.O.S. were both undone by government action. Thus, some companies may be too small to compete effectively, whereas the existing size of others may limit further growth. Within a wide range of viable sizes, however, other factors have greater impact on differential performance.

Management

Evaluating management is largely an analysis of qualitative characteristics. Useful indications of management's ability are such measures as return on equity or assets over an extended period of time and the overall growth and profitability of the business. Even this data, however, does not adequately address the largely unquantifiable nature of managerial effectiveness.

Therefore, critical variables when judging management are such factors as number of years with the company/industry, actual success in past ventures and existing commitments that would potentially distract a member of management from the task at hand. A serious investor should go even so far as to verify the educational degrees of certain management members when deemed necessary. Ideally, management should have a significant degree of ownership in the company (10% or so), one that is backed by actual invested cash. This level of ownership provides appreciably more incentive than does more modest amounts of equity obtained gratis, or with funds borrowed from the company itself. Additionally, management should devote 100% of its available time to the operation of the business, rather than being involved in various personal business ventures throughout the country.

Although a great number of bright, young individuals have been put on a fast track upward, they generally do not have the adequate experience to occupy the uppermost posts in the majority of companies. Accordingly, the presence of extremely young executives in the topmost positions should be carefully scrutinized. Additionally, companies in which the top executive makes as much as four or five times that of the number-two person may be indicative of a one-person show. Significant dependence on one person sometimes causes a great deal of difficulty in the case of his or her sudden death or departure, particularly when a successor has not been groomed.

A perceptive, aggressive, forward-looking management enhances the odds of realizing a company's full potential. The classic investment textbook by Cohen, Zinbarg and Zeikel (*Investment Analysis and Portfolio Management*) lists the following factors as relevant: motivation, R&D activity, willingness to take reasonable risks, success in integrating merged firms, effectiveness in delegating authority, information systems, use of a board of directors, relations with financial analysts and social responsibility. Other studies have noted that managers who are especially interested in stockholder welfare generally outperform those more concerned with their own well-being. Still other studies imply that highly rated managements generally do not produce unusually high returns for their shareholders but do tend to reduce risk. A broad array of information on managerial quality probably is relevant, but few investor/analysts have the resources to evaluate most of these factors effectively. Past performance is one useful guide although of less help when needed most—when leadership shifts. Investors normally can do little more than read the financial press. A few may contact some managers directly (particularly those of small local companies), however.

Qualitative Analysis:
Summary and Conclusions

High-yield credit research is very labor-intensive. The process is very demanding on the analysts or individuals who undertake it and the margin for error is always very thin and in many cases nonexistent. Subtle deviations in minor details can result in the loss or gain of millions of dollars, most times in the blink of an eye. What is most important, however, is that no relevant question be left unasked or, more importantly, unanswered. Quality research must diligently cover all of the topics mentioned here and a host of others and ultimately an investment decision must be made. The best that we can strive for is to make a reasonably informed, intelligent decision and, through constant monitoring and refinement of our investment outlook, adjust our opinions as economic, market and credit-specific environments change, hopefully to the benefit of our constituency.

Investment Information Sources

Effective investment analysis requires access to and the evaluation of significant amounts of relevant information. Various types of knowledge may be derived from a diverse set of sources. Investors who seek to review all of the relevant information must, however, know where to look. They often must do a substantial amount of digging to obtain a sufficient quantity of data to make a meaningful assessment. Furthermore, the more difficult information is to obtain, the less likely it is to be widely known. Obscure bits of information, even if publicly available, may not be fully reflected in the market price. Lack of a clear understanding of an investment's fundamentals may well cause the market to misvalue it. Finding misvaluations is what fundamental analysis is all about. Thus, serious investors must become experts at finding and assessing the relevant public information on their prospective investments. Accordingly, successful investment analysis often involves an appreciable amount of detective work. This section is designed to assist in such a search.

Investment information tends to be slanted toward the equity end of the marketplace. Thus, a company's annual and quarterly reports contain a letter from management to its shareholders. Similarly, many financial publications primarily focus on the equity end of the market. This orientation is largely a function of the numbers. Many more investors buy stocks than bonds.

Moreover, a company generally pays much more attention to relations with its shareholders (its owners) than with its bondholders (one group of its creditors who are supposed to be happy as long as their coupons and principal payments are paid when due).

High-yield and distressed-securities investors, in contrast, will tend to concentrate their investments on the debt end of the market. Such an orientation appears to put them at a bit of a disadvantage. Fortunately, however, much of the shareholder and stock market investor-oriented information also is relevant to the bond investor. Moreover, high-yield and distressed-securities investors often end up holding equity securities if their debentures default or are subject to an exchange offer. Accordingly, knowing about equity-oriented information sources is quite appropriate for an investor in high-yield and distressed-debt securities.

No one knows more about a particular company than the company itself. Thus, the company's own reports deserve careful scrutiny. Up-to-date trading information may be found in the stock and bond market quotations that appear in most daily newspapers. Even more timely information is available from electronic quotations. A number of stock indexes (also reported in most daily newspapers) are designed to reflect trends in the market and various submarkets. Generalized business and investment periodicals contain a substantial amount of ad hoc information. Several advisory services systematically cover groups of companies. Finally, computer-based information sources facilitate serious statistical analysis.

Company Reports

Company-issued reports often include particularly relevant investment information (see Figure 6.1). Annual and quarterly reports contain the basic financial statements, a letter from the chief executive officer (CEO) and a variety of additional descriptive information. The annual report also contains the auditor's statement and a section on management and analysis of operational results. This section usually offers some worthwhile commentary. More detailed financial data is included in the 10-K and 10-Q forms. The company must prepare these forms and submit them to the SEC and the listing exchange (if any of the firm's securities are listed). The 10-K is the counterpart to the annual report and the 10-Q is the quarterly equivalent. Shareholders of record automatically receive annual and quarterly reports as they are issued. Those who hold their shares in street name must depend

FIGURE 6.1 Principal Company-Issued Reports and the Nature of
Their Contents

Report	Contents
Annual Report	Financial statements, letter from the chief executive officer (CEO), auditor's report, management analysis
10-K	Annual report containing detailed financial data, required by the Securities and Exchange Commission (SEC) and the listing exchange, if any of the firm's securities are listed
Quarterly Report	Unaudited quarterly financial statements, letter from the CEO
10-Q	Quarterly report containing detailed financial data, required by the SEC and the listing exchange, if any of the firm's securities are listed
Prospectus	All relevant facts relating to a proposed action
Proxy Statement	All relevant information relating to any item requiring a shareholder vote
8-K	Information on major developments
Press Releases	Descriptive material on newsworthy events

on their brokerage firms to forward the reports. Serious investors also should obtain copies of the more detailed 10-Ks and 10-Qs. The company must honor shareholder requests for its 10-Ks and usually will send 10-Qs as well. Copies also can be bought from firms advertising this service in *The Wall Street Journal* and elsewhere. Moreover, many brokerage firms have access to a large number of such reports, which they will copy for their customers. The SEC is yet another source of 10-Ks and 10-Qs. It will supply these reports for a copying charge. The Washington Document Service (450 Fifth Street NW, Washington, DC 20001, 202-628-5200) not only will supply copies of specifically requested documents but with its "Watch Service" also will monitor particular companies, industries and situations for its clients. Anytime a relevant document is filed, the Watch Service informs the client and offers to make and send the client a copy.

A prospectus is required whenever a firm makes any major financial move that requires shareholder approval or notification. For example, a prospectus should be available if a firm publicly sells or repurchases a nontrivial amount of its securities, proposes a significant acquisition or divestiture, or begins a dividend reinvestment plan. The preparers of the prospectus (the firm's lawyers, accountants and management) are legally obligated to reveal all relevant and material information regarding the proposal. Most prospectuses, therefore, are quite detailed. Including information that is not required is safer for the preparer than excluding information that a court might later determine should have been revealed.

Proxy materials also contain interesting information about a company. Public companies must hold annual shareholder meetings. Special meetings also may be called from time to time. These meetings provide the vehicles for electing directors, approving auditors and acting on a number of other matters that require stockholder approval, such as increasing the authorized number of shares or changing the firm's legal form. Accordingly, a proxy (ballot) accompanied by relevant information on the issues (proxy statement) must be distributed to the shareholders. Proxy statements typically contain the following types of information: names and holdings of the firm's principal shareholders (more than 5% of outstanding shares), biographical information and stockholdings in the company of nominees to the board of directors, information on committees of the board and executive and director compensation as well as information relating to any issue to be voted on. As with a prospectus, the preparers of a proxy statement are liable for any damages resulting from incomplete disclosure.

Both prospectuses and proxy statements must be sent to each of the firm's shareholders. Similarly, a purchaser of an initial public offering must be given a prospectus. Brokerage houses generally receive copies of both types of documents for their street-name holdings. Most companies will send copies of their prospectuses and proxy statements to anyone who requests them.

Whenever some significant new development occurs that is not reflected in the earlier filings of a firm, the firm may file an 8-K report on the matter. For example, if the firm wins or loses a major court suit or buys or sells a substantial property, it is likely to file an 8-K.

Press releases often report additional bits of company information. Unlike the official reports just described, no stringent standards or set forms apply to press releases. Companies issue press releases to disclose newsworthy information relevant to their operations. Until such information (if material) is made public, knowledgeable insiders are legally barred from trading the stock (except under very restricted circumstances such as trades with other insiders). Some press releases are automatically sent to shareholders. Others usually are available on request. Parts of company press releases generally find their way into some newspapers (such as *The Wall Street Journal*) and appear on the Dow Jones teletype. The fuller story may, however, be obtained only from the complete release.

Reports of Large Stockholders   An owner of 5% or more of the stock of a public company is required to file a 13-D report with the SEC, the listing exchange and the company itself. This form must be filed within ten days of crossing the 5% threshold for any class of equity or convertible debt security. Rights to acquire stock through options, warrants or convertibles count toward reaching the 5% level. The document must reveal the extent of the owner's holdings, the purpose (investment, takeover, etc.), the source of the owner's funds and any relevant agreements (such as those with other investors). The 13-D must be amended whenever a material change requires an update of the prior filing. One such material change would be a change of ownership by the filer of 1% or more. Because the holdings and intentions of large shareholders often affect share values, 13-D filings are useful information sources. For example, when a particular shareholder owns 12% of the stock, reveals that he or she intends to purchase more shares and seeks an acquirer for the company, the possibility of a takeover is substantially increased.

The SEC will supply copies of 13-Ds on written request and a stated willingness to pay the copying charge. The company involved may or may not send these filings to those who ask. Most brokerage houses have access to these reports and will make copies for their customers on request. These and other SEC filings also are available "on line" through Disclosure (a data access service), but the access fees often are substantial. Finally, the person making a 13-D filing usually will send a copy if asked. These individuals normally want to maintain good relations with other shareholders.

Trading Information

Trading information is available from a variety of sources including newspaper quotations, electronic quotations and stock guides.

Newspaper Quotations   Stock market quotations appear in most daily newspapers. These quotations report relevant price and volume data plus certain other items. New York Stock Exchange (NYSE) stock quotations in

FIGURE 6.2 The *Wall Street Journal* Quotation for September 20, 1991

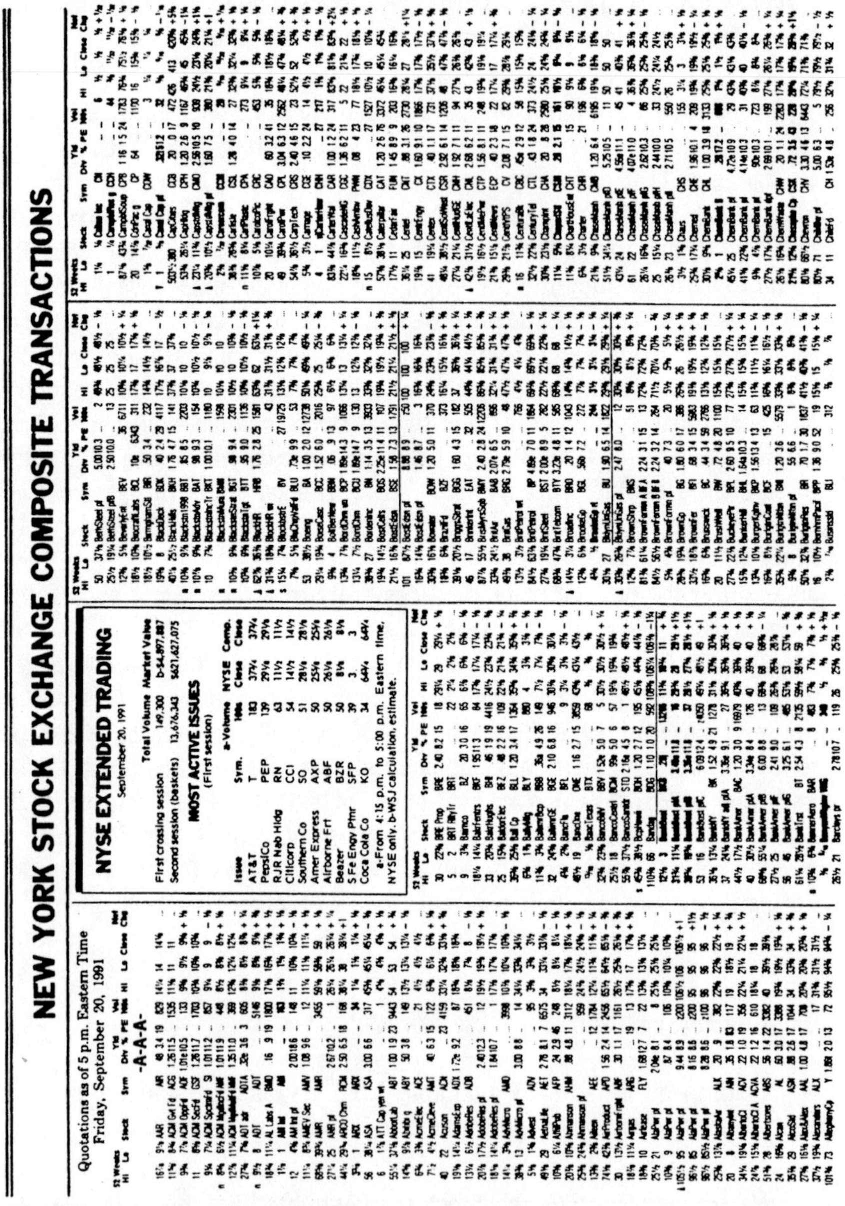
NEW YORK STOCK EXCHANGE COMPOSITE TRANSACTIONS
Quotations as of 5 p.m. Eastern Time
Friday, September 20, 1991
-A-A-A-
NYSE EXTENDED TRADING
September 20, 1991
Total Volume Market Value
First crossing session 149,300 b-$4,897,887
Second session (baskets) 13,676,343 $621,627,075
MOST ACTIVE ISSUES
(First session)
Issue Sym. a-Volume 100s NYSE Close Comp. Close
AT&T T 183 37¾ 37¾
PepsiCo PEP 139 29⅛ 29⅛
RJR Nab Hldg RN 63 11½ 11½
Citicorp CCI 54 14½ 14½
Southern Co SO 51 28⅛ 28⅛
Amer Express AXP 50 25⅝ 25⅝
Airborne Frt ABF 50 26⅛ 26⅛
Beazer BZR 50 8⅛ 8⅛
S Fe Engy Ptnr SFP 39 3 3
Coca Cola Co KO 34 64¼ 64¼
a-From 4:15 p.m. to 5:00 p.m. Eastern time.
NYSE only. b-WSJ calculation, estimate.

FIGURE 6.3 *Barron's* Stock Quotation for September 20, 1991

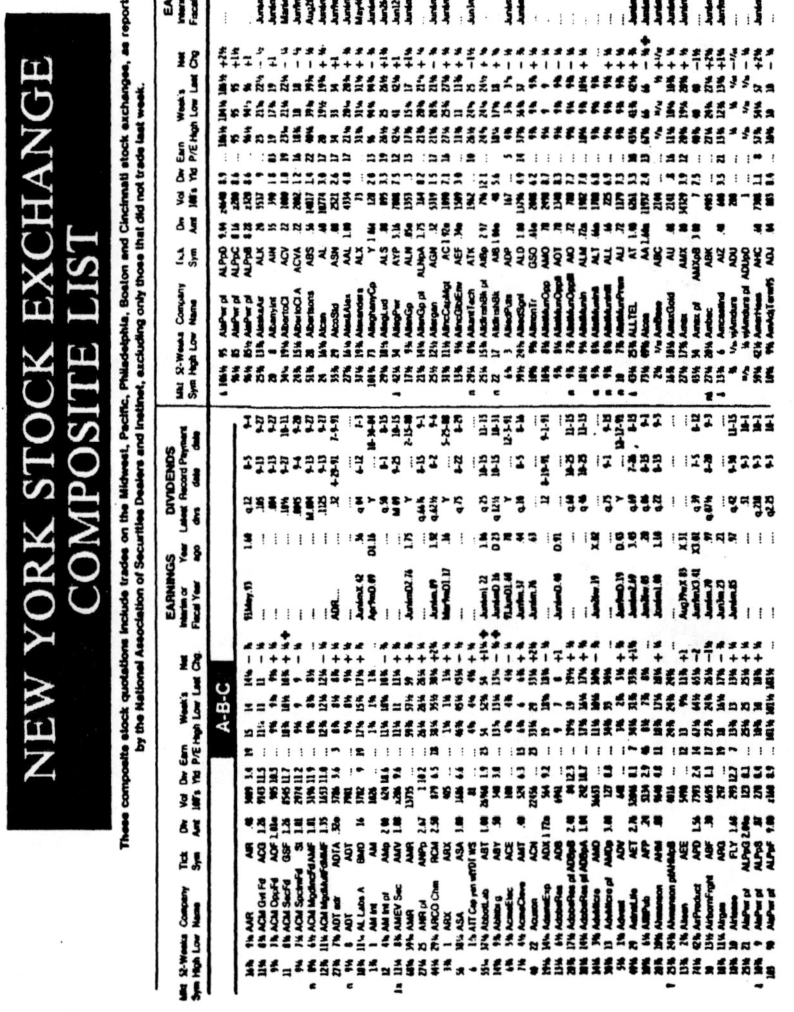

The Wall Street Journal are illustrated in Figure 6.2. The two columns at the left give the high and low prices for the most recent 52-week period, followed by an abbreviation of the company name. If no symbol follows the company name, the security listed is common stock. An additional symbol designates a security other than common stock. The possibilities include *pf* for preferred, *wt* for warrants, *rt* for rights, *un* for units, and *wi* for when issued. The reader probably is already familiar with some of these terms, but perhaps not with units and when-issued trading. When more than one security is traded as a single entity, the combination is called a unit. For example, a unit could consist of a combination of one share and two warrants. A security will trade when issued if the trade is conditional on subsequent issuance. The issuance of the when-issued security is authorized but the security itself has not actually been issued. Normally, the issuance will take place as planned on a prespecified subsequent date. The settlement (transfer of payment) of such trades occurs when and if the subject security is issued. If for some unanticipated reason the security is not issued, the when-issued transactions are reversed.

The stock quotation then indicates the dividend rate and the percentage yield. For preferred shares, the indicated rate usually is fixed by the terms stated in the prospectus when the stock was issued. For common stock, the indicated rate may be raised or lowered by the firm's directors depending on their assessment of business conditions. The percentage yield is obtained by dividing the indicated rate by the most recent stock price. Only cash dividends are used in computing the percentage yield.

Next, the stock's PE, the most recent daily sales volume in units of 100 shares and the daily high, low and closing prices are provided. Most securities without an entry in the PE column have incurred recent losses; warrants and preferred stocks also do not report a PE. The last column reports the net change in price from the previous close.

Barron's, a major investment periodical, provides a more complete stock quotation (see Figure 6.3). Many of the columns are the same as in *The Wall Street Journal*: the yearly high and low, the name of the company, the dividend rate and yield, the PE ratio and the sales. Because *Barron's* is published on a weekly basis, it also reports high, low, last sales and net change figures for the week. The quotations also include additional dividend and earnings information. The first entry of the earnings columns contains the most recent earnings report. Depending on the time that has elapsed since the end of the most recent fiscal year, earnings for 3, 6, 9 or 12 months may be reported. This entry is followed by the previous year's comparable

FIGURE 6.4   Explanatory Notes for Stock Quotations in
The Wall Street Journal

EXPLANATORY NOTES

The following explanations apply to New York and American exchange listed issues and the National Association of Securities Dealers Automated Quotations system's over-the-counter securities. Exchange prices are composite quotations that include trades on the Midwest, Pacific, Philadelphia, Boston and Cincinnati exchanges and reported by the NASD and Instinet.

Boldfaced quotations highlight those issues whose price changed by 5% or more from their previous closing price.

Underlined quotations are those stocks with large changes in volume, per exchange, compared with the issue's average trading volume. The calculation includes common stocks of $5 a share or more with an average volume over 65 trading days of at least 5,000 shares. The underlined quotations are for the 40 largest volume percentage leaders on the NYSE and the NASD's National Market System. It includes the 20 largest volume percentage gainers on the Amex.

The **52-week high** and **low** columns show the highest and lowest price of the issue during the preceding 52 weeks plus the current week, but not the latest trading day. These ranges are adjusted to reflect stock payouts of 1% or more, and cash dividends of 10% or more.

Dividend rates, unless noted, are annual disbursements based on the last quarterly, semiannual, or annual declaration. Special or extra dividends, special situations or payments not designated as regular are identified by footnotes.

Yield is defined as the dividends paid by a company on its securities, expressed as a percentage of price.

The **P/E ratio** is determined by dividing the price of a share of stock by its company's earnings per share of that stock. These earnings are the primary per-share earnings reported by the company for the most recent four quarters. Extraordinary items are usually excluded.

Sales figures are the unofficial daily total of shares traded, quoted in hundreds (two zeros omitted).

Exchange ticker symbols are shown for all New York and American exchange common stocks, and Dow Jones News/Retrieval symbols are listed for Class A and Class B shares listed on both markets. Nasdaq symbols are listed for all Nasdaq NMS issues. A more detailed explanation of Nasdaq ticker symbols appears with the NMS listings.

FOOTNOTES: ▲-New 52-week high. ▼-New 52-week low. a-Extra dividend or extras in addition to the regular dividend. b-Indicates annual rate of the cash dividend and that a stock dividend was paid. c-Liquidating dividend. e-Indicates a dividend was declared or paid in the preceding 12 months, but that there isn't a regular dividend rate. g-Indicates the dividend and earnings are expressed in Canadian money. The stock trades in U.S. dollars. No yield or P/E ratio is shown. h-Indicates a temporary exception to Nasdaq qualifications. i-Indicates amount declared or paid after a stock dividend or split. j-Indicates dividend was paid this year, and that at the last dividend meeting a dividend was omitted or deferred. k-Indicates dividend declared or paid this year on cumulative issues with dividends in arrears. n-Newly issued in the past 52 weeks. The high-low range begins with the start of trading and doesn't cover the entire period. p-Preferred. pp-Holder owes installment(s) of purchase price. pr-Preference. r-Indicates a cash dividend declared or paid in the preceding 12 months, plus a stock dividend. rt -Rights. s-Stock split or stock dividend amounting to 25% or more in the past 52 weeks. The high-low price is adjusted from the old stock. Dividend calculations begin with the date the split was paid or the stock dividend occurred. t-Paid in stock in the preceding 12 months, estimated cash value on ex-dividend or ex-distribution date, except Nasdaq listings where payments are in stock. un-Units. v-Trading halted on primary market. vj-In bankruptcy or receivership or being reorganized under the Bankruptcy Code, or securities assumed by such companies. wd-When distributed. wi-When issued. wt-Warrants. ww-With warrants. x-Ex-dividend or ex-rights. xw-Without warrants. y-Ex-dividend and sales in full, not in hundreds. z-Sales in full, not in hundreds.

number. The dividends columns begin with the amount of the latest quarterly declaration followed by the stock of record and the payment dates. Dividends are sent on the payment date to the owners as of the day of record.

The formats for the American Stock Exchange (AMEX) and NASDAQ national market quotations are identical to those for the NYSE in most newspapers. Stock quotations for regional and foreign exchanges and for over-the-counter (OTC) national and supplemental listings are less complete, however.

FIGURE 6.5   NASDAQ Symbol Explanation

NASDAQ SYMBOL EXPLANATION

All securities listed in the Nasdaq system are identified by a four letter or five letter symbol. The fifth letter indicates the issues that aren't common or capital shares, or are subject to restrictions or special conditions. Below is a rundown of fifth letter identifiers and a description of what they represent:

A-Class A. **B**-Class B. **C**-Exempt from Nasdaq listing qualifications for a limited period. **D**-New issue. **E**-Delinquent in required filings with SEC, as determined by the NASD. **F**-Foreign. **G**-First convertible bond. **H**-Second convertible bond, same company. **I**-Third convertible bond, same company. **J**-Voting. **K**-Non-voting. **L**-Miscellaneous situations, including second class units, third class of warrants or sixth class of preferred stock. **M**-Fourth preferred, same company. **N**-Third preferred, same company. **O**-Second preferred, same company. **P**-First preferred, same company. **Q**-In bankruptcy proceedings. **R**-Rights. **S**-Shares of beneficial interest. **T**-With warrants or rights. **U**-Units. **V**-When issued and when distributed. **W**-Warrants. **Y**-American Depositary Receipt (ADR). **Z**-Miscellaneous situations, including second class of warrants, fifth class of preferred stock and any unit, receipt or certificate representing a limited partnership interest.

SOURCE: Reprinted by permission of *The Wall Street Journal*, © 1991 Dow Jones & Company, Inc. All Rights Reserved Worldwide.

Explanatory Notes   Many entries in the newspaper quotations include letters that translate into explanatory notes. They alert the reader to additional information relating to the company or its quotation. For example, a note may indicate that a price is a yearly high or yearly low or that the company is in bankruptcy (see Figure 6.4).

NASDAQ's Fifth Letter   Most OTC issues traded on the NASDAQ system have ticker symbols of four letters. A fifth letter is added to signify a special status for the security. Often these letters come and go as the status of the issue changes. Fifth letters frequently convey important information. Moreover, an investor seeking a quote on an OTC issue that seems to have disappeared should check to see whether it is continuing to trade under a new five-letter ticker symbol. The principal fifth letter symbols and their meanings are listed in Figure 6.5.

FIGURE 6.6 Typical Bond Quotation from *The Wall Street Journal*

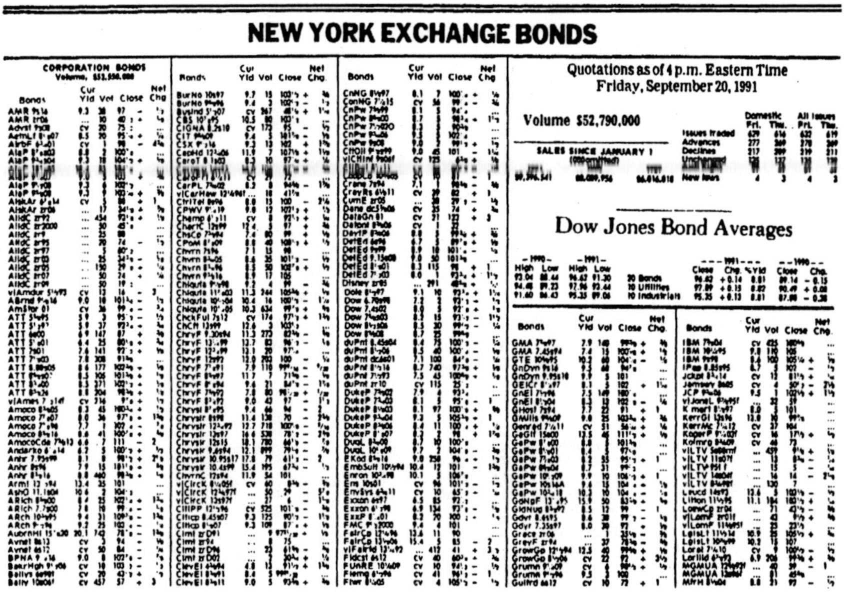
NEW YORK EXCHANGE BONDS

CORPORATION BONDS

Quotations as of 4 p.m. Eastern Time
Friday, September 20, 1991

Volume $52,790,000

Dow Jones Bond Averages

SOURCE: Reprinted by permission of *The Wall Street Journal,* © 1991 Dow Jones & Company, Inc. All Rights Reserved Worldwide.

Bond Quotations Bond quotations look relatively similar to stock quotations. Figure 6.6 is a typical quotation from *The Wall Street Journal.* The format is similar or identical in most major newspapers.

Look down the first column to the first entry for AT&T. The ATT entry identifies the issues as the American Telephone and Telegraph Company. The next two items 5⅝ 95 indicate that the bond has a coupon of 5⅝% and matures in 1995. The current yield 5.9 is simply the rounded-off quotient from dividing the coupon 5⅝ by the closing price of 95½ (5.625 + 95.5 = 5.89). The volume 3 is reported next. The volume figure is for three bonds with a face value of $1,000. Note that this represents only the volume traded on the exchange. Many more bonds probably traded OTC. The closing price of 95½ refers to parts of 100. Thus, 95½ corresponds to a price of $995 on a $1,000 face-value bond. Finally, the change from the previous close at –½ corresponds to $7.50 on a $1,000 bond valuation.

FIGURE 6.7   Abbreviated Report from the High-Yield Market

HIGH YIELD BONDS

Friday September 20, 1991

	Total Daily Return	Index Value	Average Price Change	Vol.
Flash Index	+ 0.10%	116.25	+ 0.02	M
Cash Pay	+ 0.08	111.51	− 0.02	M
Deferred Int	+ 0.21	124.36	+ 0.17	M
Distressed	+ 0.09	125.17	− 0.01	M
Bankrupt	+ 0.02	108.63	unch	M

Volume Key: H = Heavy, M = Moderate, L = Light

Index value = 100 on July 1, 1990

Key Gainers

Name	Type/Coup.	Mat.	3:00P.M. Bid Price	Price Change	Principal Return	Yld to Mat.
AdelComm	h/ 16.500	3/99	87 +	4 +	4.82	17.93
BurlgtnHldg	a/ 14.250	10/99	69 +	2 +	2.71	22.84
BurlgtnHldg	b/ 13.875	10/96	79 ½ +	1 ½ +	1.77	20.61
JonesIntcabl	a/ 13.000	5/00	100 ¼ +	1 ¾ +	1.69	12.94
FtHoward	i/ 14.125	11/04	68 +	1 +	1.49	13.66

Key Losers

Chrysler	c/ 13.000	3/97	78 ¼ −	2 ¼ −	2.77	19.68
Chrysler	c/ 9.600	7/94	79 −	1 −	1.22	19.68
RH Macy	i/ 16.500	11/06	48 −	½ −	1.03	24.14

Name	Type/Rating	Coup.	Mat.	Close	% Net Chg.	Yld. to Mat.
ARA Services	a /B+	12.500	7/01	105 ½	unch	11.54
AmerStandard	b /B-	12.875	6/00	98 ¾	unch	13.11
BurlngtnHldg	b /CCC+	13.875	10/96	79 ½ +	1 ½	20.61
CaesarsWorld	a /BB-	13.500	10/97	105 −	½	12.30
Coltecind	b /B-	12.500	10/01	103 ¾	unch	11.85
ContainerCrp	a /NR	14.000	12/01	102 ½ +	¼	13.53
FMC Corp	b /BB-	12.250	6/98	106	unch	10.95
FtHowardPpr	b /B+	12.375	11/97	100 ½ +	¾	12.25
GeorgiaGulf	b /B	15.000	4/00	111	unch	12.84
HarcourtBrac	c /CCC	13.000	11/97	99	unch	13.23
Healthtrust	d /CCC+	16.500	12/99	113 ¾	unch	13.11
JohnstonCoke	a /BB+	11.500	9/01	113 ¼	unch	9.42
Kroger	b /B-	12.875	1/99	106 −	½	11.63
McCawCell	b /CCC+	12.950	8/99	96	unch	13.79
OwensIll	b /B-	12.250	6/96	99 ½	unch	12.38
QuantumChem	b /B-	12.500	3/99	87 ½	unch	15.37
RH Macy	b /CCC+	14.500	10/98	82 ¼ −	¾	19.18
RJR Nabisco	e /BB-	15.000	5/01	119 −	⅛	13.19
RelianceElec	f /B+	14.000	4/02	94 ¾	unch	13.71
SafewayStrs	b /B	11.750	11/96	104	unch	10.71
StoneContain	b /B+	11.500	9/99	93 ¼	unch	12.88
SupermktsGen	b /CCC+	14.500	9/97	103 ½ −	½	13.62
USG	b /D	13.250	7/00	33	unch	z
ViacomIntl	b /B+	11.800	7/98	105	unch	10.74
VonsCompany	g /B+	12.875	5/97	103 ¼	unch	12.05

Volume indicators are based solely on the traders' subjective judgment given the relative level of inquiry and trading activity on any given day.

a-Subordinated. b-Senior Sub. c-Senior. d-Senior Sub, Split Cpn. e-Subordinated, PIK. f-Subordinated, Split Cpn. g-Senior Sub, VarRt. h-Senior, Split Cpn. i-Junior Sub, Split Cpn. z-omitted for reset or bankrupt bonds, or yields above 35%.

Source: Salomon Brothers

The *Journal* also contains an abbreviated report from the high-yield market (see Figure 6.7).

At the top of the high-yield quote is some aggregate data for various categories of bonds. Indexlike data is provided for cash pay, deferred interest, distressed and bankrupt bond types. The Key Gainers segment reports on bonds that have made major up moves in the past 24 hours. Key Losers have made major down moves over the past day.

For the Key Gainers section, look at the second entry, Burlington Holdings. This is a bond issued by Burlington Holdings. The entry for type reports an "a." According to the bottom of the quote, "a" refers to a subordinated issue. The coupon 14.250 is typical for a high-yield issue. The maturity, 10/99, includes the month and year. The 3:00 P.M. bid price is 69, which reflects an increase of 2 from the previous day. The principal return entry (2.71) is the annualized rate of return of principal until the issue matures. The yield to maturity entry is reported at 22.84%.

The main part of the quotation contains some of the more active high-yield issues. The third entry in this section is another Burlington issue. The type "b" indicates that this issue is senior subordinated. The CCC+ rating is at the middle for the high-yield market. A rating of BB+ would be the highest quality high-yield grade, while BBB- would be the lowest investment grade. The coupon of 13.875 is slightly below that of the other Burlington issue. Its maturity of 10/96 is similar and yet its price of 79½ is appreciably higher. This bond's senior subordinated status accounts for its higher price vis-à-vis its coupon. This issue increased 1½ and the yield to maturity is reported at 20.61%.

Clearly, the market is concerned about a possible Burlington default.

Electronic Quotations Although most investors are content to follow the prices of their securities in the newspapers, some use electronic quotations for more frequent and up-to-date reports. Thus, Trans-Lux Corporation (110 Richards Avenue, Norwalk, CT 06854) offers a ticker-tape service (each day's complete trading record for the NYSE and/or AMEX) and a service that reports sales of up to 100 stocks or futures contracts in real time (no delay in reporting). Both Quotron (1 Battery Place Plaza, New York, NY 10004) and Bunker Ramo Information Systems (35 Nutmeg Drive, Trumbull, CT 06609) provide real-time access to the stock market ticker tape plus the ability to obtain last, bid and ask quotes on specified stocks and options much like a stock exchange quotation machine. Bloomberg (Bloomberg L.P., 499 Park Avenue, New York, NY 10022) supplies very extensive on-line data for debt securities. All of these services require payments for installation and monthly service as well as additional fees to the relevant exchanges.

A less expensive system now is available to those within 50 miles of most large cities. Telenet America, Inc. (Wythe Street, Alexandria, VA 22314) offers a Pocket Quote machine about the size of a hand-held calculator. It will display the high, low and last prices for any NYSE or AMEX stock on a 15-minute delay basis. The machine also will flash whenever news appears on any of up to 20 preselected stocks.

Perhaps the least expensive source of electronic stock market data is CNBC/FNN. It provides a continuous real-time stock ticker moving across the bottom edge of the television screen. CNBC/FNN information, unlike that from other sources, is passive. Subscribers cannot obtain quotations on particular securities from CNBC/FNN. They must wait for the security of interest to trade and be reported on the tape. Most investors do not have time to sit and watch for their stock to trade.

Taking electronic quotations a step further, several services will watch for major price moves on a selection of stocks and flag the movers (Roscokrantz, Ehrenkrantz, Lyon & Ross, Hicksville, NY; and Window on Wall Street, Bristol Financial Systems, Wilton, CT). Such services require access to a personal computer and relevant computer software and incur a monthly fee.

Another category of electronic quotations utilizes the personal computer. For example, Dow Jones News/Retrieval, Quotdial, Dialog, Charles Schwab, S&P and CompuServe offer an extensive array of on-line computer investor services including stock quotations. Dowphone provides quotes for subscribers with nothing more than touch-tone telephones.

Standard & Poor's Stock and Bond Guides   The monthly *Standard & Poor's Stock Guide* and *Standard & Poor's Bond Guide* report considerably more data than the newspaper quotations. A very large number of common and preferred stocks and warrants are included in the stock guide. The S&P bond guide covers a large number of bonds. A security is covered in a single line across two pages.

Stock Market Indexes

Most investors are interested in both the price changes for their own stocks and the overall moves of the market. A number of different indexes reflect market movements. Although all market indexes are based on the average prices of a sample of securities, the samples and averaging processes differ.

The Dow Jones Industrial Average The simplest and best known of the stock indexes is the Dow Jones Industrial Average (DJIA). The Dow is an unweighted average of the market prices of 30 major ("blue-chip") industrial firms. Composition changes are relatively rare. The prices of the 30 stocks are summed and then divided by a number called the divisor. The divisor is adjusted to maintain comparability whenever a DJIA firm is split. Small stock dividends do not lead to a change in the divisor, however. Moreover, the more rapid growth of the firms that tend to split (thereby reducing their relative weight) biases the average downward. Its problems notwithstanding, the Dow remains the most widely followed market index. When people speak of the "market," they usually have the DJIA in mind. Dow Jones, Inc., also computes averages for utilities and transportation companies and a composite sample. The industrial average, however, receives by far the most attention.

Other Stock Market Averages Most other stock market averages are weighted to reflect the relative value of their components. Thus, the Standard & Poor's 500 Stock Index is a composite average of the share prices of 500 major corporations weighted according to the relative values of their outstanding shares. S&P also computes indexes of 400 industrials, 40 utilities, 40 finance firms and 20 transportation firms. The NYSE Composite Index is a value-weighted average of all stocks listed on the Big Board. Similarly, the AMEX Index is a value-weighted average of AMEX stocks and the NASDAQ Index is a value-weighted index of all domestic National Association of Securities Dealers (NASD) listed OTC stocks. Finally, the Wilshire 5000 weights stocks in all three markets. Aside from the Dow, the only other unweighted (or, more accurately, price weighted) index of consequence is the Value Line Composite Index.

Relations Between the Indexes Because stocks generally are affected by similar forces and because most of the indexes tend to have a common component, the indexes should move together. Although the various indexes do tend to move together, they also reflect somewhat different market segments. In particular, the DJIA is representative of the larger, more established blue-chip stocks, whereas the NYSE index and the S&P 500 are broader based. The AMEX and NASDAQ indexes reflect the pricing of more speculative issues. The Value Line index is a better measure of small capitalization stocks.

The Financial and Business Press

A large number of publications cater to investors and businesspeople. Most of them offer both factual news and opinions that investors may use to stay abreast of current developments. Because these published opinions are as subject to error as those of the (notoriously unreliable) investment advisory services, investors should take the advice into account but not rely on it.

Business and Investment Periodicals First and foremost among sources of current business news is *The Wall Street Journal* (WSJ), which is published five days a week. Most serious investors try to keep up with the relevant business news in the WSJ or the financial sections of major newspapers (*The New York Times*, for example). *The Wall Street Journal Index* is an excellent source for citations in the WSJ. Both the WSJ and *Barron's* are published by Dow Jones & Company, Inc., a longtime leader of the financial press. *Barron's* appears weekly and is more investor oriented than the WSJ. *Investor's Business Daily*, a relatively recent competitor in the national business newspaper field, stresses tables and statistics. It seems to have achieved a modest degree of success.

Business Week (published weekly by McGraw-Hill) appeals principally to businesspeople, but it contains some useful investment information. For example, McGraw-Hill annually surveys and forecasts business fixed investment (new spending on long-term plants and equipment). Also, the end-of-the-year issue contains an analysis of the investment climate. Another well-known business periodical is *Fortune*, which appears monthly. Compared to *Business Week*, it contains fewer but more detailed articles.

Forbes (published twice monthly) is largely investor oriented. In addition to its famous lists of interesting stocks (e.g., loaded laggers), *Forbes* contains articles on specific companies and other relevant investment subjects. Investor-oriented magazines with smaller readerships than *Forbes* include *Financial World, Finance* and the *Magazine of Wall Street.* Periodicals more oriented to general business and money management include *Money* and *Fact.* Periodicals focusing on small and start-up businesses include *Entrepreneur, Inc.* and *Venturing.*

The *Financial Analysts Journal* and the *Journal of Portfolio Management* publish serious work on investment theory and concepts. A typical article in these journals, although not easy reading, is intelligible to nonacademicians. The same cannot be said for articles in the more academic journals devoted to finance and economics such as the *American Economic Review* or the *Journal of Finance.* On the other hand, the *American Association of Individual Investors Journal* is specifically written for serious but amateur investors.

Systematic Coverage of Companies   Most of the financial press covers companies in a very unsystematic fashion. Thus, those seeking information on particular companies may wait a long time before finding an article in one of the periodicals. Several publications do, however, periodically report on a list of firms and they serve as handy references. *Moody's Industrial Manual* (published annually) contains a great deal of financial information on the past history of a large number of firms. More up-to-date information on a smaller group of firms is available quarterly in *Value Line, Standard & Poor's Stock Reports* and directly from some brokerage firms.

Moody's coverage is quite extensive. First, the capital structure is outlined, including a list of securities. This is followed by a brief history of the firm, a discussion of the business and its products and a list of its subsidiaries. Under the general heading of management is a list of managers and directors, the name of the auditor, the identity of the shareholder relations officer, the dates of the director meetings and the annual meetings, the number of stockholders and of employees and the address of the general office. This is followed by annual income statements for the past three years and cash-flow statements for the past two years. A balance sheet for the most recent four years also is included. Extensive notes accompany these financial statements. Next comes a set of financial and operating information such as per-share data and financial and operation rates. A brief description of the firm's debt and equity securities appears at the end.

In addition to its industrial manual, Moody's publishes similar manuals for other types of firms. Most publicly held companies of any consequence are included. Moody's coverage is quite extensive. The information, however, is largely descriptive and dated. Standard & Poor's publishes a set of manuals that is very similar to Moody's as well as the more investor-oriented *Standard & Poor's NYSE Stock Reports.*

The S&P report begins with a line containing information on the primary market where the stock is traded and its ticker symbol. The same line also includes a notation that options on the company's stock are traded on the Chicago Board Options Exchange (CBOE) on the February cycle and that CBS stock is in the S&P 500 index. The next block of data reports a recent stock price and the date of the quote, the price range for the current year, the PE ratio, the dividend rate, the current yield, the S&P ranking and the estimated beta. The next two blocks contain a summary and discussion of the current outlook for the company. This material is accompanied by a seven-year chart of the company's stock-price action. The most recent four years of quarterly sales revenues and common share earnings are reported next. A brief analysis of important recent developments then is presented. Annual per-share data based on the income statement and balance sheets for ten years follow. Finally, the firm's business summary, dividends and capitalization are given.

Compared with Moody's, the S&P material is briefer and more analytical, up to date and investor oriented. Most listed companies and the major OTC-traded companies are covered by S&P reports. S&P also publishes a reference book called the *Stock Market Encyclopedia*, which contains brief reports on the stocks making up the S&P 500 index.

With about 100,000 subscribers, the *Value Line* has a circulation that is several times the size of the next largest similar periodical (*Standard & Poor's Outlook*). *Value Line* coverage includes a chart of book value, cash flow and relative strength. Insider and institutional trading decisions are reported in boxes at the top. Some income and balance sheet data is reported, along with a projection for the next fiscal year and three to five years hence. *Value Line* tables include rates of return and earnings, capital structure, and quarterly sales, earnings and dividends for recent years. Projections are given for the next 12 months. Three boxes contain a description of business, an analysis of the firm's position and prospects and ratings of the firm's performance and safety and its beta ratio.

The computer-based timeliness ratings for stock selection are the most famous statistics from *Value Line*. The 1,700 stocks are grouped as follows: 100 (I), 300 (II), 900 (III), 300 (IV) and 100 (V). Group I selections (ignoring commissions) have appreciated by 1,528% over the 1965–1985 period compared with only 134% for the NYSE Composite. Even the well-known efficient market proponent Fisher Black acknowledges the past success of *Value Line*. Other more recent research has found that, although it could not be relied on to make after-commission trading profits, a buy-and-hold strategy based on the *Value Line* selections did produce above-market risk-adjusted returns.

The *Value Line* coverage is clearly investor oriented. The reports contain a great deal of analysis and prediction, although many interesting firms are not covered. On the other hand, separate services are offered for options, convertibles and new issues.

The Unlisted Market Guide   Taking up where the larger publications leave off, Scot Emerich has introduced the *Unlisted Market Guide*. This guide covers several hundred OTC companies and employs a format that is quite similar to that of S&P. To be covered in the guide, a firm must pay a $750 annual fee. Subscribers are charged $195 per year. Charging firms for inclusion may lead the guide to have divided loyalties.

Brokerage House Reports   Most full-service brokerage houses either originate or purchase research reports to distribute to their customers. The number of firms covered varies directly with the size of the brokerage house. Large companies are much more likely to be included. The reports may or may not be updated periodically and often are issued as part of an industry survey. In a study of the recommendations of one large national brokerage firm over a seven-year period, professors Stanley, Lewellen and Schlarbaum found that "the firm's investment recommendations were generally timely, and conveyed information that would have permitted its customers to earn moderately above-average portfolio returns."

Advisory Services Newsletters   Many investment services publish newsletters that deal with stock market timing and stock selection. Among the better-known names in the field are Joseph Granville (whose panic sell messages telephoned across the country led to a 24-point drop in the Dow on January 7, 1981), Martin Zweig (editor of the *Zweig Forecaster* and frequent panelist on the public television program "Wall Street Week") and Robert R. Prechter, Jr. (of the "Elliot Wave Theory"). Much advice is of a very mediocre quality. Some advisory services may be better than others, however. *Hulbert Financial Digest* tracks and evaluates advisory services' recommendations. If past results are any indicators, the digest should help investors sort out the wheat from the shaft. Investors may subscribe directly to Hulbert's (409 First Street S.E., Washington, DC 20003, 800-227-1617).

Industry Periodicals   Some publications cover particular industries. For example, *Brewers Digest*, which is published monthly (Siebel Publishing Company, Chicago, IL 60646), reports on the beer industry. Trade publications such as this may contain articles relevant to potential investors, although the industry's managers are the primary readers. Some other trade periodicals, however, specialize in the stocks of particular industries. For example, *Audits Realty Stock Review* (Audit Investment Research, 230 Park Avenue, New York, NY 10017) covers real estate investment trusts (REITs) and other real estate companies.

Computer-Based Information Sources   In the past 20 years, the computer has become an omnipresent reminder of our changing technology. Its use in investment analysis is, if anything, more extensive than its role in most other areas. Virtually all serious empirical research utilizes the computer to manipulate data in statistically meaningful ways.

Researchers employ a number of computer-based data sources. Several of these services were mentioned in the discussion of electronic data sources. They provide stock quotes and in many cases also will supply a variety of financial information. These services are designed primarily for individual and perhaps institutional investors.

Another group of data sources is designed almost entirely for serious (scholarly) research. The best known of this type of financial data bank is the COMPUSTAT service sold by a Denver subsidiary of Standard & Poor's (Investors Management Services, Box 23a, Denver, CO 80201). The primary tape contains security information listed annually for the past 20 years for each of about 5,000 companies. A second tape contains quarterly data. Specialized tapes exist for various groups of companies such as OTC companies, Canadian firms, public utilities and banks. Most companies with substantial investor interest are included. COMPUSTAT data was long suited only to those with access to mainframe computer systems. More recently, however, this information has become available on compact disks with built-in menu-driven access systems.

Also distributed through Standard & Poor's are the ISL tapes from Investors Data Corporation (122 East 42nd Street, New York, NY 10017) and the CRISP tapes from the Center for Research in Securities Prices at the University of Chicago (Graduate School of Business, Chicago, IL 60637).

The ISL tapes contain daily high, low, close and volume figures for NYSE and AMEX stocks. The CRISP tapes contain monthly price and dividend data for the NYSE from 1926 forward as well as daily NYSE stock price data from 1960 to the present.

The Value Line data base (Value Line, Inc., 711 Third Avenue, New York, NY 10017) contains annual and quarterly data for 1,600 companies beginning in 1963 (annual coverage back to 1954), plus estimated earnings and dividends for the next year. Value Line data is available on floppy disks on a monthly subscription basis.

Finally, the Media General Databank (Data General Financial Services, Box 26991, Richmond, VA 23261) includes current price, volume and financial data on 2,000 major corporations. These data bases appear to be generally, but not uniformly, accurate.

Investment Software　Programs that utilize input from these data bases can screen the data banks for certain characteristics and/or perform numerous manipulations of the available data. Some of them are marketed primarily to institutions. Others are available to people connected with an academic institution. The growth of personal computers undoubtedly will make computer analyses much more accessible to many individual investors. Indeed, a large number of investor-oriented programs have been designed to perform either fundamental or technical analysis.

The fundamental analysis packages are largely designed to sort through a large data base to find firms whose characteristics meet certain criteria. For example, the investor may set acceptable ranges for PE, past growth, dividend yield, debt/equity, beta and so on. The program then will screen for stocks meeting the specified criteria. One example of these types of programs is Stockpak II from S&P. The service offers updated information (monthly floppy disks) on 4,600 stocks and works with 75 specified criteria. The user can construct additional criteria if desired. Another example is Value/Screen Plus from *Value Line* (711 3rd Avenue, New York, NY 10017-4064), which is a condensed version of the *Investment Survey*. Subscribers receive monthly floppy disks containing information on 1,600 stocks. They may work with 37 screening and 10 portfolio management variables. Finally, the Evaluation Form is offered by the National Association of Investment Clubs. The user supplies his or her own information. The program then computes about 50 values and recommends whether to buy, hold or sell the stock.

Technical analysis programs rely heavily on current market data to analyze and forecast the market for particular securities. Most of these services require an on-line data source, a graphics card and a color monitor. The Technician (by Computer Asset Management) tracks and graphs 70 technical market indicators. MetaStock (also by Computer Asset Management) allows the user to plot data for up to four years and display up to 36 charts on a single screen. Finally, CompuTrac PC is a particularly extensive "toolbag of technical analysis tools."

Additional software packages are available for commodities, bonds, options and real estate. Before purchasing a software package and data service, an investor might wish to refer to one of the publications that review computer investment programs: *Financial and Investment Software Review* (quarterly), $45 per year, Box 6, Riverdale, NY 10471; *Wall Street Computer Review* (monthly), $139 per year, Dealer's Digest, Inc., 150 Broadway, New York, NY 10038; and *Computerized Investing* (bimonthly), $44 per year, American Association of Individual Investors, 612 North Michigan Avenue, Chicago, IL 60611.

The ultimate in computerized investing allows the investor to trade securities directly in the marketplace. A program of Instinet in New York affords direct access to the floor of the Pacific Stock Exchange (PSE). That is, one can dial into the network and first obtain a quote and then execute a trade for any security traded on the PSE.

Investment Implications of the Computer   Because the computer and computer-based data sources play a large and growing role in investment analysis, investors should be aware of their availability. Those investors simply wishing to apply the results of such research may find the computer useful but not essential. Mutual funds and other institutions in the best positions to utilize computers have not in the aggregate produced particularly impressive performances with or without them.

Investor Associations   Three associations are designed to assist individual investors. The National Association of Investment Clubs (Box 220, Royal Oak, MI 48068) helps groups of small investors establish investment clubs and provides a vehicle for investment clubs to communicate with each other. The association now has 5,000 clubs representing 90,000 members. For $25 per club plus $6 per member, investors can obtain the association's assistance in establishing a club.

The American Association of Individual Investors (612 North Michigan Avenue, Chicago, IL 60611) offers a wide variety of services for its $49 annual membership: a journal of investment theory and practice that appears ten times a year; an investor's guide to no-load mutual funds; local chapter membership (where available) in a number of metropolitan areas; a series of home computer programs for investors; a tax-planning guide; and access to a number of seminars, a variety of home-study materials and a bimonthly publication on computerized investing (optional for extra cost).

United Shareholders of America ($50 per year membership, USA, 1667 K Street, Suite 770, Washington, DC 20006) is designed primarily to represent and fight for shareholder rights. Organized and promoted by T. Boone Pickens, this association is concerned with such issues as uniform securities laws from state to state, one share/one vote, confidential proxy voting, equal access to the proxy system by both management and nonmanagement groups and restrictions on such potential management abuses as the paying of greenmail or the instituting of golden parachutes and poison pills.

At the other end of the spectrum, the Investment Company Institute (1775 K Street, Washington, DC 20006) services mutual funds and other institutional investors. The institute publishes a periodical called the *Mutual Funds Forum*.

Business News Programs

Television's only nationwide business news program during the 1970s was "Wall Street Week" (WSW). Hosted by Louis Rukeyser and a rotating series of panelists (including Martin Zweig), the program has continued to draw a substantial audience. The Public Broadcasting System (PBS) program combines a format of moderator commentary, panelist discussion, viewer questions and guest interviews.

The growth of cable systems and the "narrow casting" approach to programming led to the introduction of a rash of new business programs in the early 1980s. For example, on Friday nights, "Wall Street Week" now is accompanied on PBS by "Nightly Business Report," which appears five days a week. This half-hour program is devoted to business and particularly stock market news. It ends with a segment by one of its ten regular commentators. "Inside Business Today," a third PBS offering, is a weekly interview program.

The Cable News Network (CNN) originates a number of business news programs. "Moneyline," with a heavy concentration of economic and market information, appears daily. "Business Morning" and "Business Day" both appear in the early morning of each weekday. Among other features are their reports on market conditions around the world, especially those in Tokyo and London (where the markets open before New York's market and often influence their opening price levels). "Moneyweek" is a weekly compilation of some of the "Moneyline" stories. "Your Money" appears weekly and is devoted to financial management issues of interest to small investors and household managers. Finally, "Inside Business" and "Pinnacle" provide in-depth looks at corporate leaders.

CNBC/FNN offers 14 hours of business programs live daily, including "Business View," "Market Wrap," "Business Insiders" and "Smart Money." Other business-oriented programs include "Wall Street Journal Report," which is produced weekly by Dow Jones and broadcast by Independent Network News; "Biz Net News Today," which is produced daily by the U.S. Chamber of Commerce and broadcast by the Modern Satellite Network; and "Business Times," which the Entertainment and Sports Network offers as a daily briefing for top executives. As with other types of television programming, new shows are introduced and others are canceled. Thus, this discussion may be somewhat out-of-date by the time the reader sees it.

Sources of Investment Ideas

Readers are advised to follow up their reading by examining some of the relevant periodicals in the library. The financial press is constantly suggesting interesting investment situations. Brokers also recommend investments as part of their "service." Friends, neighbors, relatives and local businesspeople sometimes have ideas worth considering. Investors may turn up some ideas at work or even in the supermarket. For example, a product encountered in the course of business or shopping may seem interesting enough to warrant checking out the manufacturer or distributor. *Forbes*, *Value Line* and some other periodicals frequently list stocks with particular characteristics in common (very low PE ratios, large cash positions, etc.). These may serve as useful beginning points. Investors interested in a particular industry can begin with the *Value Line* sample. After identifying the company, the investor can evaluate the prospects for each of its securities.

The search for ideas even may begin with an examination of the entire list of the NYSE, AMEX or national OTC securities. For example, if an investor believes that a significant number of warrants, convertible bonds or high-yield bonds are likely to be underpriced, a quick check through the most recent edition of *The Wall Street Journal* will provide a list to investigate. Warrants are identified by *wt* after their name, convertibles by *cv* and high-yield bonds have high numbers in the yield column. A quicker approach is available to those investors with computer, software and data sources. In any case, once a preliminary list of potential investments is assembled, the investor/analyst can begin the more serious evaluation of fundamentals.

Investment Information:
Summary and Conclusions

An individual following a particular company's securities should refer to company-prepared documents such as 10-Ks, 10-Qs, prospectuses, proxy materials, press releases and annual and quarterly reports. The 13-D filings report large ownership positions. Stock quotations and indexes contain price and other information on individual securities and the market. Business news is covered in publications such as *The Wall Street Journal* and *Business Week*, whereas *Barron's* and *Forbes* offer more investor-oriented coverage. Investors seeking information about specific firms may wish to consult *Moody's Industrial Manual*, the *Standard & Poor's Stock Reports*, the *Value Line Investment Survey* or brokerage house reports. Tapes containing financial information for many firms for a number of years are almost essential for serious statistical analysis. A variety of investment-related computer software is available to those investors with personal computers.

CHAPTER 7

Types of Securities

Fixed-income securities provide the principal investment alternative to common stocks. The same brokers and similar markets are used to trade them and many companies issue both types of securities. Their similarities notwithstanding, many stock market investors largely ignore the bond markets. Such neglect was understandable when bond yields averaged 4 to 5%, and the stock market's long post–World War II rally was under way, but times have changed. Far from being a mundane backwater, the diversity and high yields of fixed-income securities now make them very competitive with common stocks. Their volatility, market attention, diversity of types, ways of participating and small investor involvement all have increased in recent years. Bonds may not belong in every portfolio, but all serious investors should at least consider them.

Here we will explore the characteristics of the various types of short- and long-term debt instruments.

Types of Debt Securities

The federal government, state and local governments, corporations, foreign governments and international organizations all issue fixed-income securities. Most debt securities promise to pay a fixed periodic coupon amount and return their face value at a prespecified time. They vary in a number of ways, including length to maturity, coupon rate, type of collateral, convertibility, tax treatment and restrictions placed on the borrower.

155

Debt instruments largely compete with other similar-maturity instruments. Securities maturing in a year or less are considered short term. High-quality, short-term debt obligations trade in what is called the money market.

The vast majority of the components of the money market never or almost never default, e.g., Treasury bills (T-bills) and government-guaranteed certificates of deposit (CDs). One category of money-market instruments that has been known to enter the category of distressed and defaulted securities is commercial paper. A second money-market category of potentially risky securities is the banker's acceptance.

The Money Market and Other Short-Term Debt Securities

Money-market instruments are highly liquid, quite marketable and very secure. The principal money-market instruments are large bank CDs, T-bills, commercial paper, bankers' acceptances and Eurodollar deposits. Very short-term lending and borrowing in the federal funds market, repurchase agreements and the Fed's discount window round out this market. In addition, money-market mutual funds, short-term unit investment trusts, short-term municipals and certain securities and accounts of banks and other financial institutions also compete in the short end of the debt security market.

Commercial Paper   Commercial paper usually is issued by large corporations with solid credit ratings to finance their short-term needs. The paper is secured only by the issuer's good name. The issuer does, however, usually have a backup line of credit at a bank. Such a credit line is available to repay the commercial paper issue if sale of new paper is not possible in the existing market environment. Commercial paper issuers generally are able to pay slightly less than bank rates (the prime rate) on their borrowings. They will incur a fee on their backup credit lines. Even adding in this fee, the commercial paper issuer's borrowing costs are typically below the alternative cost of bank borrowings. Similarly, eliminating the intermediary's (i.e., the bank's) need for compensation allows those who issue commercial paper to pay investors a slightly higher rate than the investors would receive by buying a bank's CDs.

Commercial paper is rated, but as a practical matter, only high-grade issues usually are salable. Conditions can, however, deteriorate rapidly.

Thus, what was initially marked as high-grade paper can move into the distressed category before it matures. Paper is marketed in round lots of $250,000 and seldom is available in smaller than $100,000 denominations. Some paper is registered; most is payable to the bearer.

Bankers' Acceptances A banker's acceptance involves an obligation to pay a certain amount at a prespecified time. Once the obligation is accepted (guaranteed) by a bank, it becomes an acceptance. The acceptance is a contingent liability of the bank. As such, the bank is required to redeem it whether or not the issuer funds the redemption. With this possibility in mind, banks are inclined to check out carefully the credit standing of the issuers of these obligations. Acceptances usually arise in the course of foreign trade, although they also may result from domestic trade. Acceptances tend to be about as secure as the bank that accepts them.

Long-Term Debt Instruments

A wide variety of long-term debt securities also are available to investors. Most of these securities fall into three categories: government bonds (including agencies), municipals and traditional corporate bonds. Other categories include mortgage loans and mortgage-related securities, bank CDs, bond funds, income bonds, floating-rate notes, zero-coupon bonds, Eurobonds, insurance-company debt securities and private placements and payment in kind (PIK) bonds. Preferred stock also competes for the same income-oriented investor dollars that otherwise might go into long-term debt securities.

Not since the days of the Civil War and its aftermath have U.S. government securities been considered the least bit risky. While some municipal issues indeed have fallen into the distressed category and even defaulted, these issues are not a focus of this discussion. Accordingly, our attention will center on corporate issues.

Corporate Debt Obligations

Corporations constitute a principal category of bond issuers (in addition to governments and municipals). Both convertible and nonconvertible corporate instruments, like government bonds, bear interest and mature. In addition, convertibles may, at the owner's option, be exchanged at some fixed rate for stocks of the issuing corporation.

Corporate bonds are usually sold in units with $1,000 face value while quotations are given in parts of 100. A bond trading for less than 100 is selling at a discount from its face or par value. One selling for more than 100 is trading at a premium. As expected, bonds trading below par increase the expected yields to amounts in excess of the stated coupons. Conversely, premium bonds cause the expected yields to be lower than the stated coupons.

Most bond trades involve both the price of the bond and an adjustment for accrued interest. The buyer pays and the seller receives a sum to reflect the portion of interest that already has been earned but not yet paid. Thus, a bond that is quoted at 93 initially would cost the buyer $930 principal plus the prorated amount of accrued but unpaid interest. If the bond has a 10% coupon and made its last coupon payment three months ago, unpaid interest would have accrued as follows:

$$\frac{3}{12} \times .10 \times \$1,000 = \$25$$

Interest is paid to the one who holds the bond on the day of record. When the issuer makes the coupon payment, the new owner will receive and get to keep the entire amount for that period.

A relatively small number of bonds are traded flat. Typically, bonds that are in default or whose interest payments are considered very uncertain trade flat. These bonds are traded without any adjustment for the impact of accrued interest. If such bonds do make their interest payments, they make the payments to the holder of record on the record date. Thus, the owner of these bonds on the day of record receives all of that period's interest payments regardless of the length of ownership. In the quotation tables, bonds that trade flat have an "f" following the abbreviation for their name.

Many corporate bonds are listed on an exchange, but most of the trading takes place in a much more active OTC market. Investors wishing to buy or sell a large dollar value of bonds should obtain several quotations to see which market maker offers the best price. In addition to NYSE listings, small amounts of bonds also are traded on some other exchanges including the AMEX.

High-Risk Corporates   Bonds were once thought of as very secure low-risk investments. More recently, however, many bonds are viewed as very risky and thus bear commensurate yields. Many low-rated issues have paid off and the substantial yield premiums of these issues tend to offset their default risks. Indeed, junk-bond speculators often have fared quite well. Table 7.1 illustrates some mid-1982 yield differentials. Mid-1982 was a period of relatively high rates. Risk premiums also tended to be high at that time. For comparison, some rates for January 18, 1988, and March 15, 1991, also are shown.

Clearly, these substantial indicated yield differentials reflect appreciable differences in perceived risk. Indeed, the higher the "promised" yield, the greater the default risk is likely to be. Although junk bonds are ill-suited to the needs of cautious investors, many risk-oriented investors are attracted to them. Risk and potential returns can be as great as returns with many stocks. Indeed, a risky firm's bonds sometimes offer a more attractive way of speculating than does stock. For a bond investor to realize a profit in this type of investment, the troubled firm must only avoid bankruptcy or maintain a substantial value in a reorganization. The stockholder's return, in contrast, may not be attractive unless the firm becomes relatively profitable. A study by professors Chandy and Cherry strikes a cautious note for would-be investors in junk bonds, however. The authors found that while the average realized yields on junk bonds generally exceeded those for high-grade bonds, volatility was proportionally even greater. Moreover, during periods of rising interest rates, investment-grade bonds offered both less volatile yields and higher realized returns.

While always an important investment goal, diversification is particularly crucial for junk-bond portfolios. A defaulting issue eventually may pay off, but the wait can be long and tedious. Having a diversified portfolio substantially dilutes the impact of a single default. Such risk-spreading is especially advisable for junk-bond investors. Junk-bond funds provide small investors with an effective diversification vehicle.

Corporate Bond Funds   Corporate bond funds have existed for many years. With the stock market depressed and interest rates at historic highs, bond-fund yields became increasingly attractive in the early 1970s. The very high interest environment of the early 1980s further enhanced their yields and attractiveness. Markets are, of course, always changing. Later in the 1980s, interest rates fell, making bonds and bond funds somewhat less attractive.

As with other types of securities, bond funds may be load or no-load, open-end or closed-end, and managed or unmanaged (unit trusts). As with

TABLE 7.1   Differential Bond Yields

Company	Coupon	Maturity	Price	Current Yield
May 19, 1992				
Very Secure:				
AT&T	$13\frac{1}{4}$	1991	$96\frac{1}{4}$	13.7
GE Credit	$13\frac{5}{8}$	1991	97	14.0
Risky:				
Eastern Airlines	$17\frac{1}{2}$	1998	$92\frac{7}{8}$	18.8
Rapid American	11	2005	$57\frac{5}{8}$	18.9
World Airlines	$11\frac{1}{4}$	1994	$52\frac{7}{8}$	22.3
Very Risky:				
International Harvester	9	2004	$28\frac{1}{2}$	31.6
In Default:				
Braniff	10	1986	$32\frac{1}{2}$	30.8 (if paid)
January 18, 1988				
Very Secure:				
AT&T	$8\frac{5}{8}$	2026	$89\frac{1}{2}$	9.6
General Motors	$8\frac{5}{8}$	2005	$91\frac{1}{2}$	9.4
Risky:				
Beth Steel	$8\frac{3}{8}$	2001	$74\frac{1}{2}$	11.3
Commonwealth Edison	$11\frac{3}{4}$	2015	$103\frac{1}{2}$	11.4
Very Risky:				
Texas Air	$15\frac{3}{4}$	1992	$94\frac{1}{2}$	16.7
Resorts International	$11\frac{3}{8}$	2013	62	18.3
In Default:				
LTV	$8\frac{3}{4}$	2004	25	35.0 (if paid)
March 15, 1991				
Very Secure:				
AT&T	$8\frac{5}{8}$	2026	$93\frac{3}{4}$	9.2
General Motors	$8\frac{3}{4}$	2001	98	8.9
Risky:				
Beth Steel	9	2000	$4\frac{5}{8}$	10.7
Commonwealth Edison	$10\frac{5}{8}$	1995	103	10.3
Very Risky:				
RJR Nabisco	17	2007	$109\frac{5}{8}$	15.5
Resorts International	11	1994	$50\frac{1}{2}$	21.8
In Default:				
LTV	$8\frac{3}{4}$	1998	$11\frac{1}{2}$	76.1
NV Ryan	$13\frac{3}{4}$	1997	$5\frac{1}{8}$	268.3 (if paid)

stock funds, most investors will find the no-load type of fund a generally preferable way of buying into a bond portfolio. Most closed-end funds sell at a discount from their net asset values (NAVs). Both open-end and closed-end bond funds have similar advantages and drawbacks vis-à-vis direct bond ownership, as do common stock mutual funds relative to investor-assembled stock portfolios. The bond funds offer diversification, convenience and low-denomination purchase. On the other hand, the expenses incurred in marketing and managing the funds reduce their yields somewhat. As with other types of funds, unmanaged funds have lower expenses. Thus, more of the portfolio's yields flow through to the unit holders.

Other Types of Debt Instruments

We already have discussed the most important types of debt instruments: money market, governments, municipals and traditional corporates. A number of other types of debt security also bear mentioning. Long-term CDs, income bonds, floating-rate notes, zero-coupon bonds, payment in kind (PIK) and yield-curve notes have unusual interest provisions. In addition, Eurobonds, insurance-company debt instruments and private placements have characteristics similar to other long-term debt instruments.

Income Bonds   Most bonds must either pay the agreed-on sums (coupon rates) or go into default. Income bonds, in contrast, pay interest only if the issuer earns it. Passed coupons may or may not accumulate. Bonds with large unpaid arrearage may offer attractive speculations. Specific indenture provisions indicate when earned income is sufficient to require an interest payment.

Most income bonds originate in a workout exchange or in a reorganization. Some new bond issues, however, are sold initially as income bonds. Income bonds offer issuers about as much flexibility to withhold payments as does preferred stock. In addition, the issuer has the right to deduct the (interest) payments from taxable income. Nonetheless, income bonds are much rarer than preferred stock.

Floating-Rate Notes   In 1974, Citicorp introduced a novel type of variable rate security. Soon thereafter, several other corporations offered their own floating-rate notes. For example, Citicorp issued a "floater" that matures in 2004. Its coupon is adjusted every six months to yield approximately 1% over the six-month Treasury-bill rate. The floating-rate feature of these bonds generally causes their prices to remain relatively close to their par values. The bonds are structured so that their yields adjust to market conditions. Thus, their prices can stay relatively constant as interest rates fluctuate. The more distant maturity of most "floaters" does, however, make them more risky to hold (greater default risk) than otherwise similar short-maturity debt instruments.

New issues of floating-rate notes have varied substantially over the past few years. In 1984, about $40 billion were issued, including $10 billion from U.S. issuers. The student-loan programs in Kansas, Kentucky and Minnesota have issued intermediate-term notes with taxfree interest pegged at approximately 70% of the T-bill rate. Similarly, the Student Loan Marketing Association (Sallie Mae, a government-chartered but privately owned corporation) has sold notes backed by government-guaranteed student loans whose interest rates are adjusted weekly to .75% above the 91-day T-bill rate. Floating-rate issues also are relatively common in the international market, especially in Asia. Moreover, a few companies have issued floating-rate preferreds.

Zero-Coupon Bonds and Other Types of Original Issue Discount Bonds   Most bonds' coupon rates are initially set so that they will be priced close to their face, or par, values. Original issue discount bonds are sold for appreciably less than their values at maturity (par). These bonds have either zero-coupon rates or coupon rates that are well below the market rate. As a result, such bonds initially sell for a market price that is substantially below their face values.

Bonds that do not pay coupons are called zero-coupon bonds, or zeros. The returns on these securities are derived from the differences between their purchase prices and maturity values. Treasury bills and certain other securities such as U.S. Savings Bonds have long been sold on a discount basis. For example, a one-year T-bill might be priced at 93. This means that a bill with a $10,000 face value initially would cost $9,300 and pay an additional $700 ($10,000 less $9,300) at maturity. More recently, a number of long-term corporate zeros have been issued.

Zero-coupon bonds also may be created from some types of coupon bonds. The coupons simply are separated from the principal portion and the two components are sold separately. Most bonds pay interest to the registered owner, but some have attached coupons that may be clipped and sold to an investor seeking periodic income. The bond without its coupons attached is called a strip bond.

Merrill Lynch has created yet another type of zero-coupon security that it calls Treasury Investment Growth Receipts (TIGRs). A pool of U.S. government securities is purchased and used to guarantee the issue. Like other zero-coupons securities, TIGRs pay no coupons, but they mature at face value and are sold at a discount. Other brokerage firms offer similar instruments also bearing feline names (CATS, LYONs, Cougars, etc.).

These various categories of zeros have precisely identifiable maturity values. This feature has an appeal for Individual Retirement Accounts (IRAs) and Keogh accounts. Investors in zeros know at the outset exactly what their compounded value will be at maturity. The end-period value of funds invested in coupon-yielding bonds, in contrast, is not nearly so certain. The actual compounded value of such a stream of income will depend on the rate earned on the reinvested coupon payments.

The uncertainty associated with the return on reinvested coupon payments is called reinvestment risk. Because of their lack of reinvestment risk and because of their relative scarcity, zero-coupon bonds have tended to sell for somewhat lower yields than equivalent-risk coupon bonds.

Like other long-term bonds, long-term zero-coupon bonds lock both the buyer and the issuer into a long-term rate. If rates go up after the purchase, the buyer will end up receiving a below-market return. The issuer, in contrast, will pay an above-market rate if market interest rates decline after the issue is sold. Moreover, for a given change in interest rates, the prices of zeros change proportionately more than do those of coupon bonds. Owners of coupon bonds are at least able to reinvest their coupon income at higher rates when market interest rates rise. Owners of zeros receive no coupon payments and thus have no cash income to reinvest.

Not only do zeros pay no coupons, they impose annual tax liabilities on their owners (assuming the investors are subject to the income tax). Original issue discount bonds (including zeros) are taxed in an interesting, if complicated, fashion. To determine a zero's tax liability, one first must determine the relevant amount of imputed interest. This is the amount that the government assumes is earned but not received each year. The imputed interest rate is computed as if the bond made annual coupon payments equal to its yield-to-maturity rate computed at the time of its purchase. Thus, a zero-coupon bond that was sold to yield 10% would be treated for tax purposes as if it did, in fact, yield 10% each year. Because of the effect of compounding, the imputed interest income will rise each year. The issuer is allowed to deduct the imputed interest cost each year, while the owner incurs an equivalent tax liability. As a result, the issuer obtains an early tax deduction, while the owner must pay out taxes prior to receipt of the associated income.

The tax computation on coupon-paying original issue discount bonds is even more complex. The owner, of course, is liable for taxes on the coupon payments. In addition, taxes are assessed on the appropriate imputed interest as the bond moves closer to maturity. The basis on both types of original issue discount bonds is increased each year by the amount of the accumulated imputed interest. Thus, the basis on an original issue discount bond would equal the initial purchase cost plus the sum of the imputed interest amounts.

Payment in Kind (PIK) Bonds   Payment in kind (PIK) bonds also have unusual interest characteristics. They pay interest, not in cash but in additional securities. PIK bonds will be encountered relatively infrequently, usually in conjunction with lower-rated issuers. They also might be issued or exchanged by a firm emerging from bankruptcy to ease initial cash interest requirements. PIK bonds incur many of the same tax consequences as zeros.

They, however, are different from zeros in one important aspect. Unlike zeros, PIKs do not accrete interest but receive interest in the form of additional securities that may be sold in the open market as a way of monetizing interest income. The trading market for PIK bonds in many cases is quite limited.

Eurobonds   Eurodollars are dollar-denominated accounts held by individuals, firms or governments domiciled outside the United States. Eurobonds, in contrast, are denominated either in dollars or in some other currency but traded internationally, while U.S. and foreign bonds are traded in only one country. The Eurobond issuer benefits from the wider distribution and the absence of restrictions and taxes that are placed on national bonds. Eurobond buyers may obtain greater diversification than from U.S. bonds alone. Moreover, bonds denominated in a foreign currency offer investors an opportunity to speculate against the dollar.

One of the most attractive features of Eurobonds (at least for some investors) is the ease with which they allow investors to evade taxes. Two features of Eurobonds facilitate such activity. Unlike domestic bonds, no withholding is applied to Eurobond interest and principal payments. Moreover, such bonds are issued in bearer (unregistered) form. Without either registration or withholding, Eurobond owners find that taxes are relatively easy to evade. Because of this appeal to investors wishing to evade taxes, Eurobonds tend to yield less than similar-risk domestic bonds.

Most Eurobonds are issued by multinational corporations, governments and international organizations and most are denominated in dollars or marks. By mid-1984, more than $210 billion were outstanding. They may take on any of the forms of regular bonds: straight bonds, convertibles, floating-rate notes, zero-coupon bonds and so on.

Private Placements   Approximately one-third of the debt instruments sold are placed privately to a few large buyers (often insurance companies) and publicly announced in the financial press. Such announcements generally are referred to as "tombstones" because of the large white spaces and small amount of lettering. Even if the large size (tens of millions of dollars) of typical private placements rules out direct purchases, individuals may participate indirectly through one of the closed-end funds that specialize in such investments.

Private placements generally yield ½ to 1% more than equivalent-risk bonds but lack marketability. Private placements offer issuers greater flexibility. They can be tailored for specific buyers and do not require prospectuses. Moreover, the underwriting cost savings largely offset their somewhat higher coupons. Finally, the relatively small number of owners makes terms easier to renegotiate when necessary. Figure 7.1 summarizes the various types of (nonconvertible) long-term debt instruments.

Convertibles and Other Combination Securities

Several types of securities combine option features with characteristics of other instruments. The two primary types of combination securities are convertible debentures and convertible preferreds. A host of much rarer types includes hybrid convertibles, equity notes, LYONs, payment in kind (PIKs, may be either bonds or preferreds), commodity-backed bonds and stock-indexed bonds. Convertible preferreds and PIK preferreds are equity securities. Convertible debentures, hybrid convertibles, equity notes, LYONs, PIK bonds, commodity-backed bonds and stock-indexed bonds are all debt securities. Each type of combination security has a close relationship to another type of security or other asset. Most combination securities may be exchanged for a set number of common shares or, in the case of

FIGURE 7.1   Long-Term Debt Securities

	Primary Types
Issue Type	*Characteristic*
Treasury notes and bonds	Lowest risk category
Agency issues	Slightly higher risks and yields than Treasuries
Mortgage-related securities	
Federal National Mortgage Association (FNMA)	Mortgage-backed [Veterans Administration (VA) and Federal Housing Administration (FHA)]
Government National Mortgage Association (GNMA)	Mortgage passthroughs (VA and FHA)
Freddie Mac	Conventional mortgages with Freddie Mac [Federal Home Loan Mortgage Corporation (FHLMC)] guarantee
Bank issued	Conventional mortgages, often with a private guarantee
Direct mortgage, seller financing	Risk varies, seconds usually are quite risky
Municipals	Taxfree, risk varies
Municipal bond funds	Diversified, may be open-end or closed-end
Corporates	Vary greatly in risks and yields
Corporate bond fund	Diversified, may be open-end or closed-end
Junk-bond fund	High-risk portfolio
	Specialized Types
Income bonds	Interest paid only if earned
Floating-rate notes	Coupon varies with market rates
Zero coupon bonds	Sold at a discount, pays no coupon
Eurobonds	Trade internationally
Payment in kind (PIK) bonds	Pays interest in like securities
Private placements	Large and flexible
Preferred stock	80% tax-sheltered to domestic corporations

commodity-backed and stock-indexed bonds, their redemption values or coupon rates are indexed to the price of some other asset. PIKs pay their owners a return in the form of more units of the security that now is held. Except for equity notes, conversion of the combination security is at the security owner's option.

The Appeal of Combination Securities   Combination securities derive value from their current return (interest or preferred dividends) and also as potential common stock or some other asset. If the price of the underlying common stock rises sufficiently, the convertible owner can either acquire stock at a below-market price or sell the combination security at a price that reflects the value of the underlying stock. If the stock's price does not rise sufficiently to make conversion attractive, the owners still will receive income and perhaps eventual redemption on the securities in their roles as preferreds or debentures. Convertibles do offer an attractive combination of upside potential and downside protection. The convertibility feature does, however, usually come at the cost of reduced interest or dividend income.

Convertible Terminology   A number of specialized terms are encountered with convertibles:

- Conversion ratio: Number of shares into which the security is convertible
- Conversion price: Face value of the security divided by its conversion ratio
- Conversion value: Current stock price multiplied by the conversion ratio
- Straight-debt value: Market value of an otherwise-equivalent bond lacking a conversion feature
- Conversion premium: Bond price less its conversion value
- Premium over straight-debt value: Bond price less its straight-debt value

To understand the use of these terms, consider a CVD convertible bond. It has a $1,000 face value and a 12% coupon and is convertible into 50 shares of CVD stock (its conversion ratio) any time over the next 20 years. For a $20 a share stock price, the conversion value of the convertible equals the face value of the bond ($20 × 50 = $1,000). Thus, the conversion price is $20 per share. If the stock sells for $15 a share when the bonds are issued,

TABLE 7.2   Selected Convertible Bond Data for February 1, 1983

Convertible Issue	Rating	Conversion Ratio	Stock Price	Conversion Value	Estimated Straight– Debt Value	Market Price
AVCO 5½ 93	BB–	18.52	27⅝	$ 512	$500	$ 670
GELCO 14s 01	BB–	22.13	42⅜	$ 938	$950	$1,010
GTE 5s 92	BBB	22.98	40¾	$ 936	$560	$ 962
Life Mark 11s 02	BB+	30.30	34⅞	$1,057	$840	$1,215
Ramada Inns 10s 00	B–	129.03	5¾	$ 742	$710	$ 960

SOURCE: Ben Branch, *Investments: Principles and Practices*, Second Edition (Chicago: Dearborn Financial Publishing, Inc., 1989).

the bond's initial conversion value equals $750. These bonds generally will trade at prices that more closely reflect their values as bonds (the straight-debt values of their 12% coupon rates). Thus, if the market rate on similar-risk long-term bonds is 14%, this bond should sell for at least $860 (12% ÷ 14% = .86). It actually should sell for a bit more so that its yield to maturity equals 14%.

Suppose the price of the underlying stock rose sufficiently for the conversion value to approach the straight-debt value of the convertible. In that price environment, the bond's price fluctuations would begin behaving more like that of its underlying stock. If, for example, the stock rose to $25 a share, the convertible would have a conversion value of $1,250 (50 × $25). The market price would be at or above the conversion value and would move up and down proportionately with the stock's price. Thus, if the stock's price next moved to 26, the conversion value would rise to $1,300 and the bond price would be at least that high.

Conversion and straight-debt values tend to place a floor under the price of convertibles. Because of their "equity kicker," they normally yield appreciably less than otherwise-similar nonconvertibles. A convertible with a 10% coupon therefore typically would command a somewhat higher price than a similar-quality 10% nonconvertible. The difference between the bond's conversion value and the market value is known as the conversion premium. The difference between the convertible's market price and the straight-debt value is called the premium over the straight-debt value.

Assume the CVD bonds sold for $950 when the stock traded at 15 and similar nonconvertibles were selling for $875. The conversion premium would be $200 ($950 − $750) and the premium over straight-debt value would be $75 ($950 − $875). Table 7.2 contains data on some real-world convertibles.

Because convertible bonds often are almost as risky as stocks, the same margin percentage is required: in 1992, 50% versus 30% for straight bonds. Thus, $10,000 worth of marginable convertibles could be purchased with $5,000 of investor's equity and $5,000 in margin borrowing. The convertible's coupon payments may offset part or all of the interest cost of a margin purchase. Buying convertibles on margin may be appealing if the (short-term) margin rate is low relative to the (longer-term) bond rate. Indeed, low conversion value convertibles often pay relatively high yields and sometimes even return to life.

The Advantages of Convertible Bonds   Convertible bonds offer both fixed coupons (usually a bit below the market rate on equivalent-risk straight-debt securities) and the possibilities of capital gains. They should not be bought either as income securities (straight bonds almost always offer higher risk-adjusted yield) or as pure stock plays (the stock itself will usually rise proportionately more in a strong market). Rather, convertibles appeal to investors who find the prospects of the related stock attractive but desire the income and protection of the straight-debt value.

Investing in convertibles offers two basic advantages over investments in the underlying common stock. First, the security's current return usually is higher and certainly more dependable than the corresponding common stock's dividend yield. Second, their fixed coupons give convertibles considerable resistance to the adverse effect of downward moves in the common stock's prices. Convertible prices do tend to move inversely with interest rates, however. Moreover, they normally yield less than otherwise-similar nonconvertible debentures. Finally, the conversion feature will have value only as long as the stock price has a reasonable potential of rising enough for the conversion value to exceed the straight-debt value.

Deep-discount convertibles often are particularly attractive. *Business Week* cited the following example: In the depressed market of August of 1974, the Chase Manhattan Bank's 4⅞% bond sold for $630 (a 9% yield), which equaled its estimated straight-debt value. Moreover, the market price exceeded the conversion value by only 10%. A 25% increase in the stock price would lead to a bond price increase of about 18%. A 25% fall in the stock price (assuming interest rates held steady), in contrast, probably would have produced about a 3% reduction in the bond's price. A substantial decline in the bond's price would require both an increase in interest rates and a fall in the stock's price. Even in this instance, an investor simply could hold the bond and collect a 9% yield to maturity.

Convertibles' Call Risk   While most debt securities are callable, the call feature (and corresponding call risk) is especially relevant to convertible holders. In theory, corporations should force conversion whenever the call price is safely below the bond's conversion value. Following such a policy would severely limit convertibles' upside potentials. Thus, they may offer only attractive returns (vis-à-vis nonconvertibles) if the conversion values rise above the call prices soon after the securities are issued. Moreover, calling to force conversion generally depresses the price of the underlying stock. Most companies, however, do not call their convertibles so quickly as the theoretical model predicts.

The Theoretical Value of Convertibles   Because they contain both debt and equity elements, convertibles' theoretical values are relatively difficult to define. Debt values will depend on the coupons, default risks, maturity dates and other indenture provisions. The value of the conversion feature is affected by the firm's risk and capital structure, dividend policy, calling policy, conversion terms and the current stock price.

As with call valuation, a convertible's theoretical value should not offer assured arbitrage profits to either buyers or short sellers. Values derived from the Black/Scholes contingent-claim pricing model (devised by the well-known finance theorists Fisher Black and Myron Scholes and used to derive theoretical values for options) have been applied to convertible pricing.

Calculating the prices the stocks must reach to make investments in convertibles or their associated stocks equivalent also is much more complex than with warrants. Both the premium over conversion and the difference between interest and expected dividend income must be considered.

Hybrid Convertibles   Convertible bonds and preferreds are the primary types of convertible securities, but other types of combination securities also bear mentioning. Unlike traditional convertibles, hybrids (also called exchangeable debentures) are convertible into stocks of different companies from those that issue them. For example, in 1980, Textron sold debentures convertible into Textron-owned shares of Allied Chemical (at 66). At about the same time, Mesa Petroleum sold a security convertible into General American. Companies with substantial stock portfolios may find hybrids a useful source of funds.

Hybrids are about as attractive to investors as the straight convertibles of the underlying company. The bond's default risk depends on the issuing company's financial position, however. Moreover, the conversion of a regular convertible is a taxfree exchange, whereas any profit realized when a hybrid is converted is immediately taxable.

Equity Notes Equity notes (also called mandatory convertible notes) were developed to meet the capital needs of banks. These notes are issued as debt instruments that yield fixed coupons until maturity, when they are automatically converted into common stocks. For example, Manufacturers Hanover Trust (Manny Hanny) sold $100 million in ten-year equity notes in April of 1982. These notes yield 15⅛% and in 1992 must be converted into Manny Hanny shares at a price equal to the 30-day average price prior to maturity with upper and lower limits of 55.55 and 40. Manny Hanny was selling for approximately 32 when these bonds were issued. In April of 1991, the stock was selling for about 27, a long way from the minimum conversion price of 40.

LYONs One of the most complex of the new instruments is the Liquidity Yield Option Note (LYON). LYONs differ from ordinary convertibles primarily because they are zero-coupon convertibles. In addition, they are callable and redeemable. Making the security even more complicated, both the redemption and call prices escalate through time. The first two of these issues were brought out by Merrill Lynch in 1985.

Commodity-Backed Bonds Commodity-backed bonds are debt instruments whose values are potentially related to the price of some physical commodity. For example, in 1980, Sunshine Mining (silver) sold $57.5 million in 8½% bonds whose redemption value was tied to the price of silver. For prices below $20 per ounce, the bonds mature at face value, but at higher prices, the bond's redemption value rises proportionately. Thus, these bonds allow the owner to speculate on a silver price rise while earning a modest return. The bond's price has moved up and down with variations in both the

FIGURE 7.2   Types of Combination Securities

Convertible bonds	Debt securities that may be exchanged for common stock at a fixed ratio
Convertible preferred	Preferred stock that may be exchanged for common stock at a fixed ratio
Hybrid convertibles	Debt securities of one company convertible into the common stock of another company
Equity notes	Debt securities with a mandatory conversion
LYONs	Zero-coupon, convertible, callable, redeemable bonds
Commodity-backed bonds	Debt securities whose potential redemption values are related to the market price of some physical commodity such as silver
Stock-indexed bonds	Debt securities whose yields are related to stock market volume

silver price and market interest rates. When the bonds were issued, silver sold for $14 to $15 per ounce. At year-end 1982, silver was down to $10. Still later, silver fell as low as $5. In April of 1992, silver was trading for about $5 per ounce, a substantial amount below the $20 price envisioned by the bond. Other examples include the energy bonds of Petro Lewis and the gold bonds of Refinement International and the copper-indexed bonds of Magma Copper that also are PIKs under some circumstances.

Stock-Indexed Bonds   In 1981, Oppenheimer and Company marketed a $25 million stock-indexed bond. The coupon rate was indexed to stock trading volume with a maximum of 22% compared with an initial rate of 18%. High stock volume should result in booming business for Oppenheimer. Thus, it should be able to pay a higher interest rate when stock market volume is high. Similarly, Salomon issued S&P Subordinated Index Notes whose interest is indexed to the market return. Chase has issued a CD with similar features. An interest rate of 4% is guaranteed with an additional return equal to one-fourth of the rise in the S&P 500.

Both commodity-backed and stock-indexed bonds were designed to appeal to speculative investors with options that specially positioned issuers can offer. Additional types of innovative combination securities probably will be devised as time passes. Figure 7.2 lists the various types of combination securities.

Equity Instruments

Unlike debt instruments, equity securities represent proportional ownership in an asset such as a corporation. The owners have a residual claim on its assets and earnings. Equity-related assets include publicly traded common stock, preferred stock, options, convertibles and mutual funds, as well as ownership positions in small firms and venture-capital investments. Each of these investments represents direct or indirect ownership in a profit-seeking enterprise. Equity holders' claims are junior to those of all debts but encompass all residual value and income in excess of the claims of the senior securities.

Common Stock By far the most important type of equity-related security is common stock. Approximately 50 million U.S. investors own stock directly, while many more participate indirectly in the stock market. Vehicles such as mutual funds, trust funds, insurance-company portfolios and the invested reserves of pension funds all provide indirect access.

As the residual owners, shareholders are paid dividends out of their firm's profits. The portion of profits not paid out (retained earnings) is reinvested in the company, thereby helping it grow and increase in value. Growth in sales, assets and particularly profits should lead to a higher overall value of the firm. The benefit of any appreciation in the firm's value accrues to its owners, the stockholders. A company's stockholders theoretically control it by electing its board of directors. The board, in turn, selects upper-level management and makes major policy decisions. Most stock ownership groups are, however, widely dispersed and unorganized. Existing management generally fills the resulting power vacuum by nominating and electing friendly slates of directors.

In general, stock returns compare favorably with those of most bonds and depository accounts. On the other hand, returns on certain stocks over particular periods have differed greatly from the average. Furthermore, the returns on most stocks were well below these long-term averages during much of the 1960s and 1970s. Managing a portfolio of stocks effectively is not an easy task. Many books have been written on the subject and, no doubt, many, many more will be written. Playing the stock market is and always will be a very challenging game.

Dividends are not assured and common stock never matures. Thus, shareholders are particularly dependent on their firm's future profitability and market acceptance. Investors whose holdings reduce or eliminate their dividends are likely also to see a dramatic decline in the values of their stocks. Bond prices generally fluctuate much less than stock prices. Moreover, their promised interest must be paid regardless of the firm's profit picture. Therefore, bonds almost always have less downside risk than the stocks of the same or similar-risk firms. Stocks can be bought and sold effectively in increments of as little as a few thousand dollars. Thus, the relatively low minimum cost of a stock portfolio makes stocks relatively accessible to small investors. Commissions, however, are disproportionately high on very small transactions (less than about $1,000 and/or less than 100 shares). The average (median) stockholder's portfolio was worth around $6,200 in 1985.

In summary, common stock offers somewhat higher but more risky expected returns than bonds. Stocks are not very liquid, but those of most large and medium-sized firms are quite marketable. Small investors can begin assembling a stock portfolio with relatively modest sums. Informed stock selection requires considerable skill and time, however.

Preferred Stock   While preferred stock is a type of equity security, it has much in common with debt instruments. The issuer is not required to declare preferred dividends. Payment is required, however, if common dividends are to be paid. Moreover, most preferreds are cumulative, which means that accumulated dividends (unpaid) must be made up before the common dividend can resume. Thus, the preferred dividends of many companies are almost as dependable as their bond interest. The preferreds of a weak company may, however, be almost as risky as its common stock. Some preferreds (participating) may receive an extra dividend payment if earnings or common dividends are high enough.

Preferred stockholders are residual claimants only one step ahead of common stockholders. Unless the creditor's claims are fully satisfied, nothing will be left for either class of stockholders. Unlike corporate interest payments, preferred dividends paid by domestic corporations (incorporated in the United States) to domestic corporations are 70% taxfree. That is, only 30% of dividends that one domestic corporation receives from another is taxable. This tax preference is available only to holders who retain ownership of the preferred for at least 46 days. For a corporation in the 34% tax bracket, a 9% preferred yield is equivalent to an after-tax yield of 7.98%. A fully taxable yield of 12.1%, in contrast, would be needed to generate 7.98% after taxes.

Preferreds have become very popular with corporate investors—particularly banks and insurance companies. Because their tax advantage is available only to corporations, most individual investors will not find preferreds attractive.

Preferred stocks vary greatly in risk, but, as a class, they tend to be more risky than most types of debt securities. While also a form of ownership, preferred stock generally is less risky than common stock. Preferred dividend yields usually are below the average long-term total return (dividend plus capital gains) on common stocks. As relatively fixed-income securities, preferreds are subject to the same type of interest-rate risk as bonds. Moreover, most preferred shares have relatively little long-term appreciation potential. The preferred stock of a weak company may, however, be riskier and may have a higher expected yield than the common stock of a stronger company.

The prices of preferreds vary inversely with interest rates. While dividends paid to individuals are fully taxed, only 30% of those paid to corporations are subject to federal tax. This special tax treatment is a particularly attractive feature for preferreds when dividends constitute most of the return. Like common stock, preferred stock tends to be relatively marketable. Assembling a diversified portfolio of preferred stock requires a modest amount of time, funds and effort.

Convertible Preferreds   While less popular than convertible debentures, convertible preferreds have become much more numerous in the past few years.

Convertible preferreds promise (but do not guarantee) to pay fixed dividends. Like convertible bonds, they can be converted into a stated number of common shares within prespecified periods. The convertibility feature eventually may expire, at which time the stock becomes a normal fixed-income preferred. As with convertible bonds, convertible preferreds behave more like the underlying stocks when the market price is close to their conversion values and more like straight preferreds when the conversion value is well below the value as a preferred.

The number of common shares that can be obtained by converting is called the conversion ratio. Thus, a preferred convertible into four common shares would have a ratio of 4.0. This conversion ratio may change with time. For example, an issue might be convertible into four shares for the first ten years after issue, two shares for the next ten years and then may become a straight preferred.

A preferred's conversion value is the current price of the common stock multiplied by the conversion ratio. A preferred convertible into four shares of common stock selling at $10 would have a conversion value of $40. A market price of $50 would reflect a conversion premium of $10. The conversion premium is normally expressed as a percentage:

$$\text{Conversion premium} = \frac{\text{Market price of preferred} - \text{Conversion value}}{\text{Conversion value}}$$

The conversion premium in the example is: ($50 − $40) + $40 = $10 + $40 = 25%. Knowing the size of the conversion premium may help an investor determine whether the convertible preferred stock or the common stock is the more attractive investment. For example, an investor might have a choice between a company's 10% convertible preferred stock selling at $50 and its common stock bearing a 5% dividend yield selling for $20. If the conversion ratio is 2.0 and the conversion value is $40, the conversion premium is 25%:

	CVP	Common
Price	$50	$20
Dividend	$ 5	$ 1
Yield	10%	5%

For the 25% conversion premium, an investor buying the 10% convertible preferred stock receives a higher current yield (10% versus 5%), a more stable dividend (a characteristic of preferreds) and the option of converting the issue into common stock. Of course, the higher the conversion premium, the more remote will be the chance of an attractive conversion and the lower the gain even if the conversion does become profitable. Moreover, convertible preferreds are exposed to the same kind of call risks and interest-rate risks as are convertible bonds.

Small Firm Ownership   Most people who invest in companies (e.g., as shareholders) hold very small stakes in relatively large firms. Others, however, hold relatively large stakes in small companies. These firms may be organized as sole proprietorships, partnerships or closely held corporations. An investor in such a firm may or may not take an active role in his or her company's affairs. Those who take active roles in their enterprises are much more involved in the management side of their businesses than in the investment side. This management commitment may cut deeply into the time for other activities. Moreover, joint ownership can lead to troublesome policy disputes, and nonexpert part-time owner-managers may be at a disadvantage relative to specialists—competitors. Finally, valuating and ultimately selling a small business can be especially difficult.

Silent-partner owners have different problems. A suitable manager may be difficult to find and/or keep. Managers may misuse their positions (legally or illegally) and, unless given a share in the firm's profits, may have less incentive than the owners to operate the business profitably. Moreover, the owners are personally liable for the unpaid debts of a partnership or sole proprietorship, and many creditors require the owners of a small corporation to cosign its loans.

Limited Partnerships and Master Limited Partnerships   Most businesses are organized as partnerships or corporations. The corporate form provides limited liability for owners (shareholders), but its income is first taxed at the corporate level and its shareholders are taxed again on their income (dividends) from the firm.

Unlike that of a corporation, the income of a partnership is taxed only once. Partnership profits, whether distributed or retained by the partnership, are treated for tax purposes as the imputed income of the partners. Partners are, however, individually and collectively liable for all of the partnership's obligations. Limited partnerships provide alternative ways of organizing business enterprises. They combine the benefits of a corporation's limited liability with the single taxation advantage of a partnership. A single general partner, who is usually the organizer, does have unlimited liability. The limited partners, however, are not liable for the partnership's debts and obligations beyond their initial capital contribution. Most limited partnerships do have one major drawback. Because they are relatively small, their ownership units trade in very thin markets. The master limited partnership (MLP) is designed to overcome this drawback. Most MLPs are relatively large (compared to limited partnerships). Their ownership units are designed to trade actively in the same types of markets as stock.

MLPs generally have been organized around oil and gas holdings. Others are designed for real estate. Mesa Limited Partners (oil and gas) is one of the best known of the MLPs. Investing in MLPs involves many of the same advantages and disadvantages as investing in common stock. It should be noted, however, that the stated current yields on MLPs often are inflated and unsustainable. The managers of these MLPs are depleting assets to make what appear to be attractive payouts. Moreover, the tax advantages of future MLPs have been limited by congressional action.

Venture Capital   Venture capitalists provide risk capital to otherwise undercapitalized companies that they believe have attractive growth prospects. In exchange, the venture capitalist receives a ground-floor equity position in what may turn out to be a highly lucrative venture. For example, Georges Doriot invested $70,000 of the American Research and Development's (ARD) money into what eventually grew into several hundred million dollars worth of Digital Equipment common stock when Textron acquired ARD in 1972.

Options: Calls, Puts, Warrants and Rights   Options are an interesting, if relatively complex, type of security. Most options give the holder the right to acquire or dispose of an equity-related security. The owner of a call contract has an option to buy something. The call writer sells the call buyer the right (but not the obligation) to purchase an investment asset, such as 100 shares of a particular stock. The contract will specify the price (called the striking price) at which, and the period over which, the call may be exercised. Similarly, a put is a sell-option contract for a particular security, price, quantity and period. Exercising the option privilege is solely at the owner's (not the seller's) discretion. The option buyer and option writer, in effect, have a wager on what will happen to the price of the security on which the option is written. For example, the call buyer will earn a profit if the price of the associated asset rises sufficiently. Call writers, in contrast, usually profit if the relevant price does not rise to or much above the exercise level. In that case, they generally can earn the option premium without having to deliver the stock or other optioned asset.

Suppose an investor pays $200 for an option to buy 100 shares of stock at 20 ($20 per share). If the stock's price subsequently rises to 30, the investor can exercise the option (buy the stock) at 20 and then immediately turn around and sell that same stock at 30. Such a set of transactions would yield a profit of $800 (before commissions) compared with an initial cost of $200 for the call. That amounts to a profit of 400% ($800 + $200). A similar profit would be made on $200 invested in a put if the price subsequently fell from 20 to 10. The same $200, in contrast, could have purchased only 10 shares at 20 producing a $100 gain for a 10-point price rise (50% profit). An adverse stock price move can, however, lead to a total loss for the option holder. The shareholder's potential loss, in percentage terms, generally is much less.

Standardized option trading began with the 1973 opening of the Chicago Board Options Exchange (CBOE) and soon spread to other exchanges. Options now are listed on a large number of different stocks. Other options are listed on stock indexes and commodities futures contracts. Most options have relatively short lives (nine months or less) and their prices are dominated by random market fluctuations. Accordingly, option trading is largely the preserve of relatively sophisticated investors.

Warrants and rights are traded in the same markets that trade the stocks that underlie them. A warrant, like a call, permits its owner to purchase a particular stock at a prespecified price over a prespecified period. Unlike calls, warrants generally are exercisable for relatively long periods (e.g., several years). Furthermore, warrants are issued by the company whose stock underlies the warrant. If the warrant is exercised, the issuing company simply creates more shares. In contrast, existing shares are used to satisfy the exercises of a call. Thus, warrants are company-issued securities whose exercise results in additional shares and generates cash for the issuer. Calls are contracts between individual investors that do not involve the underlying company.

Rights, like warrants, are company-issued options to buy stock. Rights differ from warrants in two ways. First, rights are issued for very short-run periods. They expire in a few weeks or at most a few months from the time of their issue. Also, rights generally are exercisable at prices that are substantially less than the current market price of the stock. The issuer sets a low enough price to make exercise attractive. Therefore, most rights are exercised, while warrant exercise is more uncertain. For example, a right might allow an investor to buy stock at 40 when the market price is 45. Failure to exercise or sell such rights is like throwing away $5 multiplied by the number of rights. Rights normally are issued to existing shareholders on the basis of their current holdings. Thus, shareholders might receive one right for each 20 shares that they owned.

Option prices tend to move in the same direction as the underlying common stock but with a considerably greater magnitude. As a result, options generally are considered relatively risky securities. On the other hand, option writing may reduce a portfolio's risk and increase its income.

In summary, most listed options are quite marketable, whereas unlisted options generally are traded in thin markets. Most types of option trading are relatively risky. At least as much expertise and time are required for profitable option trading as for trading common stock. Figure 7.3 summarizes the principal types of equity-related securities.

Hedging and Arbitraging

As markets have become more sophisticated, security types more diverse and takeover activity more widespread, hedging and arbitrage trading have risen markedly. Both brokerage firms and individual investors have gotten into the act.

Hedging involves taking opposing positions in related assets to profit (or reduce losses) from hoped-for relative price movements. For example, the hedger might buy stocks and short corresponding warrants, or vice versa. Arbitragers, in contrast, simultaneously buy and sell equivalent securities in separate markets, profiting from temporary price differences. Arbitragers generally will take advantage of any appreciable price disparities for securities traded on both the PSE and the NYSE or any other combination of exchanges. In addition to their use in debt- and equity-related securities trading, hedging and arbitraging also take place in a wide variety of other markets including those for currencies and commodities. Both hedging and arbitraging may be classified into pure and risk forms.

Hedging   A pure hedge is designed to reduce risk per se. For example, most silver mining companies generally have relatively stable extraction and processing costs. The risky part of their business stems from the volatility in the market price of silver. The price, for example, has ranged from more than $50 to under $4 per ounce in the 1979–1991 period. Establishing a price for its planned production well ahead of time would substantially reduce a silver mining firm's price-fluctuation risk. Hedge trades in the futures market would establish such a price well before the silver is ready for sale. Mining companies that hedge each projected output increment largely insulate themselves from subsequent silver spot (immediate delivery) price fluctuations. Similar types of hedge trades may be made by a variety of enterprises. Pure hedging often is advisable whenever

FIGURE 7.3   Equity-Related Securities

Direct Ownership of a Company

Common stock	Residual ownership of corporations
Preferred stock	Preferred to common in dividends and liquidation
Small firm ownership	May be organized as a corporation, partnership or sole proprietorship
Master limited partnership	Combines the tax advantage of a partnership with the limited liability and ease of trading of a corporation
Venture capital	Risk capital provided to start-up companies

Options

Call	Private option-to-buy contract
Put	Private option-to-sell contract
Warrant	Company-issued buy option
Right	Short-term company-issued option to buy

Indirect Equity Ownerships

Convertible bonds	Debt securities that may be exchanged for a prespecified amount of stock
Mutual funds and closed-end investment companies, unit investment trusts and variable annuities	Pooled portfolios of securities and other types of interest

---

establishing a forward price reduces an important business risk. Such pure hedges are incidental to hedgers' main spot-market business.

Risk hedges, in contrast, are designed to yield a relatively likely profit. Rather than reduce the impact of potentially adverse price moves, risk hedgers seek to profit from potentially favorable relative price movements while minimizing their exposure to potentially adverse moves. Put and call spreads and ratio positions are examples of risk hedges.

Arbitraging   Pure arbitragers assume opposite positions on equivalent (or convertible to equivalent) assets when prices in separate markets diverge sufficiently. Pure arbitrage produces a quick certain profit. Risk arbitragers, in contrast, take offsetting positions in potentially equivalent securities. The shares of an acquisition candidate and its proposed acquirer are the primary types of potentially equivalent securities. An exchange for debt or equity securities may or may not be hedged by the arbitrager. A tender for cash does not require the arbitrager to make an offsetting trade, however.

A proposed merger involving an exchange of shares generally will leave the relative prices of the two stocks somewhat out of line with the merger terms. For example, XYZ may offer two of its shares for each share of UVW Corporation. If preoffer prices of XYZ and UVW were 50 and 75, immediate postoffer prices might move to 52 and 85. At these levels, the UVW stock still would be underpriced relative to the XYZ offer. Assuming the merger agreement takes effect, the UVW stock is worth 104 (two times the per-share price of XYZ). That is, the arbitrager would buy in the ratio of one share of UVW at 85 while shorting two shares of XYZ for a total of 104. The net result would be a gain of 19 (104 – 85) multiplied by the number of shares of UVW purchased.

Types of Debt Securities:
Summary and Conclusions

Security market investors should at a minimum consider the wide variety of risks, returns, marketabilities, liquidities and tax treatments offered by the bond market. A well-diversified portfolio containing both equity and debt securities is likely to be less risky than a well-diversified portfolio of stocks or bonds alone. Investors should have little difficulty finding issues bearing risks corresponding to their own preferences.

The money market provides relatively attractive short-term rates on high-quality securities such as T-bills, commercial paper, large bank CDs, bankers' acceptances and Eurodollar loans. Small investors can participate in this market through money market mutual funds, short-term unit investment trusts and the money market certificates and accounts of commercial banks and thrift institutions. Larger investors can assemble their own money market portfolios.

Treasury and federal agency securities make up a large part of the long-term debt security market. Most of these issues are untaxed at the state and local levels. The agencies tend to offer slightly higher yields but are somewhat less marketable than Treasury issues. A large part of the agency security market is mortgage related. The various bonds, passthroughs and participations of FNMA, GNMA, Freddie Mac and the large bank pools offer high, safe, monthly income combined with a somewhat uncertain maturity.

State and local issues, whose interest payments are untaxed at the federal level, form another major segment of the debt security market. Most municipals offer relatively low before-tax yields. These securities primarily appeal to those investors in high tax brackets. Municipal bond funds and municipal unit investment trusts provide small investors various ways to enter this market.

Corporate securities vary greatly in risk. Some high-risk issues offer very high yields. Corporate bond funds (including high-risk bond funds) and closed-end bond funds permit a small investor to own part of a diversified debt security portfolio.

Other types of debt securities include income bonds, floating-rate notes, zero-coupon bonds, Eurobonds, privately placed issues and preferred stock (an equity asset priced primarily on its stated yield). Each of these securities appeals to specialized segments of the marketplace.

Thus, the debt security market offers a wide array of risk-return trade-offs, maturities and tax treatments. Moreover, in the past few years, a variety of new instruments have improved the access of small investors to these markets. A number of mutual funds and short-term unit trusts facilitate investing in money market, municipal, corporate, high-risk corporate and various other more specialized types of debt securities. Access, therefore, no longer is restricted by the difficulty of diversifying across a variety of high-denomination securities.

Combination securities include convertible bonds, convertible preferreds, hybrid convertibles, equity notes, commodity-backed bonds and stock-indexed bonds. Each combines a fixed-income security with an option (or in case of the equity note, an obligation) to convert the security to common stock or to some other asset. Thus, these securities offer some of the upside potential of a stock with the downside protection of a bond or a preferred.

Combination securities are priced to reflect their profit and risk characteristics. Buyers, therefore, usually obtain the upside potential at the cost of a lower yield than otherwise-equivalent straight debt or straight preferred securities. Moreover, their call risk further limits the upside potential. Pure and combination option security positions often are combined with each other and/or with nonoption securities to produce hedges and arbitrages. Clearly, investors considering investments in some company's common stock also should weight the pros and cons of taking a position in its other securities.

The Determinants of Yields

The prices of all investments (including debt securities) are affected by the general level of interest rates. That general level, in turn, is related to such factors as the supply and demand for credit, the economy's strengths and weaknesses, inflationary expectations and the state of the world economy. The relative discount rate applied to an individual debt security's promised income stream will vary with a number of other characteristics.

In this chapter, we explore the impacts of a variety of factors that affect individual debt security yields. Default risk, a primary determinant of yields, is given considerable attention. Near-default workouts, Chapter 11 and Chapter 7 bankruptcy proceedings and bond ratings are each considered. We also explore the impact of term structure, duration, coupon effect, seasoning, marketability, call protection, sinking-fund provisions, me-first rules, usability, industrial classification, condition of collateral and listing status.

Default Risk

Some investors achieve high yields from diversified portfolios of bonds in or near default. Other investors prefer simply to collect their principal and interest when it is due and not have to worry about defaults. These investors should avoid bankruptcy investing. Whether a safe or riskier investment is your goal, you must be able to evaluate the underlying security. What are you buying? One place to start this inquiry is the issuer's promises to the bondholders.

Indenture Provisions Bond indentures contain a number of provisions, the most important of which relate to each issue's interest and maturity obligations. The borrower agrees to a specified coupon payment until maturity when the principal is to be returned. The indenture also will contain a number of other provisions. For example, some debt obligations are backed by specific collateral. The indenture for such a security will specify the nature of the collateral obligation. The provision typically will state that the issuer agrees to maintain any pledged assets or acceptable substitutes in good repair.

The equipment trust certificates of railroads and other transportation companies (especially airlines) constitute a major portion of the collateralized corporate bond market. Even weak companies can issue relatively low-risk (and therefore low-yielding) equipment trust certificates. The collateral's quality protects owners of equipment trust certificates should the issuer default. For example, under Section 1110 of the Bankruptcy Code, Braniff I and Continental I & II continued to pay interest on equipment trust certificates to maintain use of certain aircraft in their fleets.

Most corporate bonds called debentures are not backed by any specific collateral. Rather, such debentures are backed by "the full faith and credit" of the issuer. This backing amounts to nothing more than a promise to pay. In most instances, the issuing firm has a strong enough credit rating so it does not have to specify any collateral to back up its debt issue. In other cases, the issuer may not have any usable collateral. Debentures can be subordinated to other debentures and/or other debt. Senior (unsubordinated) debentures generally have the same standing as the firm's other general creditors. Thus, in a bankruptcy filing, senior debenture holders and other general creditors could be treated equivalently.

In addition to interest, principal, collateral and liquidation requirements, a bond's indenture may provide for subordination to other debts, a sinking fund and call privileges, as well as restrictions on dividends and certain other matters. Subordination to other debts provides that this particular debt issue will not receive any liquidation payments until the claims of other specified debt issues are fully satisfied. Sinking funds require that a portion of the issue be retired periodically. To meet this provision, bonds may be bought in the open market, they may be called or funds may be set aside in an escrow account for the issue's eventual retirement.

A call privilege permits the issuer to redeem the securities before maturity at a prespecified price. The call price normally exceeds the bond's face value by an amount that declines over time and approaches par as maturity nears. For example, ten years before maturity, the bond might be called at 105 with the call premium declining by 0.5 per year thereafter.

Falling interest rates encourage issuers to call and refinance their debt at lower rates. The no-call feature of some bonds prohibits calls for part or all of the bond's life, however. Investors should be wary of call rights. High-coupon bonds often trade for substantial premiums over face. An early call for such a bond would cost the bondholder the difference between the precall market price and the call price. Thus, a bond selling for 115 that is called for 105 would cost the investor $100 (10 points) per bond.

Restrictions on dividend payments are designed to preserve the firm's capital. A firm that pays out too much in dividends could conceivably threaten the bondholder's interests. Dividends, therefore, might be limited to a certain percentage of profits unless and until the firm's net worth exceeds some specific level. A minimum current ratio may be set and me-first rules may restrict the future borrowing level. All of these features are designed to protect the creditors. A trustee, usually a bank, is charged with enforcing each indenture provision. Figure 8.1 summarizes the typical indenture provisions. Because the value of these provisions to the bondholder depends on how they are enforced, we must consider what usually happens in a default.

Defaults and Near Defaults   Firms rarely choose not to pay required interest and principal. Sometimes, however, they have no choice. Indeed, the 1980s and 1990s have seen a large number of financially troubled firms: Braniff, Chrysler, AM International, Lincoln Savings, First Republic Bank, International Harvester, Saxon Industries, Wickes, Mego, Manville, World Airways, LTV, Bethlehem Steel, A. H. Robins, Texas Air, Pan Am, Continental Illinois Bank, Continental Airlines (twice), First City Bank, TWA, Texaco, Bank of New England, Drexel Burnham, First Executive, Colombia Savings and so on. The experiences of these firms heightened interest in the default issue and led to the consideration of investing in the bonds of defaulting and bankrupt companies.

A firm is in technical default whenever any of the indenture provisions of its bonds are violated. Similarly, a violation of any of the terms of its other debt agreements constitutes a technical default. Many (most) debt contracts contain cross-default provisions that trigger a default in the subject instrument when a default occurs in another instrument of the same issuer. Most defaults, however, involve relatively minor matters. For example, if the working-capital ratio fell below the stipulated minimum, the firm techni-

FIGURE 8.1   Indenture Provisions

Provision	Nature of Provision
Principal and maturity	Specifies amount and timing of principal payment
Coupon	Specifies amount and timing of each coupon payment
Collateral (equipment trust certificate or other collateralized bond)	Identifies pledged collateral and specific obligation of issuer to maintain collateral's value
Full faith and credit (debenture)	Backs bond with the "good name" of the issuer
Subordination	Gives liquidation priority to other specified debt issues
Sinking fund	Provides for periodic redemption and retirement over the life of the bond issue
Call provisions schedule	Specifies length of no-call protection and of call premiums payable over the life of the bond
Dividend restrictions	Restricts dividend payments, based on earnings and amount of equity capital
Current ratio minimum	Requires that the ratio of current assets to current liabilities not fall below a specified minimum
Me-first rule	Restricts the amount of additional (nonsubordinated) debt that may be issued
Trustee	Specifies the institution responsible for enforcing the indenture provisions
Grace period	Specifies the maximum period that the firm has to cure a default without incurring the risk of a bankruptcy filing

cally would be in default of the relevant debenture provision. Rarely if ever would a default in such a matter in and of itself lead to a bankruptcy filing. The indenture trustee may grant a waiver for the violation or the matter may be quickly cured. A monetary default differs from a technical default in that some form of required payment has not been made.

Informal Reorganizations   Even a failure to pay stipulated interest and principal will not automatically force a bankruptcy proceeding. A late payment may quickly rectify the default. The indenture usually provides a grace period (generally 30 days) for curing such a default. Even after the expiration of the grace period, the trustee may not immediately institute legal proceedings. Indeed, most defaults do not lead to bankruptcy filings and most bankruptcies do not lead to liquidations. Rather, defaults (and indeed many near-defaults) usually result in a formal or informal reorganization that stops short of a long and costly liquidation.

When a few large creditors (such as banks that have extended substantial loans) can be identified, the troubled borrower may seek concessions that will give it a reasonable chance of avoiding a bankruptcy filing. Big lenders have important stakes in their creditors' survival. An interesting oversimplification of the borrower-lender relationship is seen in the following two sentences: A borrower who owes $10 and cannot pay is in trouble. A borrower who owes a million dollars and cannot pay puts the lender in trouble. The weakness of a troubled borrower is, in fact, a strength in any negotiations with the lender. Accordingly, lenders with large exposures are likely to be asked to accept a payment stretch-out, interest-rate reduction, swap of debt for equity or tangible assets, reduction in loan principal or a change or waiver of certain default provisions. Lenders often agree to such restructurings with the hopes of eventually recovering more than they would in a formal bankruptcy.

Because obtaining concessions from all of the numerous bondholders would be difficult, they only rarely are asked to make them. Accordingly, the bondholders obtain the benefit of the large lenders' concessions without making any corresponding sacrifice. If the effort fails, the bondholders still retain their priority in formal bankruptcy proceedings.

Exchange Offers   The Trust Indenture Act prohibits a change in principal, coupon or maturity provisions in a bond indenture without the unanimous approval of the bondholders. That provision effectively bans such changes. As a result, the only way to effectuate this type of change is with what is called an exchange offer. The company may offer existing bondholders a package of securities in exchange for the existing bonds. The package may contain a combination of cash, new bonds, preferred stock, common stock and warrants. The goal of the exchange is to reduce the cash-flow burden of the existing debt structure. By reducing the principal and the coupon (and partially offsetting it with equity), the company seeks to avoid a bankruptcy filing. Staying out of bankruptcy is usually in everyone's interest, including the stockholders' interest. The company, therefore, seeks to convince its bondholders to accept the exchange "voluntarily." Some bondholders, however, will hold out. They thus may achieve the benefit from the exchange but retain the benefit of their existing bonds. Each individual bondholder is likely to fare best if he or she does not exchange but everyone else does. Too many holdouts will kill the deal and force the firm into bankruptcy. Thus, the holdout problem is the Achilles' heel of exchange offers. Many are tried, but few succeed.

Bankruptcy Filings   The reorganization of a financially troubled company is not always possible. The alternative is usually a bankruptcy filing. Many troubled firms would be financially viable if their debt loads were sufficiently reduced. A major objective of most bankruptcy reorganization proceedings, therefore, is to reduce the amount and interest burden of the company's debt. Bankrupt firms generally have little or no excess cash to distribute to creditors. Indeed, bankruptcy filings often are triggered by a shortage of cash to pay bills as they come due. As a result, most creditors are prevailed on to accept lower priority securities of the reorganized firm. Senior creditors may receive debentures or preferred shares, while junior creditors could be given common stock and warrants. In some instances, the bankrupt firm may accumulate cash through asset sales and continuing operations while under court protection. Once a firm is put into bankruptcy, its obligation to pay interest and principal on its prepetition unsecured debts is deferred. Indeed, postpetition interest is a very low priority claim that rarely is paid. To the extent that this cash is not required for working capital, it may be available for distribution. The senior creditors generally demand that most or all of that cash go to them. In such circumstances, the senior creditors are likely to get packages containing both cash and various categories of securities (subordinated debentures, income bonds, preferred stock, common stock, warrants, etc.). More junior creditors get little or none of the cash. Their packages tend to be most heavily weighted toward the more junior securities (stocks and warrants).

The going-concern value of a firm in a bankruptcy process is quite subjective. The securities to be issued by the reorganized firm will not have an established market price until the firm emerges from bankruptcy. Thus, the relevant values are rather uncertain when (in the course of the bankruptcy proceeding) the securities distribution is being set. Not surprisingly, the ability of these securities to satisfy claims often is subject to dispute.

Generally, the lower-priority claimants will argue for a higher overall valuation for the company and its securities. In this way, they seek to increase the estimated value of the securities that are available for distribution to their priority class. The greater the overall estimated value of the firm, the greater is the proportion of the estimated value that is available to satisfy the lower-priority claimants. Suppose, for example, that the high-priority claimants have claims of $95,000,000 and the company's value is estimated at $100,000,000. The high-priority claimants would be awarded securities representing 95% of the firm's value. Only 5% would be available to the lower-priority claimants. Now suppose that the lower-priority claimants are able to have the estimated value raised to $110,000,000. At that valuation, the higher-priority claimants would receive about 86% (95 + 110) of the firm's value. The lower-priority claimants would, in contrast, see their share rise to about 14% (15 + 110). Clearly, the lower-priority claimants would prefer the higher-valuation estimate. The higher-priority claimants, in contrast, will argue for a more conservative valuation. They want to restrict or concentrate the distribution of the securities to the senior claimants. In addition, the legal status of each issuer may be subject to attack. Senior creditors may be challenged by the representatives of more junior issues on the theory that the senior creditors' alleged priority is invalid or subject to differing interpretations.

A given credit's priority is not always clearly established vis-à-vis all of the other credits. For example, a subordinated debenture may be clearly junior to some senior credits (e.g., bank lenders), but its status vis-à-vis others (e.g., trade creditors) may be unclear. Similarly, the validity of guarantees may be objected to by other creditors. Any transactions that occurred shortly before a bankruptcy filing may be attacked as fraudulent conveyances by anyone who was disadvantaged by them. Distributions to creditors shortly before the bankruptcy filing also may be attacked as preferences.

Whenever any uncertainty attaches to a credit's priority, the junior creditors are likely to try to take advantage of the situation. Unless the low-priority claimants are given some meaningful consideration, they are likely to use various legal maneuvers to delay and tie up the proceedings. The bankrupt estate is obligated to pick up the legal expenses of the various creditor classes as they seek to sort out their claims and agree on a reorganization or liquidation plan. Thus, the junior creditors can litigate with money that would otherwise be available for distribution to the creditors (most of which would have gone to the seniors). Not only can they delay the distribution, their actions actually can reduce the seniors' recovery. As a result of this potential weapon, most informal workouts and reorganizations

ultimately allocate lesser priority claimants somewhat more than the absolute priority of claims principle requires. In practice, unsecured and subordinated creditors generally can make enough noise to obtain some share of
the assets even when senior creditors' claims exceed the firm's remaining
asset value.

The reduced debt burden generally permits the reorganized firm to
remain solvent. New equity holders may have a long wait before receiving
any common or preferred dividend payments, however.

Bond Ratings   The default risks of both municipal and corporate bonds
are rated by several rating services. The best-known services are Standard
& Poor's and Moody's. Fitch Investors Service and Duff and Phelps, Inc.,
also rate bonds. Each service's ratings are based on its evaluation of the
firm's financial position and earnings prospects. Figure 8.2 describes the
primary rating categories. Pluses and minuses are used to discriminate
within a rating category.

These services do not release their specific rating formulas or analyses,
but a number of studies do reveal a rather predictable pattern. Ratings tend
to rise with profitability, size and earnings coverage. They decrease with
earnings volatility, leverage and pension obligations; they vary with industry classification. Ratings sometimes differ between the rating agencies,
usually reflecting a close call on fundamentals. Moody's tends to be the
more conservative of the two primary rating services. Several researchers
have found that the market price and yield of these issues are much more
closely related to the lower than the higher ratings.

For issues of the same company, a subordinate issue usually will receive
a lower rating than a more senior security. The rating services follow the
fortunes of issues over time, but rating changes occur relatively infrequently
and often take place long after the underlying fundamentals change. Accordingly, several services (including S&P's Creditwatch) now offer more
up-to-date analyses, including a prediction of rating changes. Moreover,
many brokerage firms are paying increasing attention to bond analysis.

Investors can use financial ratios and bankruptcy-prediction models to
perform their own bond analysis. Such an examination probably would
include an analysis of the level and trend in a variety of financial ratios:
current, quick, debt-equity, return on equity, times-interest-earned and other
relevant ratios. These ratios would be compared with industry and national
averages in an effort to reveal current deficiencies and/or significant long-
term risks. Clearly, high debt-equity ratios and low times-interest-earned

FIGURE 8.2   Bond Rating Categories

	Typical Ratings	Definition
Highest grade	Aaa/AAA	An extremely strong capacity to pay principal and interest
High grade	Aa/AA	A strong capacity to pay principal and interest but lower protection margins than Aaa and AAA
Medium grade	A/A	Many favorable investment attributes but may be vulnerable to adverse economic conditions
Minimum investment grade	Baa/BBB	Generally adequate capacity to pay interest and principal coupled with a significant vulnerability to adverse economic conditions
Speculative	Ba/BB	Only moderate protection during both good and bad times
Very speculative	B/B	Generally lack characteristics of other desirable investments; interest and principal payments over any long period of time are not safe
Default or near-default	Caa/CCC	Poor quality issues in danger of default
	Ca/CC	Highly speculative issues that often are in default
	C	The lowest-rated class of bonds
	C	Income bonds on which no interest is being paid
	D	Issues in default with principal and/or interest payments in arrears

percentages are not reassuring. Unfortunately, this analysis can provide only part of the story. Bondholders also should be interested in the firm's future prospects. For example, the negative perspective associated with a seemingly shaky current financial position may be offset by the positive outlook for an upcoming product introduction. Alternatively, a firm with a solid financial position may be trapped in an industry that is slowly being eliminated by changing technology.

Avoiding Bankruptcy Candidates   Avoiding or perhaps even shorting the securities of companies that are likely to go bankrupt may be a profitable strategy. Altman's (Edward Altman is a finance professor at New York University who has written extensively in the bankruptcy area) model for bankruptcy prediction facilitates such a strategy. His early warning system identifies firms with a high bankruptcy probability. Subsequent work indicates that bankruptcies are relatively predictable events. Moreover, the Altman formula seems about as accurate at forecasting failures as most of the alternatives. Whether one can profit from accurate bankruptcy predictions depends on the securities' prebankruptcy and postbankruptcy performances.

Various researchers have found significantly negative risk-adjusted returns for holding periods up to four years prior to a bankruptcy filing. Others reported that shareholders experienced large losses during the month of a bankruptcy filing especially during the three days surrounding the announcement. Taking advantage of these observed tendencies depends on having lead time relative to the market.

Using one form of risk adjustment, professors Altman and Brenner found predictable subsequent negative performance associated with deteriorating financial data, but the relationship disappeared when a second risk-adjustment procedure was used. Thus, trading signals of bankruptcy prediction models may or may not be helpful. Those who want to try them may find a simplified form of the Altman model useful. It involves the calculation of a Z-score value of creditworthiness and financial viability from the following financial data:

$$\text{Altman Z Score} = 1.2A + 1.4B + 3.3C + 1D + .6E \text{ where:}$$

$$
\begin{aligned}
A &= \text{Working capital} \div \text{assets} \\
B &= \text{Retained earnings} \div \text{assets} \\
C &= \text{Pretax earnings} \div \text{assets} \\
D &= \text{Sales} \div \text{assets} \\
E &= \text{Market value of equities} \div \text{liabilities}
\end{aligned}
$$

A firm scoring less that 1.81 is classified as troubled.

A further refinement of the Altman formula has been developed by a consulting firm called Zeta Services (Hoboken, New Jersey). Although the output of the proprietary model is sold primarily to institutional subscribers, its results sometimes appear in publications such as *Forbes*. The Relative

Financial Strength System of *Value Line* provides similar output to subscribers.

Contrary Opinion: Investing in Troubled Firms   Far from avoiding troubled firms, some investors seek them out. Indeed, the so-called "theory of contrary opinion" advises investors to concentrate on issues that are out of favor (and therefore presumably undervalued). The market eventually will return to the former favorites that now are being neglected, or so the argument goes. Contrarians may contrast their concept with what they despairingly refer to as the "greater-fool" theory. Those who follow fads often bid prices up to unrealistic levels hoping that still greater fools will pay even more.

Like many investment concepts, contrary-opinion investing is easier to discuss in the abstract than to reduce to practice. Those who favor investments in stocks with low PEs or small capitalizations, in stocks neglected by analysts or in stocks with low per-share prices are practicing a contrarian approach. Concentrating on currently unprofitable companies is another possible approach.

Conceptually, the most appealing contrary-opinion approach is to target troubled firms that are about to turn around. In this regard, professors Katz, Lilien and Nelson examined a trading strategy based on whether, according to a bankruptcy model such as Altman's, a firm was moving toward health or distress. They found that the stocks of firms moving from distress to health exhibited positive abnormal returns. Those of firms moving in the other direction were negative. Therefore, the changes in a firm's Z scores may offer useful trading signals.

An even more daring contrary approach concentrates on one of the most out-of-favor groups: the bankrupts. Thus, a *Barron's* author argued, "Equity Funding, Penn Central, Interstate Stores and Daylin all have sought the shelter of bankruptcy. But like corporate Lazaruses, each has risen from the dead." Although bankrupt companies usually decline severely around the time of their filing, a few eventually come back handsomely. Many are total or near-total losses, however. One who wishes to invest in bankrupt companies, may, however, find their bonds a more effective vehicle than their stocks.

Another contrary approach is to buy shares in a contrary-opinion mutual fund. (Contrafund, for example, rose by 300% from its 1976 founding until 1982, compared with a 150% gain for the S&P 500.) Still others seek out liquidation candidates and concentrate on the depressed issues favored by insiders.

Bond Ratings and Performance   How well do bonds of the various risk classes perform? Bonds in the top four rating categories (Aaa, Aa, A or Baa) are considered investment grade. Bonds with ratings below investment grade are referred to as junk bonds. No bonds that Moody's rated investment grade defaulted in the 1950s or 1960s. A small number of railroad bonds rated Ba or less did default, however. The experience of the 1920s and 1930s is rather different to be sure, but Pye, in a frequently referenced academic study, argued that major firms seldom go bankrupt except during major depressions. Moreover, economists and government officials now know how to avoid such depressions.

More recently, however, a number of large firms have gone under: W. T. Grant, Franklin National Bank, Penn Central, Braniff, AM International, MCorp, First Republic Bank, Bank of New England, Continental Airlines and Manville (with close calls for International Harvester and Continental Illinois Bank). Moreover, government bailouts were required to save Lockheed and Chrysler. Clearly, large firms are not immune to bankruptcy.

The issues are less clear for lower-rated bonds. The realized (after default loss) yield experience of below-Baa bonds is of considerable interest in light of the growing numbers of such issues. Many institutional investors and fiduciaries generally are not permitted to own below-Baa bonds. Accordingly, these securities may well offer superior risk-adjusted yields. Excluding a major category of investors from the marketplace may distort the supply-demand relationship and thus make pricing less efficient. Therefore, diversified portfolios of medium-risk to high-risk bonds might outperform similarly diversified high-quality bond portfolios. Diversification across industries would spread the default risk, and the higher indicated yield might more than offset any default losses. A number of researchers have found that the yield premium on junk bonds has substantially exceeded the loss from default. Such results, however, are derived from studies covering relatively prosperous times. Experience during severe recessions might be quite different. Indeed, the experience of the late 1980s and early 1990s appears to have been quite a bit less favorable for the high-yield bond market than the immediately preceding period.

The Term Structure of Interest Rates   Its term or length to maturity is one of three major determinants of a debt security's yield to maturity.

(General credit conditions and default risk are the other two.) Yields to maturity tend to vary systematically with length to maturity. This relationship can be illustrated with a yield curve. This curve emerges when the yield is plotted versus the term to maturity for issues with otherwise similar characteristics (risk, coupon, call feature, etc.). The yield curve reveals a pattern that at various times rises, falls, does not vary or rises and then falls.

Term Structure Hypotheses   The segmented markets, preferred habitat, liquidity preference and unbiased expectations hypotheses all have been advanced to explain the term structure of interest rates. Each is capable of accounting for the various shapes of the yield curve. The segmented markets hypothesis asserts that supply and demand within each market segment determine interest rates for that maturity class. According to this hypothesis, the yield curve simply reflects the supply and demand for each maturity class for that particular time frame. Some investors generally prefer to lend short, while many borrowers prefer to borrow long term. Thus, rates often are lower for short maturities.

A related but somewhat less restrictive form of the segmented markets hypothesis is called the preferred habitat hypothesis. According to this form, borrowers and lenders prefer certain maturities. They only can be induced to other maturities by more attractive rates. As with the segmented markets hypothesis, preferred habitat assumes that most investors prefer the short end and most borrowers prefer the long end of the market.

The liquidity preference hypothesis assumes that markets are not segmented per se, but that some lenders (especially commercial banks with their short-term capital sources) generally prefer to lend short. Similarly, many borrowers prefer to borrow long. Thus, a rising yield curve generally is needed to compensate lenders for their greater time commitment.

The unbiased expectations hypothesis asserts that long rates reflect the market's expectation of current and future short rates. Therefore, the one-year rate is simply the geometric average of the current six-month rate and the expected rate six months hence. Suppose that the 12-month rate is $y\%$. The unbiased expectations hypothesis asserts that current rates have embedded within them the market's anticipated six-month rate six months from now. That anticipation is, in fact, the rate necessary when coupled with the current six-month rate to yield a 12-month return of $y\%$.

Consider, for example, six-month and 12-month yields of 8% and 9%, respectively. Taken together, these yields imply a specific value for the expected six-month yield for a security whose life begins in six months.

Thus, the rate for the second six months will cause an investment that yields 8% for the first six months to generate an overall 12-month return of 9%.

An (annualized) 8% return that is earned for six months corresponds to a return relative (ratio of beginning and ending values) of 1.04. A 9% return that is earned for 12 months corresponds to a return relative of 1.09. Therefore, we first seek the return relative for the second six months that will produce the appropriate 12-month return relative. Once we obtain the return relative, the corresponding annualized return is easy to compute. The appropriate formula is:

$$1.04 \times ? = 1.09; \text{ Solving for ? yields: } ? = 1.09 + 1.04 = 1.048$$

A yield of 1.048 for six months corresponds to a 12-month return relative of 1.096. This, in turn, corresponds to an annualized return of 9.6%. Thus, the implied yield for the second six months is 9.6%. In other words, an investment that earns 8% in the first six months must earn 9.6% in the second six months to produce an overall 12-month return of 9%.

The unbiased expectations hypothesis asserts that the market signals its expectations for future interest rates by the rates it establishes for debt securities of various maturities. According to this view, potential arbitrage activity always drives the yield curve into the shape appropriate for that set of expectations.

If long rates seem too high vis-à-vis expected future short rates, some short-horizon investors will move toward longer-term issues while some longer-horizon lenders will switch toward shorter-term borrowing. This activity should quickly drive rates into the appropriate relation. All three hypotheses recognize the existence of such arbitraging activity, but only the unbiased expectations hypothesis asserts its overriding power. Figure 8.3 summarizes the four term structure hypotheses.

Each hypothesis explains the various yield-curve shapes slightly differently and has somewhat different implications. According to liquidity preference, yield curves are typically rising because, on balance, lenders prefer the short end and borrowers the long end. Segmented markets and preferred habitat also are consistent with a tendency for yield curves to rise. Lenders may be relatively more numerous at the short end.

The unbiased expectations hypothesis, in contrast, asserts that yield curves only rise when interest rates themselves are expected to increase. A flat yield curve indicates neutral expectations. A falling yield curve reflects an expectation that rates will fall. This expectation causes borrowers (bond

FIGURE 8.3   Term Structure Hypotheses

Segmented markets	Yields reflect supply and demand for each maturity class.
Preferred habitat	Investors and borrowers can be induced out of their preferred maturity structures only by more attractive rates.
Liquidity preference	Lenders generally prefer to lend short and borrowers prefer to borrow long, tending to produce an upward-sloping yield curve.
Unbiased expectations	Long rates reflect the market's expectation of current and future short rates.

issuers) to rely on short-term financing until the expected fall occurs. Accordingly, borrowers anticipating a decline in interest rates tend to shift demand from the long- to the short-term market. As a result, short rates tend to be bid up relative to long rates.

Lender expectations have a similar effect. Lenders (bond buyers) want to profit from the expected interest-rate decline by owning long-term bonds. Falling rates would cause their prices to rise relative to shorter-term issues. Thus, investors who expect rates to fall will tend to favor the longer maturities, thereby pushing downward on long rates and upward on short rates. In summary, when rates are expected to fall, the actions of both lenders and borrowers will tend to twist the yield curve downward, causing short-term rates to exceed long-term rates. The very tight monetary policy in 1974 and again in 1980–1981 created just such circumstances: very high short-term rates with lower long-term rates.

None of the term structure hypotheses has gained overwhelming acceptance or has been completely ruled out of contention. On theoretical grounds, unbiased expectation generally is favored. Liquidity preference may have a slight edge in explaining the data. Most academicians believe that modern debt markets are not segmented per se, but that appreciable numbers of borrowers and lenders may have preferred habitats. From the investor's viewpoint, the relative strengths and weaknesses of the hypotheses are less important than an understanding of the empirical relationship between yield and maturity.

The Investment Implications of the Term Structure   Yield-curve relationships may provide bond traders with two opportunities. First, securities whose yields are some distance from curves plotted with otherwise similar issues may well be misvalued. Thus, bonds whose yields exceed their respective yield-curve values may be underpriced. If their market prices adjust more quickly than the curve itself shifts, the strategy would produce an above-market return.

A second bond strategy involves what is called riding the yield curve. A steeply rising yield curve may offer an attractive trading opportunity. Suppose, for example, that one-year T-bills yield 7% compared with 5% on six-month securities. Both the six-month bill and a 12-month bill sold six months later would generate a six-month return. Suppose that six-month T-bills still are yielding 5% six months later. Under that scenario, the six-month return on the 12-month bill will be quite a bit higher than 5% and indeed above 7% as well. To yield 5% with six months to go, the 7% one-year T-bill must return approximately 9% in the first six months ($1.025 \times 1.045 = 1.07$). Undertaking a strategy of riding the yield curve does incur the risk of an adverse interest-rate move, however. Should six-month rates rise to 10%, the six-month return on the 12-month bill would only be around 3% ($1.05 \times 1.02 = 1.07$).

Duration   Up to this point, we have discussed debt securities as if the maturities of these securities were easy to determine. A 12-year bond is a bond that promises to return principal in 12 years. Not all 12-year bonds are alike, however. Debt securities vary all the way from zero-coupon bonds to fully amortized mortgages. Zeros make only one payment at maturity, while mortgages make levelized periodic payments over the life of the instrument. The final payment of a mortgage is no larger than any other payment. Thus, a 12-year zero and a 12-year mortgage have very different payment profiles. The differences are less pronounced for traditional coupon-yielding bonds. Still, measuring the length of a bond by the amount of time remaining before the principal is to be repaid may be misleading.

Bonds can have very different coupon rates even when their maturities and other characteristics are similar. The term to maturity does not fully reflect the timing of a debt security's total payment stream. The final payment on a debt security is only one of the promised payments. Most debt securities also make periodic coupon payments. Each of these coupon payments may be viewed as a partial maturity of the instrument. Each such payment is part of the entire promised cash flow of the security.

The greater the proportion of the return coming from the coupon, the more of the debt security's promised cash flow will be paid prior to its final maturity. Thus, a higher coupon is somewhat akin to a shorter maturity. The owner of such a security will receive a higher proportion of his or her promised return in the form of interest prior to the return of principal at maturity.

Bonds with coupons close to market yields sell near par. Others with coupon rates that are very low or very high compared to market rates will be priced far from par. Computed yields to maturity will have somewhat different implications for each of these issues.

On the one hand, a high coupon reduces the vulnerability to adverse interest-rate moves. At least the coupon payment of this bond can be reinvested as received. On the other hand, high coupon payments, in a period of falling yields, cannot be reinvested at rates as high as the bond's initial yield. For equivalent maturities, therefore, a high-coupon bond is less exposed to adverse interest fluctuations but has greater exposure to reinvestment risk than one with a lower coupon. At the other extreme, a zero-coupon instrument will exhibit the highest degree of price volatility (interest-rate sensitivity) given a change in interest rates, assuming other variables are constant.

The concept of duration is designed to allow the investor to make an appropriate adjustment for different maturities and coupon rates. Duration is defined as the weighted average time (measured in years) to full recovery of principal and interest payments. The weight of each of the promised payments is based on its present value relative to the sum of the present values of the payment stream. That is, each weight equals the present value of that payment divided by the bond's market price. The total of the present values equals the bond's market price. In this way, duration captures the impact of differing payback rates. The formula for duration (D) is:

$$D = \frac{\displaystyle\sum_{t=1}^{n} \frac{C_t(t)}{(1+i)^t}}{\displaystyle\sum_{t=1}^{n} \frac{C_t}{(1+i)^t}} \qquad 2$$

where:

$t \quad = \quad$ Payment period (beginning with period one) of the coupon or principal

TABLE 8.1 Duration Computation Example

			BOND A		
1	*2*	*3*	*4*	*5*	*6*
				PV as Proportion	
Year	*Cash Flow*	*PV at 14%*	*PV of Flow*	*of Price*	*1 × 5*
1	140	.877	122.78	.12278	.12278
2	140	.769	107.66	.10766	.21532
3	140	.675	94.50	.09450	.28350
4	140	.592	82.88	.08280	.33152
5	1,140	.519	<u>591.66</u>	<u>.99948</u>	<u>2.95830</u>
	Sum (Market price of bond)		999.48	.99948	3.91142
	Duration = 3.91 years				
			BOND B		
1	40	.877	35.08	.05348	.05348
2	40	.761	30.44	.04641	.09882
3	40	.675	27.00	.04116	.12348
4	40	.592	23.68	.03610	.13440
5	1,040	.519	<u>539.76</u>	<u>.82285</u>	<u>4.11425</u>
	Sum (Market price of bond)		655.96	1.00000	4.52443
	Duration = 4.52 years				

C_t = Payment in period t
i = Market yield
n = Number of periods to maturity

Now consider the durations of two bonds maturing in five years. Bond A has a 14% coupon, while bond B has a 4% coupon. Table 8.1 reports the results of computing durations of both bonds using a 14% discount rate.

Thus, bond B's lower coupon corresponds to a duration of about a half year longer than that of bond A. For equivalent maturities, the lower the coupon, the longer is the duration. In fact, the duration for a zero-coupon instrument is equal to its time to maturity. The sensitivity of bond-price movements to interest-rate changes varies proportionately with duration. A bond's duration, therefore, reflects its sensitivity to interest rate changes more accurately than does the bond's time to maturity. Duration also provides a better measure of the wait to payoff than does the time to maturity.

Other Factors Affecting Bond Prices and Yields The characteristics already discussed (general interest-rate levels, risk of default, maturity-duration, coupon effect, tax status) constitute the principal price-yield determinants of specific bonds. Somewhat less important characteristics include marketability, seasoning, call protection, sinking-fund provisions, me-first rules, usability, industrial classification, condition of collateral and listing status.

The vast majority of bond trading takes place in high-volume markets with narrow spreads and deep supply and demand. Many lower-volume issues, however, trade in thin markets with spreads of five and even ten points. A quote of 70 bid to 80 ask implies a 14% spread. Unless a limit order can be used to reduce the spread's impact, trading such an issue is extremely costly. Limit orders are only likely to be effective on any bonds that are not listed on an exchange. Other things being equal, the less marketable the issue, the higher will be the yield required to make the bond attractive to investors.

Seasoned issues are established in the marketplace. They have been traded for at least a few weeks beyond completion of the initial (offering) sale. As with new stock issues, new issues of bonds seem to be priced a bit below equivalent seasoned issues. Several authors, however, contend that the apparent yield differences can be explained by the existence of tax, call provision and other issuer-specific factors.

Call protection varies appreciably from issue to issue. Some bonds are callable when sold. Many others may not be called for the first five or ten years of their life. Callable issues that are reasonably likely to be redeemed (high yields) should be evaluated on their yield to earliest call rather than on their yield to maturity. In marginal cases, both yield figures should be computed and compared. Call protection tends to increase a bond's price, but the market may well overvalue call protection. Thus, callable issues may be superior investments.

The sinking fund's presence increases demand slightly and reduces the probability that refinancing its debts will burden the issuer. Therefore, a sinking fund generally adds modestly to the value of a bond. Providing for a sinking fund in the bond indenture does not appear to reduce the debt issuer's ex-post cost, however. Me-first rules are designed to protect existing bondholders. These rules prevent these stockholders' claims from being weakened by the issuance of additional debt with a priority higher than or equivalent to theirs. Me-first rules significantly enhance the market values of the protected bonds.

Usable bonds can be employed at their par values in exercising the firm's outstanding warrants. If these bonds sell for less than par, using them is cheaper than cash. If the stock price is near or below the point where exercising is attractive, the usability feature may add to the bond's value. The price impact of usability depends primarily on two factors: the relative magnitude of the bond's straight-debt value versus its value in exercising the warrant and the relative supply of usable bonds and warrants outstanding.

Professors Calvin Boardman and Richard McEnally, who exhaustively studied the factors that affect bond values, found that:

1. Industrial and transportation issues tend to command higher prices than otherwise equivalent utility issues.

2. The status of collateral affects values especially when the issue would otherwise have a low rating.

3. Listing has little or no price impact.

Figure 8.4 summarizes the various factors affecting bond yields.

The Elimination of Traditional Covenants

The junk-bond era was characterized by an unprecedented rush to achieve maximum yield at all costs. This led to a significant increase in the absence of traditional covenants. An article in the *Business Lawyer* showed that at the zenith of the era in 1986, only 26% of the indentures of leading corporations had limitations on the borrower incurring other unsecured debts, 32% had limitations on paying dividends and 84% had limitations incurred on secured debt (negative pledges).[1] The absence of these provisions meant that the bonds, in most cases subordinated, were potentially subordinated to an infinite amount of debt, causing the bonds to become worth less and less and lead to more and more critical default situations, hence, more bankruptcies. Clearly, the rationale behind most of these traditional provisions was to ensure the collectibility of the bonds in question at some future date. Their elimination, in the interest of achieving higher yields, has helped exacerbate the predicted disaster in the junk-bond area.

1. McDaniel, "Bondholders and Corporate Governance," 41 *Business Lawyer,* 413 (1986).

FIGURE 8.4   Factors Affecting Bond Yields

General credit conditions	Credit conditions affect all yields to one degree or another.
Default risk	Riskier issues require higher promised yields.
Term structure	Yields vary with maturity, reflecting expectations for future rates.
Duration	The average wait until payback is calculated using the duration formula.
Coupon effect	Low-coupon issues (if issued near par) offer yields that are partially tax sheltered.
Seasoning	Newly issued bonds may sell at a slight discount to otherwise equivalent established issues.
Marketability	Actively traded issues tend to be worth more than otherwise equivalent issues that are less actively traded.
Call protection	Protection from an early call tends to enhance a bond's value.
Sinking-fund provisions	Sinking funds increase demand and reduce the risk of refinancing, thereby tending to enhance a bond's value.
Me-first rules	Bonds protected from the diluting effect of additional firm borrowings are generally worth more than otherwise equivalent unprotected issues.
Usability	Bonds usable at par to exercise warrants tend to be worth more than otherwise equivalent issues.
Industrial classification	Industrial and transportation issues tend to command higher prices than otherwise equivalent utility issues.
Collateral status	Well-maintained collateral tends to enhance bond values relatively to less well-maintained collateral.
Listing	Exchange listing appears to have little or no impact on bond yields.

Assembling and Managing a Bond Portfolio   Diversified bond portfolios should be managed to meet their owners' needs. A half dozen different bond issues usually are sufficient to achieve relatively effective diversification of a portfolio of bonds. Bonds also should be selected to produce the desired level of maturity-duration, default risk–quality rating, coupon-price appreciation, etc. Moreover, bonds usually are part of a larger portfolio that also includes stocks and perhaps some other types of assets. Thus, bonds usually should be viewed as providing liquidity, dependable income and so on in the larger context of the portfolio.

Bond Swaps   Portfolio managers frequently finance a bond purchase with the funds freed up by liquidating another position. These bond swaps may be designed to increase yield to maturity or current yield, to adjust duration or risk or to establish a tax loss or gain.

The separate transactions involved with many swaps are not executed simultaneously. Therefore, swap traders risk making one side of the swap (for instance, the sell) only to encounter an adverse price move before the other side is accomplished. Moreover, transaction costs absorb some of what otherwise would be the expected benefits of the swap. Nonetheless, a variety of circumstances make swaps attractive. For example, a low-coupon, deep-discount issue might be sold and the proceeds used to purchase a higher coupon issue. The sale normally would generate a tax loss. Presumably, the purchased issue is designed to offer a higher yield. On the other hand, the swap probably would increase both the call risk and the reinvestment risk. In addition to increasing current income, swaps of this type also require a "payup" or the infusion of additional cash to purchase a par amount equal to that sold.

In another type of swap, an investor might sell one issue that had been held at a loss and then purchase another very similar issue. This pure tax swap establishes a tax loss while leaving the portfolio's basic character unchanged. In yet another type of swap, a bond originally purchased as a long-term issue may have moved much closer to maturity. Swapping it for a longer-term bond would restore the desired maturity and duration level and possibly enhance the yield as well (if long rates are above short rates). Possible bond swaps are illustrated with the help of the quotations in Table 8.2.

Investors owning the AT&T 3⅞s of 1990 at the end of 1981 could have greatly increased their current yield with a swap into the 10⅜s of 1990 (10.5% versus 5.6%). The yield to maturity also would have risen (10.6%

versus 9.4%). To be effective, a tax swap requires a switch to a different bond issuer. Thus, one holding the AT&T 3⅞s or 10⅜s of 1990 at year-end 1981 could have swapped them for the GM Acceptance 11⅝s of 1990. The maturities are similar and the GMAC quality was only slightly below that of AT&T (AA+ versus AAA). Maturity swaps could have been made between either AT&T 1990 issues and the 8.80s of 2005 or between the GMAC 11⅝s of 1990 and the GMAC 11¾s of 2000.

Six years later, new prices and yields were obtained for this group of bonds. The changes are interesting. First, two of the bonds no longer are listed. Unfortunately for those who owned them, they were called by the issuer and the outstanding borrowings refinanced at a lower interest rate. Second, the remaining three bonds all have been downgraded. The ratings of the AT&T issues were down to AA (year-end 1987) compared with AAA on the earlier date. The divestiture of AT&T's operating companies had increased their risks. Similarly, the GMAC bond was (year-end 1987) rated AA− compared with AA+ at the earlier date. General Motors' share of the automobile market had slipped as had its profitability. Third, notwithstanding the ratings downgrades, each of the bonds was priced higher on the later date. Market interest rates had declined.

Similar bond swaps are possible with the more recent bond quotes. For example, the investor could execute a maturity-yield swap between the AT&T 3⅞s and the 8.80s. Tax swaps are possible between the AT&T and GMAC issues.

Other Aspects of Bond Portfolio Management   Managing a bond portfolio effectively can involve much more than the simple types of swaps mentioned previously. The investor, for example, might speculate on a bond upgrade by buying an issue that the market views pessimistically. Margin borrowing may be used to magnify potential gains and/or to leverage a high yield. Some bonds may have higher promised long-term yields than the current cost of margin money. Whether such apparently attractive yield spreads should be exploited depends on both the likelihood that they will persist and the default risk of high-yielding issues. If market interest rates rise, the margin borrowing rate will increase and bond prices will decline.

Still more complicated maneuvers involve the use of interest futures and hedges between a company's bonds and its other securities. For example, a long bond position in a company with a high default risk might be hedged with a short position in the firm's stock. If the firm goes bankrupt, the stock could become almost worthless while its bonds still might retain some value

TABLE 8.2   Selected Bond Quotations

| | | | December 31, 1981 | | Current | Yield to |
Issuer	Rating	Coupon	Maturity	Price	Yield	Maturity
AT&T	AAA	3⅞	1990	69½	5.6%	9.4%
AT&T	AAA	10⅜	1990	98⅞	10.5	10.6
AT&T	AAA	8.80	2005	79⅝	11.1	11.3
GMAC	AA+	11⅝	1990	101¾	11.4	11.3
GMAC	AA+	11¾	2000	97	12.1	12.2
			December 31, 1987			
AT&T	AA	3⅞	1990	90⅞	4.3%	8.0%
AT&T	AA	8.80	2005	91½	9.6	9.8
GMAC	AA–	11¾	2000	104½	11.3	11.1

in a reorganization or liquidation. If the company avoids bankruptcy, the bonds eventually will pay off, although the stock may not do well unless the company prospers. Finally, portfolio managers can trade on the basis of their interest-rate forecasts. If interest rates are expected to fall, portfolio maturities should be lengthened. An expected rise should cause the manager to shift toward near-cash securities. This strategy assumes that the manager can accurately forecast interest-rate changes, however.

Transaction Costs for Bonds   As with stocks, investors in bonds must be aware of the costs associated with trading these securities. The costs can vary enormously, depending on the nature of the trade. In addition to the basic price of the debt security, bond traders must be aware of three charges: commissions, spreads and accrued interest.

Compared to stocks, commissions on bond trades tend to be relatively low. A trade of ten bonds or more typically will incur a commission of $5 per bond. A large trade or large trader is likely to qualify for a discount from this rate. Five dollars per bond amounts to 0.5% of a $1,000 face value. Retail commissions on stock trades, in contrast, average closer to 3%. Thus (compared to stocks), trading bonds that sell near to their par values normally will incur rather modest commissions.

Two circumstances in which the commissions may be of concern are very small trades and bonds that sell for a small fraction of their par value.

Most brokers charge a minimum commission that overrides their per-bond formula. An investor who purchases three bonds, therefore, may be charged a $50 commission because $50 is the brokerage firm's minimum. Similarly, a trade involving deep-discount or zero-coupon bonds may incur a high commission relative to the dollar value of the trade. That is, $5 per bond is a much higher percentage of the money involved for a bond trading at 20 (2.50%) than for one trading at 95 (0.53%).

Bid-ask spreads are another important consideration in bond trading. Spreads on actively traded bonds tend to be quite narrow. For example, the spreads on most government bonds are measured in 32nds. A spread of $\frac{3}{32}$ on a $1,000 bond amounts to $0.9375, which is less than 0.1% of the price. On the other hand, less actively traded issues may have much wider spreads. For example, a small inactively traded corporate bond might be quoted 80-85. A five-point spread on a bond with a bid of 80 corresponds to a spread of 6.25% of the bid price. The spreads can be even wider. For instance, an inactively traded deep-discount bond might be quoted 30-40. This quote corresponds to a spread of 33% of the bid.

The final matter for bond traders to consider is the accrued interest assessed of the buyer. Between coupon payments, bonds may be seen as building up an accrual for the forthcoming interest payment. For example, a bond with an 8% coupon will make a semiannual payment of 4% of its par ($40 on a standard $1,000 face value bond). Midway between coupon payments, the bond will have accrued half of the coupon ($20). According to standard trading practice, a buyer of the bond at that point would pay the seller the price of the bond plus the amount of accrued interest. When the next coupon is paid, the new owner will keep the entire payment and thereby recoup the accrued amount advanced to the seller.

Not all bonds are traded this way but most are. The remainder are traded flat, which means no allowance is made for accrued interest. Bonds are likely to trade flat only if they have defaulted on a prior coupon payment, if the amount of the interest payment is uncertain (income bonds and floating-rate notes, for example) or if the issuer has announced that it does not expect to make the scheduled payment.

Two potential concerns with the accrued-interest component of a bond's cost should be borne in mind. First, the buyer earns no interest on the amount of the accrued-interest advance. The seller receives his or her share of the coupon payment at settlement, while the buyer is not reimbursed until the next coupon is received. Thus, the accrued interest is analogous to an interestfree loan from the buyer to the seller. Normally, the amounts advanced are relatively small so this concern is rarely a major consideration. Moreover, the market price paid for the bond may take the impact of accrued interest into account. The buyer should, however, realize that the cost of the purchase will include this allowance for accrued interest. The trader should be sure of having enough money to cover the full amount due at settlement.

The second concern with the accrued-interest advance is potentially more serious. Bonds that default on their interest obligations during a given interest-payment period leave the new buyer without any coupon payment and with no recourse to reclaim the accrued interest paid to the seller. Accrued interest on bonds is not returned in the event of a default. Once the bond defaults on a payment, it will begin to trade flat so that accrued interest no longer will be collected from the seller. During the payment period when the bond defaults, however, the interest will have been accrued and then lost to an investor who bought at that time. The owner will have a claim for interest against the issuer, but that claim goes with the owner of the bond as it continues to trade. Moreover, how much is a claim for back interest worth on a defaulted bond? Normally, bonds default on their interest payment by failing to make the payment and announcing that they are unable to do so. Thus, the default action itself frequently occurs at the end of the coupon payment period. Accordingly, a full-coupon payment of accrued interest is potentially lost. Because a default on coupon payment generally causes the bond price to fall, the newer buyer of a quickly defaulting bond typically suffers two losses: the bond price decline and the lost accrued interest.

The Determinants of Yields: Summary and Conclusions

A variety of factors influence bond yields. General market forces affect both the level and term structure of rates. For a given maturity class and market environment, rates differ primarily with default risk. Informal work-outs may reduce the impact of technical defaults and near-defaults, while Chapter 11 proceedings are less costly than the more formal Chapter 7 process. Rating services assess the default risks of bonds and their issuers' financial strengths.

Various hypotheses attempt to explain the term structure of interest rates. Segmented markets ascribe rates to supply and demand for each maturity class. Preferred habitat sees investors and borrowers preferring particular maturity structures and only able to be induced out of them by more attractive rates elsewhere. Liquidity preference asserts that borrowers generally prefer the long end, while lenders prefer the short. The unbiased expectations hypothesis holds that the term structure reflects a contiguous set of short-term interest-rate expectations. Investors may use the term structure relationship to identify securities that are potentially mispriced. Moreover, some investors may ride a yield curve that is expected to remain approximately stable.

Duration, the weighted average term of the payment stream, is a more accurate measure of repayment timing than is length to maturity. Investors and portfolio managers may utilize the duration concept in a strategy designed to immunize their portfolios from reinvestment risk. Specifically, they may minimize the potentially adverse impacts of being unable to reinvest coupons at attractive rates by assembling a portfolio with durations equal to their planning horizons.

Prices tend to be higher for more marketable, seasoned issues with sinking funds, me-first rules and call protection. Usable bonds also may command higher prices. Industrial classification and condition of collateral may have some minor price impacts, while listing status probably does not.

G L O S S A R Y

absolute priority of claims rule   The rule in bankruptcy law that each class of liability claims is repaid in full before the next highest priority category can receive even a partial payment.

accelerated depreciation   Writing off assets at a more rapid rate than is proportional to their pro rata life expectancy.

acceptance   *See* banker's acceptance.

accrued interest   The pro rata interest obligation on a bond or other debt instrument that has accumulated since the last payment date. Most bonds trade at a price that reflects their net market price plus accrued interest. Defaulted and certain other bonds, however, trade "flat." *See also* flat.

acid-test ratio   Cash and accounts receivable divided by current liabilities; used to measure short-term liquidity. Also called quick ratio.

actuarial tables   Tables reporting particular age groups' probabilities of death; based on past experience, with separate tables for men and women and certain hazardous occupations. An actuarial table might indicate that at age 25 a male would have 1 chance in 350 of dying within the next year and is expected to live 49 more years (to age 74). A 65-year-old male's chance of dying in the next year might be reported as 1 in 25 and his future life expectancy as 12 years (to age 77).

adequate protection   Not specifically defined in the Bankruptcy Code, but generally refers to the concept of protecting a creditor's interest in property owned by the debtor. Several nonexclusive methods for

providing adequate protection for creditors are specified including
periodic cash payments to a lien creditor equal to a decrease in the
value of the creditor's interest in the collateral. Another example
would be an additional lien or substitute lien on other property to
protect against a decline in value. An additional concept would be
providing a secured creditor with the "indubitable equivalent" of its
bargain with the debtor.

adjusted gross income (AGI)   An interim figure that is reached on the way
to computing tax liability; consists of total income less allowed adjustments, which include such items as moving expenses, IRA and Keogh
contributions and employee business expense. Taxable income then
results from subtracting deductions and the allowance for exemptions
from adjusted gross income.

ADR (American depository receipt)   A U.S.-traded security representing
stock in a foreign corporation.

affiliate   Includes an entity that directly or indirectly owns control or holds
power to vote 20% or more of the debtor for an entity that operates the
business or substantially all the property of the debtor under a lease
agreement.

after-tax cash flow   The difference in the actual cash income and outgo
for an investment project after taking account of the tax impact.

after-tax return   The rate of return an investor receives after adjusting for
inflation. Thus, a 10% before-tax return corresponds to a 7.2% after-
tax return for one in the 28% marginal tax bracket.

adviser's sentiment index   A technical market indicator based on a composite of investment adviser's forecasts; index users believe that a
bullish adviser's sentiment forecasts a market decline.

agency security   A debt security issued by federal agencies such as GNMA
or Freddie Mac.

air rights   The right to build over someone else's property; for example,
an office complex above a downtown rail switching yard.

all-or-nothing order   An order to purchase securities that must be executed in its entirety or not at all.

alpha   The intercept term in the market model; provides an estimate of a
security's return for a zero-market return.

alternative minimum tax (AMT)   Tax that may be applicable to those with
large amounts of otherwise sheltered income (preferences) such as
accelerated depreciation deductions; applies when the tax liability

computed by disallowing these preferences exceeds the liability when the tax is computed the normal way.

amalgamation Combining more than two firms into a single firm.

American Association of Individual Investors (AAII) Organization designed to help and promote the interests of small investors.

American Stock Exchange Index A value-weighted index of AMEX stocks.

Americus Trust certificate A type of security that divides the ownership of certain stocks into two categories of instruments: the primes receive dividends and are entitled to a liquidation value equal to the price of the stock at termination or a predetermined value, whichever is lower; the scores are entitled to the remaining termination values.

AMEX (American Stock Exchange) The second largest (in terms of primary security listings) U.S. stock exchange (after the NYSE); occasionally abbreviated as ASE; listed firms tend to be of medium size compared with the larger NYSE issues and the typically smaller OTC issues.

amortization The process of writing off the value of an asset or liability, particularly a paper asset or liability.

annual percentage rate (APR) The yield to maturity on a fixed-income investment or the interest rate charged on a loan; computed using a compounding factor reflecting the balance still due.

annual report A yearly report to shareholders containing financial statements (balance sheet, income statement, changes in financial position statement and funds statement), auditor's statement, president's letter and various other information.

annuity An asset that usually promises to pay a fixed amount periodically for a predetermined period, although some pay a sum for an individual's lifetime; certain annuities' values are variable depending on the issuer's investment experience. Most are sold by insurance companies.

antidilution clause A provision in a convertible bond or other security indenture restricting new share issues.

anxious trader effects Short-run price distortions caused by sales or purchases of impatient large traders.

appreciation Increase in the value of an investment over time.

appreciation mortgage A mortgage in which the lender is given the rights to a percentage of any price appreciation derived when the property is sold. In exchange for giving up part of the profit potential, the borrower usually receives a more attractive rate than that charged on a standard loan.

arbitrage (pure)   Simultaneously buying in one market and selling equivalent assets in another for a certain, if modest, profit. *See also* risk arbitrage.

arbitrage pricing theory (APT)   A competitor to the capital asset pricing model that introduces more than one index in place of (or in addition to) CAPM's market index.

arithmetic mean return   The simple average return found by dividing the sum of the separate per-period returns by the number of periods over which they were earned.

ARM (adjustable rate mortgage)   A type of mortgage in which the interest rate is adjusted periodically as market rates change.

arrearage   An overdue payment, as in passed preferred dividends; if the dividends on the senior security are cumulative, arrearage must be made up before common dividends are resumed.

ask   The lowest price at which a security currently is offered for sale; may emanate from a specialist (exchange), market maker (OTC) or unexercised limit order.

asset   Any item of value; often income producing; appears on left of balance sheet.

asset allocation   A compromise approach to market timing. The asset allocator divides his or her portfolio among a number of categories such as low-risk stocks, high-risk stocks, short-term bonds and long-term bonds. The percentage of the portfolio invested in each of these categories will vary, depending on whether the asset allocator's outlook is positive or negative.

asset play   A firm whose underlying assets are worth substantially more (after deducting the firm's liabilities) than the market value of its stock.

at-the-close order   An order that must be executed near or at that day's close.

at-the-opening order   An order that must be executed at that day's opening.

auditor's statement   A letter from the auditor to the company and its shareholders in which the accounting firm certifies the propriety of the methods used to produce the firm's financial statements.

Auto Ex   A division of Xerox that attempts to forecast large block trades for institutional clients.

back testing Trying out a proposed investment strategy on prior period data to see if it would have been profitable to employ in the past. Successful back testing does not necessarily prove that the tested rule will work (be profitable) in the future; the past experience may not reflect the future market environment.

balanced fund A mutual fund that invests in both stocks and bonds.

balance of payments The difference between a country's international payments and its international receipts.

balance of trade The difference between a country's expenditures on imports and its income from exports.

balance sheet A financial statement providing an instant picture of a firm's or individual's financial position; lists assets, liabilities and net worth.

balloon payment A final large principal payment on a debt instrument whose interim payments either incompletely amortized or did not amortize the initial principal at all.

banker's acceptance A money market instrument usually arising from international trade; made highly acceptable by a bank's guarantee or acceptance. Also called acceptance.

bankruptcy proceeding A legal process under Title 11 of the United States Code for dealing formally with an entity seeking protection; may result in a liquidation or reorganization.

bankruptcy trustee Generally, a representative of the estate. The filing of a bankruptcy petition, in a sense, creates an estate consisting of all of the property of the debtor at the time of bankruptcy that is not exempt. This is a separate legal entity and the trustee is the representative of this entity. Also called trustee.

bar chart In technical analysis, a type of graph that plots the price over time; typically contains data on the high, low and volume.

Barron's A major weekly investment periodical published by Dow Jones, Inc.

Barron's Confidence Index A technical indicator based on the yield differential between high-grade and average-grade corporate bonds, with a small differential signifying confidence in the future and a large differential signaling a lack of confidence.

basis (commodity) The difference between the spot price and the futures price.

basis (taxable) The acquisition cost of an asset less any capital distributions. The difference between the basis and the sale proceeds is the taxable gain.

basis point   One-hundredth of one percentage point; primarily used with interest rates.

basis risk   The risk that the basis of a commodity contract will move adversely.

BCG   *See* Boston Consulting Group.

bear   One who expects a declining market.

bearer bond   An unregistered bond whose ownership is determined by possession.

bear market   A declining market.

bear raid   An attempt to drive prices down by selling short.

benefactor   A person named to receive property or other resources as in a will or insurance policy.

Bernhard and Company (Arnold)   The firm that owns Value Line and manages the Value Line mutual funds.

beta   A parameter that relates stock performance to market performance; for a $z\%$ change in the market, a stock will tend to change by (beta) $z\%$.

bid   The highest currently unexercised offer to buy a security; may emanate from a specialist (exchange), market maker (OTC) or limit order.

Big Board   A popular term for the New York Stock Exchange, the largest U.S. stock exchange.

bills   Government debt securities issued on a discount basis by the U.S. Treasury for periods of less than one year.

Billy Martin indicator   A whimsical indicator that hypothesized that any time the New York Yankees named Billy Martin to be their manager, the stock market would decline.

black knight   A potential acquirer opposed by existing management and to which management would prefer to find an alternative (i.e., a white knight).

Black/Scholes formula   An option pricing formula based on the assumption that a riskless hedge between an option and its underlying stock should yield the riskless return; thus, an option's value is a function of the stock price, striking price, stock return volatility, riskless interest rate and length to expiration.

blind pool offerings   Bonds issued, the proceeds of which are to be used for some as yet to be stated purpose.

block trade   A trade involving 10,000 shares or more; usually handled by a block trader.

block trader   One who assembles the passive side of a block trade.

Bloody Monday October 19, 1987, when the market experienced its worst one-day decline in its history; the Dow Jones Industrial Average dropped by 508 points, which was equivalent to a 23% decline.

blue-chip stock Shares of a large, mature company with a steady record of profits and dividends and a high probability of continued earnings.

blue-sky laws State laws designed to protect investors from security frauds.

Blume adjustment A method of adjusting estimated betas toward unity to improve their general accuracy.

boiler-room operations High-pressure selling programs often associated with investment scams such as Ponzi schemes; characterized by aggressive sales forces utilizing banks of telephones to extract "investments" from unsophisticated individuals for risky and often worthless ventures.

bond A debt obligation (usually long term) in which the borrower promises to pay a set coupon rate until the issue matures, at which time the principal is repaid; sometimes secured by a mortgage on a specific property, plant or piece of equipment. *See also* debenture, collateral trust bond and equipment trust certificate.

bond rating An estimated index of the bond's investment quality and default risk.

bond swap A technique for managing a bond portfolio by selling some bonds and buying others; may be designed to achieve benefits in the form of taxes, yields, maturity structure or trading profits.

book value (of common shares) The total assets of an enterprise minus its liabilities, minority interests and preferred stock par, divided by the number of outstanding common shares.

borrower life insurance An insurance policy on the borrower's life equal to the outstanding loan principal and naming the lender as the beneficiary.

Boston Consulting Group (BCG) A strategic planning consulting firm famous for its growth-share matrix (BCG matrix).

box spread A type of option spread in which the investor assembles a vertical spread with calls and a similar but offsetting spread with puts.

Brady Commission One of a number of commissions that studied the causes for the stock market crash of October 19, 1987; set up by the U.S. Congress and named after Nicholas Brady, former New Jersey senator.

breakup value   The sum of the values of a company's individual assets if sold separately.

broker   An employee of a financial intermediary who acts as an agent in the buying and selling of securities. A broker, like a dealer, never owns the securities that he or she trades for his or her customers.

brokerage firm   A firm that offers various services such as access to the securities markets, account management, margin loans, investment advice and underwriting.

broker call-loan rate   The interest rate charged by banks to brokers for loans that brokers use to support their margin loans to customers; usually scaled up for the margin loan rate.

bull   One who expects a rising market.

bullion   Gold, silver or other precious metals in the form of bars, plates or certain coins minted to contain a specific unit of weight (bullion coins).

bull market   A rising market.

business cycle   The pattern of fluctuations in the economy.

Business Week   A major business periodical published weekly by McGraw-Hill, Inc.

butterfly spread   A type of spread in which two calls are sold at one striking price and one call each is purchased at striking prices above and below the sold calls.

buying power   The dollar value of additional marginable securities that can be purchased with the current equity in the account.

call   An option to buy stock or some other asset at a prespecified price over a prespecified period; also, a feature on bond or preferred stock—an option of the issuing company to repurchase the securities at a set price over a prespecified period (prior to maturity).

callable   The property of a security that allows the issuer to redeem it prior to maturity.

call-loan rate   *See* broker call-loan rate.

call price   The price at which a bond, preferred, warrant or other security may be redeemed prior to maturity; usually begins at a significant premium to the face value and then the premium declines as the instrument approaches its stated maturity. Also called the redemption price.

call protection   An indenture provision preventing a security (usually a bond or preferred stock) from being redeemed earlier than a certain time after its issue; for example, a 20-year bond might not be callable for the first five years.

call risk The danger that a callable bond or preferred will be redeemed early (called) by the issuer.

capacity effect The tendency of inflationary pressures to accelerate when the economy approaches the full employment level.

capital asset Virtually any investment asset. To qualify as a capital asset (and thus be subject to the advantages, if any, of long-term capital-gains treatment), an asset must be held as an investment rather than in inventory as an item of trade.

capital asset pricing model (CAPM) The theoretical relationship that seeks to explain returns as a function of the riskfree rate and market risk.

capital distribution A dividend paid out of capital rather than from earnings. Such distributions are not taxed when received but do reduce the investment's basis.

capital gains (losses) The difference between the basis and sales price of an investment asset held for a period specified by the IRS; long-term gains received special tax treatment until 1988.

capitalizing of expenses Placing current business expenses on the balance sheet and writing them off over time.

capital market line The theoretical relation between an efficiently diversified portfolio's expected return and risk derived from the capital asset pricing model.

CAPM *See* capital asset pricing model.

carry The cost of holding a physical commodity until it is deliverable on a futures contract; primary components are storage and financing costs.

cash cow A company or subsidiary of a company that in the normal course of its operations throws off a substantial cash surplus.

cash flow Reported profits plus depreciation, depletion and amortization.

cash management account An individual financial account that combines checking, credit card, money fund and margin accounts to maximize returns and minimize interest charges on transaction balances.

cash market A market in which physical commodities (spot) are traded for cash.

cash surrender value The accumulated savings element of a life insurance policy that can be recovered by canceling the policy or can be borrowed against at a specified interest rate.

CBOE (Chicago Board Options Exchange) The largest of the option exchanges; originator and promoter of organized options trading.

CBT (Chicago Board of Trade)   The largest of the commodity exchanges; lists futures in a variety of physicals including wheat, corn, oats, soybeans, plywood, silver, stock indexes, GNMA and long-term bonds.

CD (certificate of deposit)   Special redeemable debt obligation issued by a bank and other depository institution.

CEA (Commodity Exchange Authority)   A former government agency that had regulatory authority over agricultural futures markets; now regulated by the CFTC.

Central Certificate Service   An organization that allows clearing firms to effect security deliveries with computerized bookkeeping entries.

central market   A congressionally mandated concept for a complete linkup of the various markets trading securities; the development was under way but incomplete as of 1992.

central unemployment rate   The unemployment rate for males in the 25 to 45 age group or some similar high-employment grouping.

certificate of deposit   *See* CD.

CFTC (Commodity Futures Trading Commission)   The federal regulator of the futures markets.

changes in financial position statement   An accounting statement that reports on a firm's cash inflows and outflows. Formerly called source and application of funds statement.

Chapter 7 bankruptcy   Contemplates a liquidation under the Bankruptcy Code.

Chapter 11 reorganization   Contemplates a rehabilitation and restructuring under the Bankruptcy Code.

characteristic line   The relationship between a security's expected return and the market return; defined by the security's α (intercept) and β (slope parameter).

chart reading   Attempting to forecast security price changes from charts of past price and volume data.

Chicago Board of Trade   *See* CBT.

Chicago Board Options Exchange   *See* CBOE.

Chicago Mercantile Exchange (the Merc)   The second largest of the commodity exchanges; lists futures in a variety of physicals including cattle, hogs, pork bellies, fresh broilers, lumber-stock indexes, currencies and debt securities.

churning   Overactive trading of customer accounts designed to generate commissions for the manager/broker.

circuit breakers A procedure for stopping trading when a market move reaches a prescribed threshold; for example, stock trading might be halted for 30 minutes whenever the market moved 150 points on the DJIA during a single day.

claim A right to payment.

classified common stock Different categories of stock, some of which may be nonvoting and others nondividend receiving.

clearinghouse An organization that keeps track of and guarantees fulfillment of futures contracts or options contracts.

Clifford trust A device for shifting tax liability on income, usually from parent to dependent child; trusts set up since the Tax Reform Act of 1986 do not achieve the desired goal.

CLOB (consolidated limit order book) A composite book of limit orders that could be executed in any market where a security is traded; a feature of the proposed central market.

closed-end fund A type of investment company organized as a corporation with its stock traded in the same markets as other stocks; price may vary appreciably from fund's net asset value.

closing costs Costs associated with obtaining a real estate loan and completing the purchase; may include title search, points, transfer taxes and various other fees.

Coffee, Sugar and Cocoa Exchange A commodity exchange located in New York City that lists futures contracts for coffee, sugar and cocoa.

collateral Asset pledged to assure repayment of debt; the lender may take ownership of the collateral if the loan is not repaid as promised.

collateral trust bond A secured bond; for example, an equipment trust certificate secured by such collateral as railroad rolling stock or airplanes.

combination security An asset combining characteristics of more than one type of security; includes convertible bonds, convertible preferred stocks, hybrid convertibles, equity notes, commodity-backed bonds and stock-indexed bonds.

commercial paper Short-term, usually low-risk debt issued by large corporations with very strong credit ratings.

commingled real estate fund (CREF) In effect, a self-liquidating unit investment trust with a managed portfolio of real estate.

commissions Fees charged by brokers for handling investment transactions such as security or real estate trades.

commodity   In general, any article of commerce; in investments, any of a select group of items traded on one of the commodity exchanges either spot (for immediate delivery) or in the futures market (for delivery at a prespecified future date).

commodity board   An electronic sign in the trading room of a commodity exchange that displays current market statistics.

Commodity Exchange Authority   *See* CEA.

Commodity Futures Trading Commission   *See* CFTC.

commodity option   A put or call option to purchase or sell a futures contract.

common stock   Stock that represents proportional ownership of an incorporated enterprise; common stockholders are the residual claimants for earnings and assets after all holders of debt and preferred stock have received their contractual payments.

company analysis   Evaluating the strengths and weaknesses of a company and its investment appeal vis-à-vis its markets and competitors. Also called firm analysis.

composition of creditors   A contract between a debtor and two or more creditors in which the creditors consent to take a specified partial payment in full satisfaction of their claims. This generally is outside of the bankruptcy law and frequently is referred to as a "formal workout."

compound interest   Interest earned on interest as a result of reinvesting one period's income to earn additional income the following period; compounding may take place as frequently as daily. For example, compounded annually, $100 earning 9% will yield $9 the first year. In the following year, the 9% will be applied to $109 for a return of $9.81. In the third year the principal will have grown to $118.81 (100 + 9 + 9.81) and another 9% will add about $10.62. This process continues with the interest rate being applied to a larger and larger principal.

compound value   The end-period value of a sum earning a compounded return.

COMPUSTAT Data Tape   A data source containing balance sheet, income statement and other information on a substantial number of companies for the most recent 20 years.

concentrated position   A margined portfolio having most of its value represented by one or a few securities; may have a higher margin maintenance percentage than that set by brokerage firms for more diversified accounts.

conditional forecast   A forecast based on some exogenous factor such as a stock performance forecast relative to market performance.

Conference Board   An organization that compiles quarterly capital appropriations statistics and reports them in *Manufacturing Industrial Statistics*.

conglomerate   A company with a diversified portfolio of business units; particularly one formed through a merger of a diverse array of formerly independent companies.

consol   A perpetual debt instrument that pays interest but never matures and thus never returns principal.

consolidated limit order book   *See* CLOB.

consumer credit   Personal debt as represented by credit card loans, finance company loans or similar debts.

consumer durables   Long-life assets such as furniture or appliances.

Consumer Price Index (CPI)   A monthly cost-of-living index prepared by the Bureau of Labor Statistics, U.S. Department of Labor.

Consumer Reports   A periodical that frequently contains articles oriented to personal finance.

consumption expenditures   Spending by individual consumers on final goods and services.

contingent liability   A potential claim against a company or other entity; for example, a lawsuit claiming damages would represent a contingent claim against the defendant.

contrary opinion   An investment approach that concentrates on out-of-favor securities; contrarians assert that what is not wanted today may be quite desirable in the future.

conversion   A complicated maneuver that involves purchasing options, shorting the underlying stock and reinvesting the sale proceeds; a technique used by brokerage firms to earn substantial returns when option and stock prices are appropriately related.

conversion price   The face value of a convertible bond divided by the number of shares into which it is convertible.

conversion ratio   The number of common shares into which a convertible bond or preferred stock may be converted.

conversion value   The market price of a stock multiplied by the number of shares for which the convertible may be exchanged.

convertible   A bond or preferred stock that may be exchanged for a specific number of common shares.

convertible debenture   A debenture that may for the bond's life be exchanged for a specific number of shares of the issuing firm's common stock.

convertible preferred   A preferred stock that may be exchanged for a specific number of shares of the issuing company's common stock.

corner   The act of acquiring a large, often controlling, interest in a security issue or other specific type of asset that pushes the market price to a very high level and restricts supply; especially damaging to shorts, who may need to cover at very disadvantageous prices.

corporate bond fund   A mutual fund holding a diversified portfolio of corporate bonds.

corporates   Corporate bonds.

correlation coefficient   A measure of the comovement tendency of two variables, such as the returns on two securities.

cost of carry   The excess of a company's cost of funds over its return on available investments.

country fund   A type of mutual fund that assembles and manages a portfolio of securities in a single country, such as the Japan Fund or the Mexico Fund.

coupon bond   A bond with attached coupons that must be clipped and sent in to receive interest payments.

coupon clipping   Claiming income on coupon bonds by detaching each physical coupon and presenting it for payment when due.

coupon effect   The price impact of differential yield components derived from coupon versus price appreciation as a bond moves toward maturity. Thus, a deep-discount, low-coupon bond will offer a yield to maturity that includes a substantial component of tax-deferred capital gains; such a bond's price usually will be affected favorably by the coupon effect.

coupon-equivalent yield   Yield on an investment computed to correspond with a bond that pays a semiannual coupon.

coupon rate   The stated dollar return of a fixed-income investment.

covariance   The covariance of variables x and y is: $Cov = E[x - E(x)][y - E(y)]$ where $E(z)$ is the expected value of z. If x and y tend to be above their means simultaneously and below their means simultaneously, the covariance is positive. If one is above, when the other tends to be below, the covariance is negative. If they are independent, the covariance is zero.

covenants Legally binding pledges between bond issuers and bondholders contained in indentures.

covered writing Writing options against existing stock holdings.

covering Repurchasing securities or other assets sold short.

CPI *See* Consumer Price Index.

crack Combination commodity trade in which the trader buys crude oil futures and sells corresponding amounts of heating oil and gasoline futures.

cramdown The acceptance of a plan when less than every class of creditors votes in favor of the plan. Certain additional requirements exist that must be satisfied, including (a) at least one impaired class of claims has accepted the plan; (b) the plan does not discriminate unfairly; and (c) the plan is fair and equitable.

Crash of 1987 The largest one-day decline in stock market history; on October 19, 1987, the Dow Jones Industrial Average dropped 508 points, which corresponded to 23% of its value the previous close.

credit In this context, "credit" is used as a synonym for "company" or "high-yield issuer."

credit balance A positive balance, as in a brokerage account.

creditor An entity that has a claim against a debtor.

creditors' committee A committee that the United States Trustee is instructed to appoint of the largest unsecured creditors willing to serve. This committee consults with the trustee or debtor in possession and investigates the debtor's acts and financial condition as well as participating in the formulation of the plan.

credit union A cooperative association in which the members' pooled savings are available for loans to the membership.

Creditwatch One of several short-term credit analysis services. A bond in danger of being downgraded would be likely to be placed on S&P's Creditwatch list once some degree of trouble is spotted.

CREF *See* commingled real estate fund.

CRISP data tape A data source containing daily stock price information.

crown jewel option Antitakeover defense in which the most sought after subsidiary of a target firm is spun off.

crown loan Interestfree loan, usually from parent to dependent child, designed to shift taxable income from a high- to low-bracket individual. The Tax Reform Act of 1986 ended the tax advantage of this maneuver.

crush   A combination trade, especially a commodity trade in which soybean futures are bought and corresponding amounts of soybean oil and meal futures are shorted.

cum-rights period   The time prior to the day of record that determines when shareholders receive a rights distribution; securities that sell cum rights will reflect the imputed value of the rights to be distributed.

cumulative preferred   A preferred stock for which dividends in arrears must be paid before common dividends can be resumed.

cumulative voting   A method of voting for corporate directors that gives each shareholder votes equal to the product of the number of shares held multiplied by the number of director slots; allows a group of shareholders with a substantial but minority position to concentrate their votes on one or a few candidates and thereby elect at least their proportional share of directors.

Curb exchange   The American Stock Exchange, which until 1953 was called the New York Curb Exchange.

currency   Any form of money accepted by a country and in actual use within that country as a medium of exchange.

current assets   Assets that are expected to be used up or converted to cash within the next year or next operating period, whichever is longer; primarily cash, accounts receivable and inventory.

current liabilities   Liabilities that will become due and payable in the next year or the next operating cycle, whichever is longer; includes accounts payable, short-term bank loans, the current portion of long-term debt and taxes payable.

current ratio   The ratio of current assets to current liabilities; a measure of short-term liquidity.

current yield   A bond's coupon rate divided by its current market price or a stock's indicated dividend rate divided by its per-share price.

day of record   The date on which ownership is determined for that quarter's dividends or for the issuance of some other distributions such as rights.

day order   An order that is canceled if it is not executed sometime during the day that it was entered.

day trader   A commodity trader who closes all of his or her positions by the end of the day; thus all transactions are opened and closed on the same day.

DCF   *See* discounted cash-flow analysis.

dealer A security trader who acts as a principal rather than as an agent; thus, a specialist or a market maker but not a broker (brokers are agents).

debenture A long-term debt obligation that unlike a collateralized bond only gives the lender a general claim against the borrower's assets. In a default, the debenture holder has no claim against any specific assets.

debit balance A negative balance in a margin account.

debt A liability on a claim.

debt-equity ratio The ratio of total debt to total equity.

debtor A person concerning whom a case under the Bankruptcy Code has been commenced.

debt securities Bonds and similar securities that call for the payment of interest until maturity and principal at maturity. A firm that defaults on its interest or principal obligations eventually may be forced into bankruptcy.

decreasing term A type of term insurance in which protection decreases with the insured's age.

deduction In tax computation, an amount that may be subtracted from the adjusted gross income to determine taxable income; for example, if the taxpayer itemizes, state income taxes, charitable contributions, mortgage interest expenses and certain other costs.

deep-discount bond A bond selling for substantially less than its par value.

default Failure to live up to any of the terms in an agreement.

default risk The risk that a debt security's contractual interest or principal will not be paid when due.

defeasance The process whereby a debtor offsets the impact of a portion of its debt by purchasing high-quality debt instruments (usually governments) whose payments cover the payment obligations of the debt issue.

defensive recapitalizations A form of leveraging a company where the majority of historical equity ownership is maintained. Assets are not generally written up to fair market value.

deferred compensation plan A procedure whereby employees are permitted to set aside and defer the tax liability on a portion of their wages and salaries into approved deferred compensation plans.

deflation An increase in the purchasing power of the dollar or some other currency unit; the opposite of inflation.

depletion   The writing off of assets, particularly mineral assets such as oil or natural gas, as they are exploited.

Depository Trust Company   A firm that facilitates exchange members' securities trading with one another by using bookkeeping entries rather than physically delivering the stock certificates.

depreciation   A deduction from income that allocates the cost of fixed assets over their useful lives.

depression   An economic collapse with high unemployment and negative growth.

designated order transmission   *See* DOT.

dilution   Issuing additional shares and thereby reducing proportional ownership of existing shareholders.

disability insurance   Insurance protection designed to provide an offset to potential income loss from a health condition that reduces or ends the insured's ability to earn income.

discharge   Bankruptcy gives a release of and forgives certain debts of a debtor. Certain debts (e.g., tax liens, environmental liabilities, etc.) are not dischargeable. In general, a discharge protects a debtor from any further personal liability on account of the debts that are discharged.

discount brokers   Brokers who charge below-retail commission rates and usually offer a more limited set of investment services.

discounted cash-flow analysis (DCF)   The method of discounting a projected stream of cash flows to its present worth. Similar to interest in reverse. The worth of dollars to be received in the future in terms of their present worth.

discount loan   A loan from the Federal Reserve System to a member bank to cure a temporary reserve deficiency.

discount rate (for Fed members)   The interest rate charged by the Federal Reserve System on loans to member banks.

discount rate (for income stream)   The interest rate applied to an income stream or expected income stream in estimating its present value.

discount yield   A yield computation in which the return is based on the final value of the asset; thus, a bill that sells for $100(1-x)$ and matures in one year for 100 has a yield of x.

disinflation   A slowing in the rate at which prices increase.

disintermediation   The tendency, for example, of high interest rates to draw funds out of thrift institutions and therefore away from the mortgage market.

diversifiable risk Firm-specific or industry-specific risk; such risks tend to offset one another and thus average out in an efficiently diversified portfolio.

diversification The technique of spreading an investment portfolio over different industries, companies, investment types and risks; used to reduce risks by not having "all of your eggs in one basket."

dividend capture A strategy in which an investor purchases securities to own them on the day of record and then quickly sells them; designed to capture the dividend but avoid the risk of a lengthy hold.

dividend discount model An approach to stock valuation that evaluates stocks on the basis of the present value of their expected stream of dividends; the basic formula is $P = d + (r - g)$ where P = stock price, d = initial year dividend, r = appropriate discount rate and g = expected growth rate.

dividend exclusion An amount of qualifying dividends that an individual may exclude from taxable income. The Tax Reform Act of 1986 ended the exclusions.

dividend reinvestment plan A company program that allows dividends to be reinvested in additional shares, which often are newly issued and may be sold at a discount from the current market price.

dividend restriction The limitation placed on dividend payments in a bond indenture.

dividends Payments made by companies to their stockholders; usually financed from profits.

divisor The number divided into the sum of Dow Jones 30 stock prices to determine the average. The divisor is adjusted to preserve consistency when any of the components is split.

dollar averaging A formula-investment plan requiring periodic (such as monthly) fixed-dollar-amount investments. This practice tends to "average" the unit purchase cost of an investment made over time.

DOT (designated order transmission) A system on the New York Stock Exchange in which orders are routed electronically to the trading posts where the securities are traded; often used by program traders. Also called Super Dot System.

Dow *See* Dow Jones Industrial Average.

Dow Jones & Company, Inc. The firm that publishes *The Wall Street Journal* and *Barron's* and also compiles Dow Jones stock indexes.

Dow Jones Industrial Average The most commonly referred to index of stock prices; computed as the sum of the prices of 30 leading industrial firms divided by a divisor that is adjusted to reflect splits of its components. Dow Jones indexes also are computed for utilities and transportation companies. Also called simply Dow.

Dow Theory   A charting theory originated by Charles Dow (Dow Jones & Company, Inc.). According to Dow Theory, a market uptrend is confirmed if the primary market index (such as the Dow Jones Industrial Average) hits a new high that soon is followed by a high in the secondary index (such as the Dow Jones Transportation Index). A downtrend is signaled in a similar fashion.

draft   A checklike instrument that calls for payment on receipt.

dual fund   A type of closed-end investment company that divides its returns between dividend-receiving fund holders and capital-gains holders.

dual listing   A security listed for trading on more than one exchange.

Dun & Bradstreet   A firm that rates the creditworthiness of many borrowers and generates financial ratios on many industry groups.

Dupont equation   A profitability relationship that relates return on equity to several components; $ROE = ROS \times Sales + Assets \times Assets + Equity$.

duration   The weighted average rate of return of a bond's principal and interest; a superior index of the payback rate compared to length to maturity, which ignores returns prior to principal repayment.

earnings per common share (EPS)   The net income of a company, minus any preferred dividend requirements, divided by the number of outstanding common shares; provides the investor or potential investor with information on the stability of dividends and capital gains potential; is considered one of the most important indications of the value of common stock.

econometric model   A model based on an analysis of economic data; particularly models of the economy.

econometrics   The statistical analysis of economic data.

economic analysis   An evaluation of a firm's investment potential within its economic setting.

efficient frontier   A set of risk-return trade-offs, each of which offers the highest expected return for a given risk.

efficient market hypothesis   The theory that the market correctly prices securities in light of the known relevant information. In its weak form, the hypothesis implies that past price and volume data (technical analysis) cannot be profitably used in stock selection. The semistrong form implies that superior manipulation of public data is impossible;

thus, such data cannot be used to improve stock selection over what is possible through random selection. In the strong form of the hypothesis, even inside (nonpublic) information is thought to be reflected accurately in prices.

efficient portfolio   Portfolio on the efficient frontier that offers the highest expected return for that risk level.

election-year cycle   The alleged tendency for the stock market to reach a peak about seven months after a presidential election and then fall to a low about 11 months later.

Employee Retirement Income Security Act   *See* ERISA.

Employee Stock Ownership Plan   *See* ESOP.

EPS   *See* earnings per common share.

equipment trust certificate   A type of bond collateralized by equipment, particularly railroad rolling stock or airplanes.

equity   *See* net worth.

equity accounting   Partially consolidating income and equity of affiliates that are 20% or more owned by the parent firm.

equity kicker   A sweetener designed to make a debt issue more attractive by giving its owner an opportunity to benefit from the borrower's success.

equity notes   Debt securities that are automatically converted into stock on a prespecified date at a specific price or one based on a formula that is prespecified. Also called mandatory convertible notes.

equity security   A share in a corporation whether or not transferable as stock, or a similar security.

ERISA (Employee Retirement Income Security Act)   A 1974 federal law that protects workers' pension funds.

escrow account   In general, an account designed to hold a sum of money for a specific purpose; in real estate, the fund normally set up for monthly deposits of the expected pro rata real estate taxes.

ESOP (Employee Stock Ownership Plan)   A program in which a corporation contributes newly issued company stock worth up to 15% of employee payrolls into what amounts to a tax-sheltered profit-sharing plan.

estate   A person's total worth as determined by his or her vested interests in property and other assets, exclusive of any liabilities.

estate tax   A progressive tax on the assets left by deceased parties.

Eurobonds   Bonds that may be denominated in dollars or some other currency but must be traded internationally.

Eurodollars   Dollar-denominated deposits held in banks based outside the United States, mostly in Europe, but some in Asian and other area banks.

Euromarkets   Financial markets that operate outside any national jurisdiction and deal in securities that may pay unusually high interest rates. The securities usually are based on deposits of large, international corporations or governments of nations involved in extensive foreign trade.

examiner   A court-appointed individual that the United States Trustee selects that does not run the debtor's business but merely examines certain facts concerning the debtor and files a report of the investigations.

ex ante   Before the fact; thus, a procedure that consistently identifies attractive investments ex ante generally would facilitate a profitable trading strategy.

ex-dividend date   The day after the day of record. Purchases completed on or after the ex-dividend date do not receive that period's dividend even if the stock is held on the payment date.

executor   The person appointed to carry out the provisions of a will.

exemptions   In tax laws, a dollar sum per dependent that may be used to reduce an individual's taxable income.

exempt property   *See* reaffirmation agreement.

exercise value (put)   The striking price of a put less the price of the associated stock or zero if the difference is negative. Also called intrinsic value.

exercise value (warrant, call or right)   The price of the associated stock less the striking price of the option or zero if the difference is negative. Also called intrinsic value.

exordium clause   The introductory portion of a will or other legal document.

expected value   The sum of the probabilities multiplied by their associated outcomes; the mean or average value.

expense deferral   An accounting technique whereby expense recognitions are spread over time.

explanatory notes   Additional information in the form of notes; keyed to stock and bond quotations by letter symbols.

ex post   After the fact; thus, a procedure that identifies attractive investments but relies on ex post data to do so would not by itself facilitate a profitable trading strategy.

ex-rights period The time subsequent to the day of record for a rights distribution.

extraordinary gain (loss) An unusual nonrecurring gain (loss).

face value The maturity value of a bond or other debt instrument; sometimes referred to as the bond's par value.

FASB (Financial Accounting Standards Board) An accounting organization that establishes rules for preparing financial statements.

FDIC (Federal Deposit Insurance Corporation) A federal agency that insures deposits at commercial banks and thrifts up to $100,000 per depositor.

Fed *See* Federal Reserve System.

Federal Deposit Insurance Corporation *See* FDIC.

Federal Funds Market The market where banks and other financial institutions borrow and lend immediately deliverable reservefree funds, usually on a one-day basis.

Federal Home Loan Mortgage Corporation *See* Freddie Mac.

Federal Housing Administration *See* FHA.

Federal National Mortgage Association *See* FNMA.

Federal Reserve Board of Governors The governing body of the Federal Reserve System, comprised of seven members appointed by the president for long and staggered terms.

Federal Reserve System The federal government agency that exercises monetary policy through its control over banking system reserves. Also called the Fed.

FHA (Federal Housing Administration) A federal government agency that insures home mortgages.

FIFO (first in, first out) An inventory valuation method whereby items taken out of inventory are assumed to have cost the amount paid for the earliest unused purchase.

fill-or-kill order A type of security market order that must be canceled unless it can be filled immediately.

filter rules Any mechanical trading rule, such as a rule to buy stocks when their PE ratio falls below some predetermined value or to trade whenever a particular price pattern is observed.

Financial Accounting Standards Board *See* FASB.

financial ratio A ratio such as the debt-equity or times-interest-earned ratio designed to reflect a firm's long-term financial strength.

firm analysis *See* company analysis.

first in, first out *See* FIFO.

fiscalist A type of economist who believes that fiscal (not monetary) policy is the primary economic tool.

fiscal policy Government tax and spending policy that affects the economy.

Fitch Investors Service A bond rating service that is considerably less well known than Moody's or Standard & Poor's.

fixed assets Tangible assets with a relatively long expected life (greater than a year) that are not intended for resale and that are used in the operation of the business; includes plant and equipment but not inventories or accounts receivable.

fixed-asset value The present value of the free cash flows expected to be generated by a business, plus the residual asset value.

fixed costs Costs that do not vary with the firm's output in the short run.

fixed-income security Any security that promises to pay a periodic nonvariable sum, such as a bond paying a fixed-coupon amount per period.

fixed-rate mortgage A mortgage having a constant interest rate for the life of the debt.

flat Term used to describe a type of trade; bonds trading for a net price that does not reflect any accrued interest are said to trade flat.

flipping The act of quickly selling a recently acquired investment; thus, an investor who subscribed to a new issue and then sold in the immediate aftermarket could be described as a flipper.

floating rate notes A type of debt security whose coupon rate varies with market interest rates.

floating rate preferred A type of preferred stock whose indicated dividend rate varies with market rates.

floor trader One holding a seat on an exchange who trades for his or her own account. Also called a registered competitive market maker (RCMM).

Florida land boom A 1920s speculative real estate boom followed by a crash in the price of Florida property.

flower bonds Government bonds that may be used at their par value for estate tax payments.

flowthrough A method of handling investment tax credits in which benefits are taken into income statements as they are incurred rather than spread over the acquired asset's life (normalization).

FNMA (Federal National Mortgage Association) A previously government-owned but now privately owned corporation that operates a secondary market in mortgages. FNMA issues its own debt securities to finance its mortgage portfolio.

focal point   A round number value that is generally agreed on or recognized.

footnotes (to a financial statement)   Notes that explain or expand on entries; an integral part of a financial statement.

Forbes   A twice-monthly popular investment periodical famous for its Forbes lists, such as the list of loaded laggers.

Form 10-K   A detailed annual report that must be submitted to the SEC, to the listing exchange and to any shareholders who request it.

Form 10-Q   A detailed quarterly report that must be submitted to the SEC and the listing exchange and may be sent to shareholders who request it.

Form 13-D   A required SEC filing of any individual or group owning 5% or more of any public corporation; the form must disclose a number of matters, including the actual ownership percentage, its cost, the intentions of the owner and any relevant agreements of the owner with any other party.

four-nine position   A holding of approximately 4.9% of the outstanding shares of a company, which is about the limit for a quiet holding. At 5%, the holder must file a Form 13-D with the SEC revealing his or her position.

fourth market   Direct trading of listed securities between institutions.

fraudulent conveyances   Defined differently by the several uniform state statutes and the Federal Bankruptcy Statutes. All have their origin in the statute of 13 Elizabeth enacted in 1570 that provided that "Covinous and fraudulent feoffments, gifts, grants . . . devised and contrived of malice, fraud, coven, collusion or guile, to the end, purpose and intent, to delay, hinder or defraud creditors and others . . . shall be utterly void. . . ."

Freddie Mac (Federal Home Loan Mortgage Corporation)   A government agency that assembles pools of conventional mortgages and sells participations in a secondary market.

free cash flow   As used in this text, the amount of cash flow remaining after funding required levels of capital expenditures.

front-end loading   Taking a large portion of the sales fee from the early payments of a long-term purchase contract.

front running   An illegal trading strategy in which the trader (usually an employee of a brokerage firm) learns that a large trade is about to take place (usually placed by a substantial customer) and runs ahead of that trade to place an order at the pretrade price. If the large trade causes a major price change, the position can be reversed at a nice profit. In effect, the front-runner is trading on inside information (knowledge of the forthcoming trade).

full employment   The unemployment rate that is thought to be the minimum level before inflationary pressures accelerate and the maximum level the public will view as reasonable. Opinions on this level have over time varied from around 4 to 6%.

full faith and credit   In economics, the promise backing a debenture or other type of uncollateralized debt instrument; the borrower promises to pay and pledges its full faith and credit.

fundamental analysis   The evaluation of firms and their investment-attractiveness based on their financial, competitive, earnings and managerial position or similar evaluation of other investment types.

futures   Deferred delivery commodities contracts.

GAAP (generally accepted accounting principles)   A set of accounting principles that are supposed to be followed in preparing accounting statements.

gambler's ruin   The wiping out of an individual's original capital by a series of adverse events. Often used in the context of the risk of gambler's ruin.

gamma factor   The number of years of above-average growth at a rate equal to that of the recent past that is necessary to justify the current multiple on growth stocks.

generally accepted accounting principles   *See* GAAP.

general mortgage bond   A bond having a generalized claim against the issuing company's property.

general obligation   A municipal bond secured by the issuer's full faith and credit.

general unsecured creditor   A creditor whose loan is not secured (is uncollateralized) by any specific assets; debts are evaluated based only on the credit of the borrower.

geometric mean return (GMR)   The value obtained by taking the nth root of the product of n per-period returns; the return that if earned over the entire set of periods produces the same ending compound value as the separate per-period returns applied period by period.

GIC (guaranteed interest contract) An investment sold by an insurance company that offers high yields plus the opportunity to earn similar returns on additions to the plan.

gift tax A progressive tax on gifts; now incorporated with estate taxes.

gilt-edge security A very secure bond or other asset.

Ginnie Mae *See* GNMA.

give up A now-prohibited practice whereby brokers making trades for a mutual fund were directed to pay a portion of their commission fees to brokers who had sold the fund's shares.

Glass-Steagall Act A 1933 federal act that required the separation of commercial and investment banking.

GMR *See* geometric mean return.

GNMA (Ginnie Mae) (Government National Mortgage Association) A government agency that provides special assistance on selected types of home mortgages; securities are backed both by GNMA mortgage portfolios and by the general credit of the government.

GNP *See* gross national product.

go-go fund A type of mutual fund popular in the late 1960s that sought short-term trading profits. Also called a performance fund.

going private The process of a company's buying back all of its publicly held stock so that ownership rests with a few owners and it becomes a privately held company.

going public The process of a start-up or heretofore private firm selling its shares in a public offering.

golden handcuffs An employment agreement that makes the departure prior to normal retirement age of upper-level managers very costly to themselves; they may lose attractive stock options.

golden handshake A provision in a preliminary merger agreement in which the target firm gives the acquiring firm an option to purchase its shares or assets at attractive prices or to receive a substantial bonus if the proposed takeover does not occur.

golden parachute A very generous termination agreement for upper management that takes effect if control of their firm shifts.

good till canceled order (GTC) A type of order that remains in effect until executed or canceled.

goodwill The amount by which a firm's going concern value exceeds its book value.

Government National Mortgage Association *See* GNMA.

governments   U.S. government bonds issued by the Treasury Department and backed by the full faith and credit of the federal government.

grace period   Time period in which offensive action is stayed until a defaulting debtor has an opportunity to cure the default.

Graham and Dodd approach   A type of securities analysis that stresses fundamentals. Its originator, Benjamin Graham, coauthored the investment text that dominated the market from the 1930s to 1950s. Also called the Graham approach.

grantee   The individual receiving property under a grantor deed.

grantor   The conveyor of property under a grantor deed; the one who transfers property to another.

Gray approach   An investment timing device that seeks to identify overvalued and undervalued market phases on the basis of interest rates relative to market PE ratios.

Great Crash   1929 stock market decline.

greater-fool theory   The tongue-in-cheek view that a still "greater fool" will come along to bail out a foolish investment.

greenmail   The practice of acquiring a large percentage of a firm's stock and then being bought out at a premium after threatening to take over the firm.

gross income   Total income, either actual or estimated.

gross margin   The net sales of an enterprise minus its cost of goods sold.

gross national product (GNP)   The sum of market values of all final goods and services produced annually in the country.

growth fund   A common stock mutual fund that seeks price appreciation by concentrating on growth stocks.

growth share matrix   A relationship popularized by the Boston Consulting Group that seeks to explain a large part of interfirm profit differences as due to the combined impacts of market share and growth.

growth stock   The shares of a company that is expected to achieve rapid growth; often carries above-average risks and PE ratios.

GTC   *See* good till canceled order.

guarantee bond   A bond with a guarantee from a company other than the issuer.

guaranteed interest contract   *See* GIC.

guarantee preferred   A preferred stock with a guarantee from a company other than the issuer.

head-and-shoulders price formation   A technical pattern that looks like a head and shoulders and is said to forecast a price decline.

hedge fund   A type of mutual fund that seeks to offset some of its long positions with short positions.

hedging   Taking opposite positions in related securities in the hope of profiting from relative price movements (risk hedging) or of reducing an existing risk (pure hedging).

hemline indicator   A whimsical technical market indicator that forecasts stock market moves on the basis of women's hemlines.

histogram   A discrete probability distribution display.

holding company   A company set up to maintain voting control of other business enterprises.

holding period return (HPR)   The rate of return over some specific time.

holding period return relative (HPRR)   The end-period compound value for a specific holding period.

horizontal integration   The process of a business buying or building from scratch a business that is complementary in nature to existing lines of business.

horizontal spread   Short and long option positions on the same security with the same strike price but different expirations.

HPR   *See* holding period return.

HPRR   *See* holding period return relative.

Hulbert Financial Digest   A publication containing ratings of investment advisory services.

hypothecation   The pledging of securities as loan collateral.

immunization   The process of buying bonds with durations equal to one's investment horizon or using interest futures to accomplish the same purpose.

inactive post   NYSE trading post for inactively traded securities.

in and out   The purchase and sale of the same security within a short period.

income anticipation   An accounting practice whereby a profit is reflected in the income statement before it is received.

income approach   Valuing real estate or some other asset as the discounted value of its expected income stream.

income bond   A bond on which interest is paid only if the issuer has sufficient earnings.

income fund   A common stock mutual fund that concentrates on stocks paying high dividends.

income statement   A financial statement of interim earnings; provides a financial accounting of revenues and expenses during a specified period, i.e., three months, one year and so on. Also called profit-and-loss statement.

income stock   A stock with a high indicated dividend rate.

incorporation   The forming into a legal body endowed with various rights and duties.

increasing rate notes   Bond issues whose interest rate automatically increases by some predetermined amount at predetermined times.

indenture (bond)   The statement of promises under the Trust Indenture Act the company makes to its bondholders, including a commitment to pay a stated coupon amount periodically and return the face value (usually $1,000) at the end of a certain period (such as 20 years after issue). A trustee, such as a bank, is charged with overseeing the issuing firm's commitments.

indenture trustee   The trustee under an indenture for the benefit of the holders of the debt represented by the indenture. Also called trustee.

independence (statistical)   The relationship between two variables if knowledge of one's value does not help explain the other's value. Thus, if IBM and AT&T stock returns are totally unrelated, knowing that AT&T stock returned x% over the most recent 12 months would not help explain IBM stock's return over the same period.

index arbitrage   A trading strategy involving offsetting positions in stock index futures contracts and the underlying cash market securities (stocks making up the index). If, for example, the index futures contract is priced above the stocks making up the index, the arbitrager would buy the stocks and sell the index. If, in contrast, the index was priced below its corresponding stocks, the arbitrager would short the stocks and buy the index.

index fund   A mutual fund that attempts to duplicate the performance of a market index such as the S&P 500.

Individual Retirement Account   *See* IRA.

industry analysis   The evaluation of an industry's position and prospects as they relate to its component firm's investment attractiveness.

inflation   The rate of rise in the price level; for example, if on the average, $1.06 will buy what $1 would buy a year earlier, inflation has equaled 6%.

inflation hedge   An asset whose value varies directly with the price level.

informal workout   An approach to dealing with a troubled firm that seeks to avoid the problems of a bankruptcy proceeding by obtaining sufficient lender concessions to allow the obliger to continue.

in play   The status of being an actively pursued takeover candidate.

input-output model   A model that relates various industries' outputs to their derived demands from other industries.

insider trading   The buying or selling of securities by traders with access to relevant nonpublic information relating to the company in question.

insolvency   Can be defined in several ways depending on the particular statute to be applied. One common classification is simple balance sheet insolvency. A second test is the ability to pay one's debts as they become due.

installment sale   In general, any sale that calls for payments to be made over time; in real estate transactions, an installment sale may reduce and postpone the tax liability if the payments are stretched out over a sufficiently long period.

Instinet   An automated communications network among block traders.

institutional investor   An organization that invests the pooled assets of others; includes pension funds, mutual funds, bank trust departments, insurance companies and investment companies.

intercorporate dividend   Dividend payment from one corporation to another; 70% of such dividends are not subject to the corporate income tax.

interest   The amount a borrower pays for the use of a lender's funds; frequently expressed as an annual percentage of the principal balance outstanding and may be compounded on a monthly, quarterly, annual or some other periodic basis.

interest futures   A commodity futures contract calling for delivery of a debt security such as a T-bill or long-term government bond.

interest-rate risk   The risk that an interest-rate rise will take place, thereby reducing the market value of fixed-income securities.

interest spread   The cost of carry, measured in percentage points.

international fund   A mutual fund that invests in securities of firms based outside the fund's home country.

International Monetary Market   A futures exchange associated with the Chicago Mercantile Exchange that trades futures contracts on gold, T-bills, Eurodollars, CDs and several foreign currencies.

in-the-money option   An option whose striking price is more favorable to option holders than the current market price of the underlying security.

intraday dependencies   Nonrandom price movements of transactions taking place over the course of a single day.

intrinsic value (option)   *See* exercise value.

intrinsic value (stock)   The underlying value that a careful evaluation would produce; generally takes into account both the going-concern value and the liquidation or breakup value of the company. An efficient market always would price stocks at their intrinsic values, although an inefficient market would not necessarily do so.

inverted market   A futures market in which the futures price exceeds the spot.

investment banker   A firm that organizes a syndicate to underwrite or market a new issue of securities.

Investment Companies   Periodical that reports on mutual funds; published by Weisenberger.

investment company   A company that manages pooled portfolios for a group of owners; may be either a closed-end company, whose fixed number of shares outstanding are traded like other shares, or an open-end company (mutual fund), whose shares outstanding change by the amounts bought and sold.

Investment Company Institute   Organization of mutual funds and other institutional investors; publishes *Mutual Fund Forum*.

investment manager   One who manages an investment portfolio.

Investor's Daily   A national business newspaper that competes with *The Wall Street Journal*.

involuntary bankruptcy   A bankruptcy petition filed by the creditors of a debtor forcing the commencement of a case under Chapter 11 or 7.

IRA (Individual Retirement Account)   A retirement plan that allows employees to set aside up to $2,000 annually in a tax-sheltered instrument. Earnings are not taxed until they are withdrawn. The contributed sum also is deductible from taxable income if the individual is not covered by a company pension or has a relatively low income.

itemizing   One of two basic approaches to filing income taxes; involves taking deductions for specific allowed expenses. Taxpayers who do not itemize take a standard deduction.

January indicator   A technical timing device utilizing the assertion that as January goes so goes the year.

junk bonds   High-risk bonds usually promising a very high indicated return coupled with a substantial default risk.

Kansas City Board of Trade   A futures exchange listing wheat and Value Line stock index futures.

Keogh account   A retirement account that allows self-employed individuals to set aside (1992) up to $30,000 or 20% of their income in a tax-sheltered fund. Neither the contribution nor the earnings on it are subject to tax until they are withdrawn.

key-person life insurance   Life insurance on key employees with their employer as the beneficiary; designed to assure creditors and suppliers and customers that the firm would survive the loss of the insured.

Krugerrand   A South African gold coin containing one ounce of gold that often is traded by gold speculators.

kurtosis   The degree to which a distribution departs from normal. *See also* platokurtosis and leptokurtosis.

lagging indicators   Government-compiled data series whose movements are identified as tending to follow turns in the overall economy.

last in, first out   *See* LIFO.

law of one price   The principle that, whenever two assets offer equivalent payoff matrices, their prices must be identical.

LBO   *See* leveraged buyout.

leading indicators   Government-compiled data series whose movements are identified as tending to precede turns in the overall economy.

leakages   Funds that "leak" into savings, import purchases or taxes during each round of stimulatory spending or tax reduction, reduced each round, thus reducing the impact of fiscal policy.

learning curve   A relationship popularized by the Boston Consulting Group that hypothesizes that manufacturers are able to reduce costs substantially as they increase their cumulative volume; in one formulation, costs are said to decrease by 20% with each doubling of cumulative volume.

legal lists   Lists of stocks authorized by various states for fiduciary investing.

leg on   The process of assembling a spread or other combination position one side at a time.

leptokurtosis   The degree to which a distribution differs from the normal by having more probability in the peak and tails.

lettered stock   Newly issued stock sold at a discount to large investors prior to a public offering of the same issue; in accordance with SEC Rule 144, buyers agree not to sell their shares for a prespecified period.

leverage   Using borrowed funds or special types of securities (warrants, calls) to increase the potential return; usually increases both the risk and the expected return.

leveraged buyout (LBO)   The takeover of a company financed largely by debt secured by the acquired firm's own assets.

liabilities   Debts; appear on right side of a balance sheet.

lien   A charge against or interest in property to secure payment of a debt for performance of an obligation.

LIFO (last in, first out)   An accounting method that for income reporting purposes values items taken out of inventory at the most recent unused invoice cost.

limited liability   Property that under most circumstances limits shareholders' liabilities for their corporation's debts to their initial investments.

limit order   An order to buy or sell at a prespecified price.

linear model   A method of estimating portfolio risks that requires only alpha and beta estimates of the components.

line of credit   Prearranged agreement from a lender to supply up to some maximum loan at prespecified terms.

liquidation   The process of selling all of a firm's assets and distributing the proceeds first to creditors and then any residual to shareholders.

liquidation value   The value of a going concern's assets if sold piecemeal.

liquidity   The ease with which an investment can be converted to cash for approximately its original cost plus its expected accrued interest.

liquidity preference hypothesis   The term structure of interest rates hypothesis that asserts that most borrowers prefer to borrow long and most lenders prefer to lend short; implies that long rates generally exceed short rates.

liquidity ratio   A ratio (e.g., current or quick) of a firm's short-run financial situation.

liquidity risk   The degree to which an asset's holding period return varies with interest-rate moves.

listed stocks   Stocks approved for trading by one or more of the stock exchanges.

listing   The act of obtaining exchange approval for trading.

listing requirements   The qualifications that a company must meet to be listed on an exchange.

load   The selling fee applied to a load mutual fund purchase.

loaded lagger   A stock of a company whose assets, particularly its liquid assets, have high values relative to the stock's price.

load fund   A type of mutual fund sold through agents who receive fees that are typically 8.5% on small purchases and somewhat less on trades above $10,000.

lock-up agreement An agreement between an acquirer and a target that makes the target unattractive to any other acquirer; similar to a golden handshake.

long interest The number of futures or options contracts outstanding (owned and sold).

long position The ownership of stocks or other securities as opposed to a short position, in which the investor has sold securities that are not owned.

long-term assets *See* fixed assets.

long-term capital gain (loss) Gain (loss) on a capital asset held for at least six months.

long-term liabilities Liabilities that are not due in the next year or next operating period, whichever is shorter; usually include outstanding bonds, debentures, mortgages and term loans.

loss Net revenues minus costs when costs exceed revenues.

low PE stocks Stocks with low price-earnings ratios; sought out by value-oriented investors.

LYON (liquidity yield option note) A complicated type of zero-coupon convertible debt security that is both callable and redeemable at prices that escalate through time.

M1 The basic money supply; includes checking deposits and cash held by the public.

M2 A broader based money supply definition than M1; includes everything in M1 plus most savings and money market deposit accounts.

M3 A still broader based money supply definition than M2; includes everything in M2 plus large certificates of deposit and money market mutual funds sold to institutions.

maintenance capital expenditures The amount a business must spend just to maintain the efficiency and appearance of its plant and equipment. No additions to the plant and equipment are contemplated.

management control A situation in which no group owns enough of the firm's stock to exercise control and control thus is abdicated to the managers.

management-oriented company A firm that is largely run in the interest of management as opposed to that of the shareholders.

mandatory convertible notes *See* equity notes.

manufactured call A call-like position generated by a combination put and a long position in the underlying stock; position with a similar payoff matrix to a call.

manufactured put   A put-like position generated by a combination of a call and a short position in the underlying stock; position with a similar payoff matrix to a put.

margin   Borrowing to finance a portion of a securities purchase; regulated by the Fed. For example, if a 60% margin rate is set, $10,000 worth of stock may be purchased with up to $4,000 of borrowed money. Only securities of listed and some large OTC companies qualify for margin loans.

marginal tax rate   The percentage that must be paid in taxes on the next income increment.

margin call   A demand by a brokerage firm for more collateral or cash to support existing margin debt; a call is required when the borrower's equity position falls below a preset percentage (e.g., 35%) of the value of margined securities.

margin maintenance   The minimum percentage that an equity account must maintain to avoid a margin call.

margin rate   The percentage of the cost of a purchase of marginable securities that must be paid for with the investor's own money.

marketability   The ease with which an investment can be bought or sold without appreciably affecting its price; for example, blue-chip stocks usually are highly marketable because they are actively traded.

market approach   Estimating the value of properties (particularly real estate) based on what similar properties are selling for.

market indexes   An average of security prices designed to reflect market performance. The Dow Jones Industrial Average, the best known and most closely followed, is calculated by adding the market prices of 30 leading industrial companies and dividing by a divisor; the divisor is changed periodically to reflect stock splits. Dow Jones & Company, Inc., also compiles averages for utility and transportation stocks. Standard & Poor's Investor Service, the NYSE, NASD and AMEX all compute their own indexes. Indexes also are compiled for bonds, commodities, options and various other investment types.

market indicator   *See* technical indicator.

market maker   One who creates a market for a security by quoting a bid and ask price.

market model   Relating the price of individual security returns to market returns with a linear equation of the form: $R_{it} = \alpha_i + \beta_i R_{mt}$ where $R_{it} =$ return of security i for period t; $R_{mt} =$ market return for period t; and α_i and β_i are firm i parameters.

market on close order   An order that is to be held until just before the close and then executed.

market order   An order to buy or sell at the market price; requires immediate execution.

market portfolio   A hypothetical portfolio representing each investment asset in proportion to its relative weight in the universe of investment assets.

market price   The current price at which willing buyers and willing sellers will transact.

market risk   The return variability associated with general market movements; not diversifiable within the market. Also called systematic risk.

mark to market   Practice of recomputing equity position in a margin account (stock or futures) on a daily basis.

master limited partnership (MLP)   A method of organizing a business that combines some of the advantages of a corporation with some of the advantages of a limited partnership. Shares of ownership trade much like corporate stock, yet the MLP is taxed like a partnership; that is, profits are imputed to the owners and taxed only once.

matched and lost   Term applied to the outcome for the loser when two traders simultaneously arrive at the relevant trading post with equivalent orders, only one of which may be filled within the current market situation; they flip a coin to determine whose order is to be filled.

maturity   The length of time until a security must be redeemed by its issuer.

maturity date   The date at which a security's principal must be redeemed.

mean   The average or expected value of a sample or distribution.

me-first rules   Restrictions in a bond's indenture that limit a firm's ability to take on additional debt with similar standing to that of the bonds in question.

merger   The act of combining two firms into a single company.

MGIC (Mortgage Guarantee Insurance Corporation)   One of a group of companies that for a fee guarantee the timely payment of a portion of certain mortgages' obligations.

middle-of-the-road fund   A mutual fund that invests in a balanced portfolio of stocks (some blue chips and some more speculative).

MLP   *See* master limited partnership.

mode   The high point or most likely outcome of a distribution; for a symmetrical distribution, the mode and mean (average value) are identical.

modern portfolio theory (MPT)   The combination of the capital asset pricing model, efficient market hypothesis and related theoretical models of security market pricing and performance.

Monday-Friday stock pattern   The observed tendency of stock prices to decline on Mondays and rise on Fridays.

monetarist   One who emphasizes the powerful economic role of monetary (as opposed to fiscal) policy.

monetary asset   An investment that is denominated in dollars.

monetary policy   Government policy that utilizes the money supply to affect the economy; implemented by the Fed through its control of bank reserves and required reserves.

money fund   *See* money market mutual fund.

money illusion   Failure to take account of inflation's impact; thus, an individual who received a 10% raise and thought his or her financial situation had improved would suffer from money illusion if prices had risen by 20%.

Money Magazine   A monthly personal finance periodical published by Time, Inc.

money market   The market for high-quality, short-term securities such as CDs, commercial paper, acceptances, Treasury bills, short-term tax-exempt notes and Eurodollar loans.

money market account   A type of bank or thrift institution account that offers unregulated money market rates.

money market mutual fund   A mutual fund that invests in short-term highly liquid securities. Also called money fund.

money multiplier   The ratio of a change in reserves to the change in the money supply; thus, a money multiplier of five would imply that a $1 billion increase in reserves would result in a $5 billion increase in the money supply.

money supply   Generally defined as the sum of all coin, currency (outside bank holdings) and deposits on which checklike instruments may be written. *See* M1, M2 and M3.

mood indicators   Technical market indicators designed to reflect the market's pessimism or optimism.

Moody's Industrial Manual   An annual publication containing detailed historical information on most publicly traded firms.

Moody's Investor Service   A firm that publishes manuals containing extensive historical data on a large number of publicly traded firms. Moody's also rates bonds.

mortgage A loan collateralized by property, particularly real estate; the lender is entitled to take possession of the property if the debt is not repaid in a timely manner.

mortgage-backed security A debt instrument representing a share of ownership in a pool of mortgages (e.g., GNMA passthroughs) or backed by a pool of mortgages (e.g., FNMA bonds).

mortgage bond Debt security for which specific property is pledged.

mortgagee The lender under a mortgage loan.

Mortgage Guarantee Insurance Corporation *See* MGIC.

mortgages—secured claims The law governing real property mortgages and mortgages on chattel; governed by various laws and different statutes in various jurisdictions. No central federal bankruptcy law exists on the subject.

mortgagor The borrower under a mortgage loan.

MPT *See* modern portfolio theory.

multi-index model A method of estimating portfolio risk that utilizes a market index and indexes for various market subcategories.

multiplier The ratio of the change in government spending to the resulting change in the GNP.

municipal bond fund A mutual fund holding a portfolio of municipal bonds.

municipals Taxfree bonds issued by state and local governments.

mutual fund A pooled investment in which managers buy and sell assets with the income and gains and losses accruing to the owners; may be either load (with sales fee) or no-load (no sales fee); stands ready to buy back its shares at their net asset value.

mutual fund cash position A technical market indicator based on mutual fund liquidity; high fund liquidity is said to be associated with subsequent market rises.

NAIC *See* National Association of Investment Clubs.

naked option writing Writing options without owning the underlying shares; the naked writer satisfies the contract with the option holder, if it is exercised, by buying the required shares on the market.

NASD (National Association of Securities Dealers) The self-regulator of the OTC market.

NASDAQ (National Association of Securities Dealers Automated Quotations) An automated information system that provides brokers and dealers with price quotations on securities that are traded OTC.

NASDAQ Composite Index A value-weighted index of OTC issues.

NASDAQ National List   The secondary list of OTC issues carried in many newspaper stock quotations. Stocks that are not sufficiently active for the NASDAQ list may appear on the National List.

NASDAQ National Market System List   The primary list of OTC issues carried in most newspaper stock quotations. Membership is determined by criteria similar to the AMEX listing.

NASDAQ Supplemental List   The tertiary list of OTC stocks carried in some newspaper stock quotations. Stocks not active enough to be on either of the two major NASDAQ lists may be included on the supplemental list.

National Association of Investment Clubs (NAIC)   Organization that fosters and assists in the setting up of investment clubs.

National Association of Securities Dealers   *See* NASD.

National Association of Securities Dealers Automated Quotations   *See* NASDAQ.

National Bureau of Economic Research   *See* NBER.

NAV (net asset value)   The per-share market value of a mutual fund's portfolio.

NBER (National Bureau of Economic Research)   A private nonprofit research foundation that dates business cycles and sponsors economic research.

near money   Assets such as savings accounts and Treasury bills that can quickly and easily be converted into spendable form.

negotiable order of withdrawal account   *See* NOW.

net asset value   *See* NAV.

net equity value   The value of a firm after subtracting outstanding debt obligations.

net-net   A stock whose market price is very low relative to the value of its liquid assets; more specifically, stock whose per-share price is less than the pro rata amount of both short- and long-term debt subtracted from the company's per-share liquid assets.

net worth   The dollar value of assets minus liabilities; the stockholders' residual ownership position. Also called equity.

new issue   An initial stock sale, usually of a company going public; also an initial sale of a bond issue.

new listing   A stock that recently has been listed on an exchange; may be the company's first listing on the particular exchange or the first on any exchange.

New York Curb Exchange   The former name for what now is called the American Stock Exchange.

New York Futures Exchange   *See* NYFE.

New York Stock Exchange   *See* NYSE.

nifty fifty   A list of about 50 companies, with high multiples and rapid growth rates, that are preferred by many institutional investors.

no-load (mutual) fund   A fund whose shares are bought and sold directly at the fund's NAV. Unlike a load fund, no agent or sales fee is involved.

nonmarket risk   Individual risk not related to general market movements; the total risk of an investment may be decomposed into that associated with the market and that which is not. Also called unsystematic risk.

nonnormal distribution   A distribution, such as a skewed distribution of returns, that differs from the normal shape. *See also* leptokurtosis and platokurtosis.

nonparticipating insurance   A type of insurance sold by a stockholder-owned company as opposed to participating insurance, which is sold by an insurance company owned by its policyholders (mutual).

normal distribution   A distribution corresponding to the normal shape.

normalization   Spreading the benefits of investment tax or other types of credits across the life of an asset. *See also* flowthrough.

notes   Intermediate-term debt securities issued with maturity dates of one to five years.

NOW (negotiable order of withdrawal) account   A special type of deposit account that draws interest and allows checklike instruments to be written against it.

NYFE (New York Futures Exchange)   A futures exchange associated with the NYSE; lists futures and option contracts on the NYSE Composite Index.

NYSE (New York Stock Exchange)   The largest U.S. stock exchange.

NYSE Composite Index   A value-weighted index of all NYSE-listed securities.

odd-lot short ratio   A technical market indicator based on relative short trading by small investors; when such trading is heavy, the market is said to be near a bottom.

odd-lotter   One who trades in odd lots.

odd-lot trade   A transaction involving less than one round lot of stock; usually 100 shares, although a few stocks are traded in ten-share lots.

off-board trading   Trading that takes place off an exchange, particularly OTC trading in NYSE-listed securities. NYSE rule 390 restricts such trading by member firms.

one-decision stocks   A now largely discredited concept of the early 1970s that certain high-quality growth stocks should be bought and held; supposedly, the only decision necessary was to buy.

open-end investment company   A mutual fund or other pooled portfolio of investments that stands ready to buy or sell its shares at their NAV or NAV plus load if the fund has a load.

open interest   The number of option or commodity contracts outstanding; analogous to shares outstanding for stock.

open market committee   The Federal Reserve Board committee that decides on open market policy; consists of all seven of the Federal Reserve Board governors plus five of the presidents of the regional Fed Banks including the president of the New York bank.

open market operations   Fed transactions in the government bond market that affect bank reserves and thereby influence the money supply, interest rates and economic activity.

option   A put, call, warrant, right or other security giving the holder the right but not the obligation to purchase or sell a security at a set price for a specific period.

ordinary least squares   A method of estimating regression parameters by choosing linear coefficients that minimize the square of the residuals.

organizational slack   Wasted firm resources due to managerial deadwood, lack of aggressiveness, carelessness and so on.

OTC (over the counter)   The market in unlisted securities and off-board trading in listed securities.

out-of-the-money option   An option whose striking price is less attractive than the current market price of its underlying stock.

overbought   An opinion that the market has risen too rapidly and therefore is poised for a downward correction.

oversold   An opinion that the market has fallen too rapidly and therefore is poised for an upward correction.

over the counter   *See* OTC.

Pac Man defense   Tactic to avoid takeover by attempting to take over the attacking firm.

paper   *See* commercial paper.

paper loss   An unrealized loss.

paper profit   An unrealized gain.

par (bond) The face value at which the issue matures.

par (common stock) A stated amount below which per-share equity (net worth) may not fall without barring dividend payments.

par (preferred stock) The value on which the security's dividend and liquidation value is based.

parking The illegal practice of holding a security for another in an attempt to conceal the owner's true identity. Sometimes stock is parked during the period prior to launching a takeover attempt.

par ROI equation An empirically estimated profitability equation of the Strategic Planning Institute.

participating bond Bond that may pay an extra coupon increment in years in which the issuing firm is especially profitable.

participating life insurance Life insurance sold by a mutual company, which is owned by and shares its profits with its policyholders.

participating preferred Preferred stock that may pay an extra dividend increment in years in which the issuing firm is especially profitable.

passed dividend The omission of a regular dividend payment.

passthrough A share of a mortgage pool whose interest and principal payments are flowed through to the holders.

payback period The length of time until an original investment is recaptured.

payment in kind securities *See* PIKs.

payout ratio Dividends per share as a percentage of earnings per share.

PE (price-earnings ratio) The stock price relative to the most recent 12-month earnings per share.

penny stock market A market for low-priced stocks (under $1 per share); especially active in Denver.

penny stocks Low-priced stocks usually selling for under $1 per share; normally are issued by small speculative companies.

pension A periodic or lump-sum payment to a person following retirement from employment or to surviving dependents of a deceased former employee.

PE ratio model A model designed to explain PE ratios.

percentage order A market or limit order that is entered once a certain amount of stock has traded.

performance fund *See* go-go fund.

per-period return (PPR) The return earned for a particular period.

physical The underlying physical delivery instrument for a particular futures contract.

PIKs (payment in kind securities)   Securities whose yield is at the issuer's option, payable in additional securities of like kind to the existing securities; thus, a preferred stock may choose to pay the dividend in additional preferred shares.

Pink sheets   Quotation source for most publicly traded OTC issues.

Pink-sheet stocks   OTC stocks not traded on the NASDAQ system; issued by very small, obscure and often speculative companies.

Pit   The name of the physical location where specific commodity contracts are traded.

planning horizon (portfolio management)   The time frame in which a portfolio is managed.

platokurtosis   The degree to which a distribution differs from the normal by having less of the distribution concentrated at the peaks and tails.

point (stocks and bonds)   Pricing units; for stocks, a point represents $1 per share; for bonds, a point is equivalent to $10.

point-and-figure chart   A technical chart that has no time dimension. An x is used to designate an up move of a certain magnitude while an o denotes a similar size down move. The xs are stacked on top of each other as long as the direction of movement remains up; a new column is begun when direction changes.

points (real estate)   A fee charged for granting a loan, especially for a mortgage on real estate.

poison pill   Antitakeover defense in which a new diluting security is issued if control of the firm is about to shift.

Ponzi scheme   An investment scam promising high returns that are secretly paid out of investor capital; usually exposed when incoming funds are insufficient to cover promised outpayments. The scam depends on fresh investor capital to pay its promised return.

pooling of interest accounting   A type of merger accounting in which an acquired firm's assets and liabilities are transferred to the acquiring firm's balance sheet without any valuation adjustment.

portfolio   A holding of one or more securities by a single owner (institution or individual).

portfolio insurance   A service in which the "insurer" endeavors to place a floor on the value of the "insured" portfolio. If the portfolio value falls to a prespecified level, the insurer neutralizes it against a further fall by purchasing an appropriate number of index puts or selling an appropriate number of index options.

portfolio risk   Risk that takes account of the diversifying impact of portfolio components.

position trader   A commodity trader who takes and holds futures position for several days or more.

post   One of 18 horseshoe-shaped locations on the NYSE floor where securities are traded. Also called trading post.

postponable expenditures   Purchases of long-term assets such as consumer durables.

PPR   *See* per-period return.

preemptive rights   Shareholder rights to maintain their proportional share of their firm by subscribing proportionally to any new stock issue.

preferences   In general, a preference consists of a transfer of the debtor's property to or for the benefit of a creditor on account of an antecedent debt at a time in which the debtor was insolvent, the purpose of which was to permit the creditor to receive more than the creditor would receive in a Chapter 7 case.

preferred habitat   One of four hypotheses for explaining the term structure of interest rates based on a tendency for borrowers and lenders to gravitate toward their preferred loan lengths.

preferred stock   Shares whose indicated dividends and liquidation values must be paid before common shareholders receive any dividends or liquidation payments.

premium (bond)   The amount by which a bond's price exceeds its par.

premium (option)   The market price of an option; confusingly, the term also is sometimes used to refer to time value.

premium over conversion value   The amount by which a convertible's price exceeds its conversion value.

premium over straight-debt value   The amount by which a convertible's price exceeds its value as a nonconvertible debt security.

prepayment penalty   The fee assessed for early liquidation of an outstanding debt.

present value   The value today of a dollar to be received at some future point, using appropriate discount rates.

present-value factor   The factor used when deriving the present value of a future cash flow. For the first year, it is calculated as one divided by one plus the discount rate, or $1 \div (1 + \text{Discount})$. In subsequent years, it is calculated as one divided by one plus the discount rate raised to the power of the year in question. For example, in Year 5, the present value factor would be $1 \div (1 + \text{Discount rate})^5$.

price dependencies   Price movements that are related to past price movements.

price-earnings ratio   *See* PE.

price floor   The support level of a convertible bond provided by its straight-debt value.

price stability   The absence of inflation or deflation.

primary distribution   The initial sale of a stock or bond (new issue).

primary market   The market for initial sales of securities; later, the securities are traded in the secondary market.

prime   One of the two component securities created when appropriate shares are deposited into an Americus Trust. The prime receives the stock's dividends and up to some prespecified liquidation payment at the termination date; the score receives any value in excess of the amount assigned to the prime.

prime rate   The rate that banks advertise as their best (although some very secure borrowers may receive a still lower super prime rate).

principal (in a trade)   The person or institution for whom the broker acts as an agent.

principal (of a bond)   The face value of a bond.

priorities   Certain claims such as taxes and the costs of administering a bankruptcy estate are paid ahead of the general claims of other creditors, all as particularized in the Bankruptcy Code.

private market value   The value that a private buyer would pay for an entire company to control the disposition of its cash flow as determined by using discounted cash flow analysis.

private placement   A direct security sale to a small number of large buyers.

probability distribution   A display of possible events along with their associated probabilities.

professional corporation pension plans   Pension plans as a means to shelter income from taxes; set up by professionals such as doctors, lawyers and architects after organizing their businesses as corporations. The 1982 tax act severely limited the amount of tax-sheltered contributions that may be put into such plans.

profit   Net revenues minus costs when revenues exceed costs.

profitability models   Models designed to explain company profit rates.

profitability ratio   A ratio such as return on equity and return on sales designed to reflect the firm's profit rates.

profit-and-loss statement   *See* income statement.

programmed trading   *See* program trading.

programs   The actual trades instituted by a program trader. Market watchers, for example, might see a series of large trades in stocks making up the S&P 500 and conclude that programs are moving the market in a particular direction.

program trading   A type of mechanical trading in large blocks by institutional investors; usually involves both stock and index futures contracts as, for example, in index arbitrage or portfolio insurance. Also called programmed trading.

proof of claim   Creditors having a desire to participate in the distribution of the proceeds of a bankruptcy estate must file a claim with the court within the time periods provided to receive a payment and distribution from the Bankruptcy Court.

proprietorship   The condition of ownership of a business entity, usually referring to sole ownership.

prospectus   An official document that all companies offering new securities for public sale must file with the SEC; spells out in detail the financial position of the offering company, what the new funds will be used for, the qualifications of the corporate officers and any other material information.

proxy   A shareholder ballot.

proxy fight   A contest for control of a company.

proxy material   A statement of relevant information that the firm must supply to shareholders when they solicit proxies.

public offering   A security sale made through dealers to the general public and registered with the SEC.

purchase accounting   A type of merger accounting in which the net assets of the merged firm are entered on the books of the acquiring firm at amounts that sum to the firm's acquisition price. As opposed to the "pooling of interest" method of accounting for a business combination, the purchase method allows assets to be written up to fair market value. Under the pooling method, assets continue to be carried at their historical basis. Earnings under the purchase method are included only from the date of acquisition, whereas under the pooling method they are restated as far back as necessary.

pure arbitrage   An arbitrage that involves no element of risk.

pure hedge   A hedge whose purpose is to reduce the risk on an existing position.

pure risk premium   The portion of the expected yield above the riskless rate that is due to pure risk aversion as opposed to the expected default loss.

put   An option to sell a stock at a specified price over a specified period.

put bond   A bond with an indenture provision allowing it to be sold back to the issuer at a prespecified price.

put-call parity   A theoretical relation between the value of a put and a call on the same underlying security with the same strike and expiration date.

quarterly earnings   Profits, usually per-share profits, for a three-month period.

quarterly report   A report to shareholders containing three-month financial statements.

quick ratio   *See* acid-test ratio.

raider   A hostile outside party that seeks to take over companies.

rally   A brisk general rise in security prices usually following a decline.

random walk   The random motion of stock prices, analogous to the movement of a drunk who at any time is as likely to move in one direction as another; implies that the next price change is as likely to be up as down regardless of past price behavior. This type of behavior is called Brownian motion in the physical sciences.

rate of return   A rate that takes into account both dividends and capital appreciation (increases in the price of the security); for example, a 9% rate of return implies that the owner of $100 worth of stock will earn a total of $9 in dividends and capital appreciation over the forthcoming year.

rating (bond)   A quality or risk evaluation assigned by a rating service such as Standard & Poor's or Moody's.

ratio analysis   Balance sheet and income statement analysis that utilizes ratios of financial aggregates.

RCMM (registered competitive market maker)   *See* floor trader.

reaffirmation agreement   An agreement by a debtor to pay a debt that would otherwise have been dischargeable in a bankruptcy proceeding. Under state law and the bankruptcy law, all prebankruptcy property of the debtor generally becomes property of the estate. However, an individual is permitted to exempt certain properties from the property of the estate. This is called "exempt property." Property designated through certain exemption statutes cannot be reached by creditors through judicial collection efforts.

real estate investment trust   *See* REIT.

real estate limited partnership (RELP)   A type of investment organized as a limited partnership that invests directly in real estate properties.

Real Estate Mortgage Investment Conduit   *See* REMIC.

real estate sales company   A firm that sells property, especially at marketing events such as complimentary dinners; the property is often in a distant location and part of a projected retirement or vacation development.

real return   A return adjusted for changes in the price level; for example, if the nominal rate of return were 7, a 3% inflation rate would reduce the real return to 4%.

rebate   A return of a portion of a payment.

receivership   A prejudgment collection remedy that exists outside of the Bankruptcy Code. The court appoints a receiver as an equitable remedy to prevent the deterioration or impairment of the value of property of a defendant.

recession   An economic downturn categorized as a recession by the National Bureau of Economic Research (NBER); in the past, two successive quarters of decline in real (noninflationary dollars) GNP have signaled the start.

record date   The shareholder registration date that determines the recipients for that period's dividends.

redemption fee   A charge sometimes assessed against those who cash in their mutual fund shares.

redemption price   *See* call price.

refinancing   The selling of new securities to finance the retirement of others that are maturing or being called.

registered bond   A bond whose ownership is determined by registration as opposed to possession (bearer bond).

registered competitive market maker (RCMM)   *See* floor trader.

registered representative   A full-time employee of a NYSE member firm who is qualified to serve as an account executive for the firm's customers.

registered trader   An exchange member who trades stocks on the exchange floor for his or her own account (or account in which he or she is part owner).

registrar   A company such as a bank that maintains the shareholder records.

registration statement   A statement that must be filed with the SEC before a security is offered for sale; must contain all materially relevant information relating to the offering. A similar type of statement is required when a firm's shares are listed. Referred to in the trade as a "red herring" because of the disclaimers written in red ink on its cover. Describes the terms of the bond issue, the business operations of the company and other relevant information required by the SEC.

regional exchange   A U.S. stock exchange located outside New York City.

regression   An equation that is fitted to data by statistical techniques; computers often used to perform the calculations. In the simplest case, a regression will have one variable to be explained (dependent variable) and one variable to explain it (independent variable) and would take the form: $x_t = a + by_t$ (where x_t = dependent variable; y_t = independent variable; and a and b are parameters selected by the computer that best fit the data). Graphically, one can envision a scatter diagram relating x_t and y_t with a line drawn through the points close to the line on the average) as the regression line. The a is the intercept and b the slope coefficient of this line. More complicated regression equations of the form $x_t = a + by_t + cz_t + dw_t + ev_t \ldots$ containing more than one explanatory variable also may be estimated. Again the computer can be used to select the best values of a, b, c, etc.

regression toward the mean   The tendency of many phenomena to migrate toward the average over time.

regulated investment company   A company such as a mutual fund or closed-end fund that qualifies for exemption from federal corporate income tax liability as a result of meeting the requirements set forth in Subchapter M of the Internal Revenue Code.

Regulation Q   A federal rule that at one time limited interest rates that banks and thrifts could pay on certain types of deposits/investments; rendered ineffective by deregulation.

Regulation T   A federal rule that governs credit to brokers and dealers for security purchases.

Regulation U   A federal rule that governs margin credit limits.

reinvestment risk   The risk associated with reinvesting coupon payments at unknown future interest rates. The yield to maturity generally is computed for the assumption that coupons will be reinvested at the same rate as the bond's current yield to maturity; thus, if interest rates decline prior to the bond's maturity, the coupons will not generate the expected return.

REIT (real estate investment trust)   Companies that buy and/or manage rental properties and/or real estate mortgages and pay out more than 95% of their income as dividends; no corporate profit taxes are due on their income.

relative strength   A technical analysis concept based on an assumption that stocks that have risen relative to the market exhibit relative strength, and this tends to carry them to still higher levels. Tests of the concept are largely negative.

RELP   *See* real estate limited partnership.

REMIC (Real Estate Mortgage Investment Conduit)   A type of mortgage-based debt security that restructures the payment streams into bondlike components. Thus, the short-term REMICs receive most of the initial cash flows in a pattern similar to a short-term debt security. Similarly, the longer-term REMICs are promised a cash flow much like a long-term bond. The uncertain portion of the cash-flow stream is left with a residual security called the resid.

reorganization   Restructuring a firm's capital structure and operating facilities in the face of a default, near default or bankruptcy.

replacement-cost approach   The valuing of real estate or other assets on the basis of the cost of producing equivalent assets.

repo   *See* repurchase agreement.

repurchase agreement   A type of investment in which a security is sold with a prearranged purchase price and date designed to produce a particular yield. Also called repo.

reserve requirement   The percentage of reserves the Fed requires each bank to have on deposit for each increment of demand or time deposits.

resid   The residual security left as the various cash flows are assigned to the various term REMICs.

residual asset value   The present value of the amount in which the assets of a business are to be sold at some specified future date.

resistance level   A price range that, according to technical analysis, tends to block further price rises.

retained earnings   On the income statement, annual after-tax profits less dividends paid; on the balance sheet, the sum of annual retained earnings to date.

return on assets (ROA)   Profits before interest and taxes as a percentage of total assets. Also called return on investment.

return on equity (ROE)   Profits after taxes, interest and preferred dividends as a percentage of common equity.

return on investment (ROI)   Profits before interest and taxes as a percentage of total assets. Also called return on assets.

return on sales (ROS)   Profits as a percentage of sales.

revenue bond   A municipal bond backed by the revenues of the project that it finances.

reverse crush   A commodity trade involving buying oil and meal and selling soybean futures.

reverse split   A security exchange in which each shareholder receives a reduced number of shares but retains the same proportional ownership; thus a 10-for-1 reverse split would exchange 10 new shares for each 100 old shares.

revolving credit facility   Similar to working capital facilities but may be used for other corporate purposes. Similar in nature to credit cards in that they typically provide for some minimum repayment schedule.

riding the yield curve   A bond portfolio management strategy of taking advantage of an upward sloping yield curve by purchasing intermediate-term bonds and then selling them as they approach maturity.

right   A security allowing shareholders to acquire new stock at a prespecified price over a prespecified period, generally issued proportional to the number of shares currently held; normally exercisable at a specified price that usually is below the current market price. Rights generally trade in a secondary market after they are issued.

risk   The variance of the expected return, i.e., the degree of certainty associated with the expected return.

risk arbitrage   The taking of offsetting positions in the securities of an acquisition candidate and the would-be acquirer when the combined position should show a profit if the merger takes place.

risk averse   The property of preferring security and demonstrating a willingness to sacrifice return to achieve a more secure yield.

riskfree rate   The interest rate on a riskless investment such as a Treasury bill.

risk hedge   A hedge position undertaken from scratch that seeks to profit from relative price moves in the underlying positions; spreads are an example.

riskless investment   An investment having an expected return that is certain; that is, if a riskless asset is expected to yield 6%, the chance of a 6% return is 100%.

risk neutral   The property of preferring the highest return without regard to risk; indifference to risk.

risk premium   The return in excess of the riskfree rate reflecting the investment's risk.

risk-return trade-off   Tendency for more risky assets to be priced to yield higher expected returns.

risk-reward ratio   A measure of the amount of risk assumed in seeking a specific level of profit.

ROA   *See* return on assets.

Robert Morris Associates   An organization of bankers that compiles averages of financial ratios for various industry groups.

ROE   *See* return on equity.

ROI   *See* return on investment.

rollover   A change from one type of investment to another.

ROS   *See* return on sales.

round lot   The basic unit in which securities are traded; usually 100 shares, although some stocks trade in ten-unit lots.

Rule 144   An SEC rule restricting the sale of lettered stock.

Rule 390   A NYSE rule restricting members from off-board trading (not on an exchange).

Rule 415   An SEC rule allowing shelf registration of a security, which then may be sold periodically without separate registrations of each part.

Rule of 20   Market timing rule that asserts that the Dow Jones Industrial Average's PE plus the inflation rate generally tend toward a value of 20; thus, departures in either direction tend to forecast a market move.

run   An uninterrupted series of price increases or of price decreases.

Sallie Mae (Student Loan Marketing Association)   A federal government agency that sells notes backed by government-guaranteed student loans.

saturation effect   The impact on revenues and profits when a heretofore rapid-growth firm or industry largely satisfies its market's demand.

savings bonds   Low-denomination Treasury issues designed to appeal to small investors.

scalper   A commodity trader who seeks to profit from very short-run price changes.

scorched-earth defense   An antitakeover tactic in which the defending company's management engages in practices designed to reduce the firm's value to such a degree that it no longer is attractive to the potential acquirer.

S corporation   *See* Subchapter S corporation.

seasoning The process of new issues acquiring market acceptance in after-issue trading.

seat A membership on an exchange.

SEC (Securities and Exchange Commission) The government agency with direct regulatory authority over the securities industry.

secondary distribution A large public securities offering made outside the usual exchange or OTC market; those making the offering wish to sell a larger quantity of the security than they believe can be easily absorbed by the market's usual channels. A secondary offering spreads out the period for absorption.

secondary market The market for already-issued securities that may take place on the exchanges or OTC.

secondary stocks Relatively obscure stocks not favored by institutional investors; thus, individual investors are the primary market. May trade on the AMEX, NASD and regional exchanges or be among the smaller companies listed on the NYSE market.

second mortgage A mortgage debt secured by a property's equity after the first mortgage holder's claim has been subtracted from the pledged asset's value.

sector fund A type of mutual fund that specializes in a narrow segment of the market; for example, an industry (chemicals), region (Sunbelt) or category (small capitalization).

securities Paper assets representing a claim on something of value, such as stocks, bonds, mortgages, warrants, rights, puts, calls, commodity contracts or warehouse receipts.

Securities Amendment Act of 1970 An act restricting the front-end loading fees that mutual funds can charge.

Securities and Exchange Commission *See* SEC.

Securities Investors Protection Corporation *See* SIPC.

securitization The process of turning an asset with poor marketability into a security with substantially greater acceptability; for example, a security that looks like a standard bond but is derived from real estate mortgage loans, automobile loans or credit-card balances.

security agreement An agreement that creates or provides for a security interest.

security interest A lien created by an agreement.

security market line The theoretical relation between a security's market risk and its expected return.

segmented markets hypothesis   A theory that explains the term structure of interest rates as due to the supply and demand of each maturity class.

self-tender   A firm tendering for its own shares; often used as an antitakeover defense.

seller financing   A procedure in which the real estate seller is used to finance part of the purchase price.

selling short   The act of selling a security that belongs to someone else and is borrowed; the short seller covers by buying back equivalent securities and restoring them to the original owner.

semistrong form of the efficient market hypothesis   The view that market prices quickly and accurately reflect all public information; implies that fundamental analysis applied to public data is useless.

semiweak form of the efficient market hypothesis   The view that market prices cannot be successfully forecast with technical market indicators.

SEP (Simplified Employee Pension Plan)   Pension plan in which both the employee and the employer contribute to an Individual Retirement Plan.

serial bond   A bond issue portions of which mature at stated intervals rather than all at once.

serial correlation   Correlation between adjacent time series data.

shark repellent   Antitakeover provisions such as a poison pill.

shelf registration   An SEC provision allowing preregistration of an amount of a security to be sold over time without specific registration of each sale; permitted by SEC Rule 415.

short against the box   The short selling of stock that is owned; usually employed as a tax device for extending the date of realizing a gain.

short covering   Buying an asset to offset an existing short position.

short interest (commodities and options)   The number of futures or options contracts written and outstanding.

short interest (stocks)   The number of shares sold short.

short position   To have sold an asset that is not owned in the hope of repurchasing it later at a lower price.

short squeeze   The result when powerful forces driving up the price of a stock have the effect of squeezing a substantial short interest.

short-swing profit   A gain made by an insider on stock held for less than six months; such gains must be paid back to the company.

short-swing rule   A tax rule that prevents a trader from realizing a tax loss on a sale and immediately repurchasing the issue in question; stock must be held at least 30 days before the sale and repurchase must be delayed at least 30 days after the sale.

short-term gains (losses)   Gains (losses) on capital assets held less than six months.

short-term trading index   A technical market indicator based on the relative percent of advancing versus declining stocks.

short-term unit trust   A unit investment trust made up of an unmanaged portfolio of short-term securities; usually self-liquidating within six months of issue.

simple interest   Interest paid and computed only on the principal.

Simplified Employee Pension Plan   *See* SEP.

single-index model   A method of estimating portfolio risk that utilizes only the market index and market model as opposed to the full variance-co-variance matrix.

single-premium deferred annuity contract   An annuity with a defined future value; sold by insurance companies.

sinking fund   An indenture provision requiring that a specific portion of a bond issue be redeemed periodically; required by many bond indentures so that all of the debt will not come due simultaneously.

SIPC (Securities Investors Protection Corporation)   A federal government agency that guarantees the safety of brokerage accounts up to $500,000, no more than $100,000 of which may be in cash.

skewed distribution   A nonsymmetrical distribution that is spread out more on one side of its mode than the other.

skewness   The degree to which a distribution is skewed.

SMA (special miscellaneous account)   A sum associated with a margin account; normally equal to the account's (margin) buying power. The account is increased when stock is sold and decreased when stock is purchased. At times the SMA of an account can become inflated (above the account's buying power) when the equity of the account is near or below the minimum for margin maintenance.

smokestack companies   Companies in basic industries whose profits and sales are cyclical with the economy.

social responsibility fund   A type of mutual fund that avoids investments in allegedly socially undesirable companies such as those involved with tobacco, alcohol, pollution, defense, South Africa and so forth.

source and application of funds statement   An accounting statement reporting a firm's cash inflows and outflows. Now called changes in financial position statement.

S&P (Standard & Poor's Corporation)   An important firm in the investment area that rates bonds, collects and reports data and computes market indexes.

S&P 500 Index   A value-weighted stock index based on the share prices of 500 large firms.

special miscellanous account   *See* SMA.

specialist   An exchange member who makes a market in listed securities.

specialized dependencies   Predictable return patterns related to some specific type of event such as a new issue or tax-loss trading.

special offering   A large block of stock offered for sale on an exchange with special incentive fees paid to purchasing brokers. Also called spot secondary.

speculating   The act of committing funds for a short period at high risk in the hope of realizing a large gain.

SPI (Strategic Planning Institute)   A strategic planning consulting firm that is best known for its par ROI equation.

split   An exchange of securities whereby each shareholder ends up with a larger number of shares representing the same percentage of the firm's ownership. In a 2-for-1 split, a shareholder with 100 old shares would receive an additional 100 shares.

spot market   The market for immediate delivery of some commodity such as wheat or silver.

spot secondary   *See* special offering.

spread (bid-ask)   The difference between the bid and the ask price.

spread (trade)   A type of hedge trade such as a vertical or horizontal spread (options) or some comparable combination trade in the futures market; offsetting positions taken in similar securities in the hope of profiting from relative price moves.

Standard & Poor's Corporation   *See* S&P.

Standard & Poor's Corporation Reports   An investment periodical containing quarterly analyses of most publicly traded firms.

Standard & Poor's Encyclopedia   A book containing analyses of S&P 500 stocks.

Standard & Poor's Investor Service   An important firm in the investment area that rates bonds; also computes market indexes, compiles investment information and publishes various investment periodicals.

Standard & Poor's Stock Guide   A monthly publication with a compact line of data on most publicly traded corporations.

standard deviation   A measure of the degree of compactness or spread of a distribution. About two times out of three, the actual value will be within one standard deviation on either side of the mean value; about 19 out of 20 times, it will be within two standard deviations. One standard deviation is the square root of the variance. *See also* variance.

standstill agreement   A reciprocal understanding between a company's management and an outside party that owns a significant minority position in the company's stock, with each party giving up certain rights in exchange for corresponding concessions by the other party. For example, the outside group may agree to limit its ownership position to some prespecified level. In exchange, management may agree to minority board representation by the outside group.

stays   A restraining of creditors from taking action against the debtor or the debtor's property to collect claims and enforce security interests.

Stein estimators   Statistical techniques for estimating a variable that assume a regression toward the mean tendency.

Stock Clearing Corporation   A NYSE subsidiary that clears transactions for member firms.

stock dividend   A dividend paid in the form of additional stock; similar to a stock split although usually proportionately less new stock is distributed.

stock exchange   An organization for trading a specific list of securities over specific trading hours usually at a single location.

stockholder-oriented company   A company whose management is particularly responsive to the interest of its stockholders; a large ownership group may exercise effective control or management itself may own a large block of the stock.

stock split   The division of a company's existing stock into more shares (for example, 2 for 1 or 3 for 1); usually done to reduce the price per share in the hope of improving the shares' marketability.

stop-limit order   An order to implement a limit order when the market price reaches a certain level.

stop-loss order   An order to sell or buy at market when a certain price is reached.

straddle (in commodities)   Another name for a spread, where offsetting positions are taken in similar contracts such as adjacent expirations of the same physical.

straddle (in options)   A combination put and call on the same stock at the same striking price.

straight-debt value   The value of a convertible bond as a straight-debt (nonconvertible) bond.

straight-line depreciation   A method of writing off assets at a constant dollar rate over their estimated lives.

strap   A combination of two calls and a put each having the same strike and expiration date.

Strategic Planning Institute   *See* SPI.

street name   Securities held in customer accounts at brokerage houses but registered in the firm's name.

strike   *See* striking price.

striking price   The amount an option holder has to pay (or will receive) to exercise an option. Also called strike.

strip   A combination of two puts and a call each having the same strike and expiration date.

strip bond   A coupon bond with its coupons removed; returns only principal at maturity and thus is equivalent to a zero-coupon bond.

strong form of the efficient market hypothesis   The view that market prices quickly and accurately reflect all public and nonpublic information; implies that inside information is useless in security selection.

Student Loan Marketing Association   *See* Sallie Mae.

Subchapter M   The section of the Internal Revenue Code that sets forth the criteria for a regulated investment company. *See also* regulated investment company.

Subchapter S   The section of the Internal Revenue Code that sets forth the criteria for a Subchapter S corporation.

Subchapter S corporation   An arrangement whereby a corporation may be taxed as a partnership under the provisions of the Internal Revenue Code. Also called S corporation.

subordination provisions   Bond indenture provisions that give an issue a lower priority than other issues.

sum of the years' digits depreciation   A method of accelerated depreciation that assigns depreciation equal to the ratio of the number of years remaining to the sum of the years in the asset's estimated life.

Super Bowl indicator   A whimsical technical market indicator based on whether the Super Bowl is won by a former member of the old American Football League (AFL) or the National Football League (NFL). An NFL victory forecasts an up market for the coming year; an AFL victory forecasts a down market. No forecast is derived from an expansion team win.

Super Dot System *See* DOT.

superNOW account An interest-bearing checking account with no set maximum interest rate; most banks require a $2,500 minimum balance.

support level A floor price that, according to technical analysis, tends to restrict downside price moves.

Survey Research Center Research institute at the University of Michigan that surveys and publishes statistics on consumer sentiments.

swap fund A type of mutual fund that allows purchases with shares of other companies at their market prices.

sweep account A type of bank account that daily sweeps the portion of the balance exceeding some preassigned minimum into a money fund where rates are not limited by federal restrictions.

syndicate A group of investment bankers organized to underwrite a new issue or secondary offering.

systematic risk *See* market risk.

takeover bid A tender offer designed to acquire a sufficient number of shares to achieve working control of the target firm.

tangible investments A broad group of commodities that includes precious metals, gemstones, artifacts and some types of collectibles.

tangibles *See* tangible investments.

tax credit Amounts applied against computed taxes on a dollar-for-dollar basis, reducing the amount otherwise due.

Tax-Exempt Bond Fund *See* TEBF.

tax-loss carryforward Unutilized prior-period losses that may be employed to offset subsequent income.

tax-loss trading Year-end selling of depressed securities designed to establish a tax loss.

tax-managed fund A type of investment company that sought to convert dividend income into capital gains; prior to IRS rulings disallowing the practice, such funds organized themselves as corporations rather than as mutual funds and reinvested their portfolios' dividends.

tax shelter An investment that produces deductions from other income for the investor with a resulting savings in income taxes. The Tax Reform Act of 1986 severely restricted most types of tax shelters.

tax swap A type of bond swap in which an issue is sold to yield a tax loss and replaced with an equivalent issue.

T-bill *See* Treasury bill.

TEBF (Tax-Exempt Bond Fund) A mutual fund that invests in municipal bonds, offering taxfree income to its holders.

technical analysis (broad form)   A method of forecasting general market movements with technical market indicators.

technical analysis (narrow form)   A method of evaluating securities based on past price and volume behavior; largely debunked by evidence favorable to the efficient market hypothesis.

technical indicator   A data series or combination of data series said to be helpful in forecasting the market's future direction. Also called market indicator.

Templeton approach   A fundamental approach to investment analysis named after renowned mutual fund manager John Marks Templeton; emphasizes a worldview to finding undervalued issues.

tender offer   An offer to purchase a large block of securities made outside the general market (exchanges, OTC) in which the securities are traded; often made as part of an effort to take over a company.

term insurance   A type of life insurance that does not have a savings feature and for which rates rise with age to reflect the greater probability of death. *See also* whole life insurance.

term loan   Bank loans that are generally of a longer-term nature and have preset amortization schedules and a stated maturity.

term structure of interest rates   A pattern of yields for differing maturities (risk controlled). *See also* liquidity preference, preferred habitat, segmented markets and unbiased expectations hypotheses.

term to maturity   The length to maturity of a debt instrument.

tertiary stocks   The most obscure group of stocks; much less popular than even the secondary stocks; trade on the pink sheets.

testator   *See* testor.

testimonium   The concluding portion of a will.

testor   A person who leaves a will in force at his or her death. Also called testator.

thin market   A market in which volume is low and transactions relatively infrequent.

third market   The OTC market in listed securities.

thrifts   Institutions other than commercial banks that accept savings deposits, especially savings and loan associations, mutual savings banks and credit unions.

tick   The minimum size price change on a futures contract.

ticker symbols   Symbols for identifying securities on the ticker tape and quotation machines; listed in *Standard & Poor's Stock Guide* and several other publications.

ticker tape   A device for displaying stock market trading.

tight money   Restrictive monetary policy.

TIGRs (Treasury Investment Growth Receipts)   Zero-coupon securities assembled by Merrill Lynch and backed by a portfolio of Treasury issues.

times-interest-earned ratio   Before-tax, before-interest profit relative to a firm's interest obligation.

time value (option)   The excess of an option's market price over its intrinsic value.

time value (present value)   The value of a current as opposed to a future sum.

title search   A process whereby the validity of a title to a real estate parcel is evaluated.

TOLSR (Total Odd-Lot Short Ratio)   A technical market indicator that relates odd-lot short sales to total odd-lot trading.

top-tier stocks   Established growth stocks preferred by many institutional investors.

Total Odd-Lot Short Ratio   *See* TOLSR.

total return   Dividend return plus capital-gains return.

total risk   The sum of market and nonmarket risk.

trading post   *See* post.

transfer   Every mode, direct or indirect, absolute or conditional, voluntary or involuntary, of disposing of or parting with property or with an interest in property.

transfer agent   The agent who keeps track of changes in shareholder ownership.

transfer tax   A New York State tax on the transfer of equity securities.

Treasury bill   Government debt security issued on a discount basis by the U.S. Treasury. Also called T-bill.

Treasury Investment Growth Receipts   *See* TIGRs.

treasury stock   Previously issued stock reacquired by the issuing company.

trust   A property interest held by one person for the benefit of another.

trustee   *See* bankruptcy trustee; also, under an indenture, a bank or other third party that administers the provisions of a bond indenture; *see also* indenture trustee.

turnover   Trading volume in a security or the market.

Turov's formula   A formula for computing the amount by which a stock price must change to produce equivalent returns on its options.

12b-1 fund   A type of mutual fund that does not charge a load but does take out a selling fee on an annual basis.

two-tier tender offer   Takeover tactic in which one offer is made for controlling interest of the target (usually cash) and a second generally less attractive offer (usually securities) is made for the remainder.

unbiased expectations hypothesis   A theory explaining the term structure of interest rates as reflecting the market consensus of contiguous forthcoming short rates.

underwriter   An investment dealer who agrees to buy all or part of a new security issue and plans to sell the securities to the public at a slightly higher price.

underwriting fee   The difference between the price paid and the selling price on an underwritten issue.

unemployment rate   The percentage of those actively seeking employment who are out of work.

United Shareholders of America (USA)   A shareholder rights organization sponsored by T. Boone Pickens, advocating such issues as equal voting rights for all classes of stock, secret proxy votes and prohibition of poison pills.

United States Trustee   An employee of the Department of Justice who attends to certain administrative functions in terms of the administration of the bankruptcy case. This is not the same as a bankruptcy trustee who is an individual assigned to manage and run a debtor's estate.

unit investment trust   A self-liquidating unmanaged portfolio in which investors own shares.

universal life   A type of life insurance in which the cash value varies with the policyholder's payments and the company's investment returns.

Unlisted Market Guide   An investment publication that periodically covers small companies that are not found in larger periodicals such as *Value Line* and Standard & Poor's publications.

unlisted security   A security that trades only in the OTC market.

unsystematic risk   *See* nonmarket risk.

uptick   A transaction that takes place at a higher price than the immediately preceding price.

urgent selling index   A technical market indicator based on the relative volume in advancing and declining issues.

USA   *See* United Shareholders of America.

usable bond   A bond that may be used at face value to exercise corresponding warrants.

VA (Veterans Administration)   A federal government agency that guarantees mortgage loans of veterans.

Value Line   A firm that publishes quarterly analyses on approximately 1,700 firms and compiles the Value Line Index; owned by Arnold Bernhard and Company.

Value Line Index   An unweighted broadly based stock price index.

value-oriented investor   Investor who seeks to assemble a portfolio of stocks that sell at low prices relative to their underlying values; that is, to their earnings, cash flows, book values, breakup values and liquid assets.

variable annuity   An investment vehicle similar to a mutual fund but sold by insurance companies.

variable life   A type of life insurance in which the cash value varies with the return of the policyholder's portfolio.

variable-rate mortgage   A mortgage in which the interest rate is allowed to vary with market rates.

variance   The expected (average) value of the square of the deviation from the mean; variance of $X = E(X - \overline{X})^2$ where $\overline{X}$ is the mean of X and E is the expected value.

variance-covariance model   A method of estimating portfolio risk that utilizes the variances and covariances of all of the potential components.

Vasicek adjustment   A method of adjusting estimated betas based on the uncertainty of the mean and specific beta estimates.

venture capital   Risk capital extended to start-up or small going concerns.

versus purchase order   Sale order that specifies purchase date of securities to be delivered for sale.

vertical integration   The process of a business either buying or building from scratch a supplier or customer.

vertical spread   Short- and long-option positions on the same security with the same expiration but different striking prices.

vested benefits   Pension benefits that are retained even if the individual leaves his or her employer.

Veterans Administration   *See* VA.

volume   The number of shares traded in a particular period.

Wall Street Journal, The   A business/investments newspaper published five days a week by Dow Jones & Company, Inc.

"Wall Street Week" (WSW) A popular and long-running weekly business news television program.

warrants Certificates offering the right to purchase stock in a company at a specified price over a specified period.

wash sale A sale and repurchase made within 30 days, thereby failing to establish a taxable loss.

weak form of the efficient market hypothesis The view that market prices move randomly with respect to past price return patterns; implies that the broad form of technical analysis is useless.

Weisenberger A major publisher of mutual fund investment information, including *Investment Companies.*

when issued Trading in as yet unissued securities that have a projected future issue date.

white knight defense Finding an alternative and presumably more friendly acquirer than the immediate takeover threat.

white squire defense Finding an important ally to purchase a strong minority position of the firm now controlled by existing management but threatened by an outside group; presumably, the white squire will oppose and hopefully block the efforts of the outsider to take control of the vulnerable company.

whole life insurance A type of policy that couples life insurance with a savings feature. Premiums are fixed with a surplus built up in the policy's early years to meet claims that exceed premiums when the policyholders are older.

will A legal statement of a person's wishes with regard to the disposition of his or her property or estate at the time of death.

Wilshire 5000 Index A value-weighted stock index based on a large number of NYSE, AMEX and OTC stock.

wire house An exchange member electronically linked to an exchange.

withholding tax A portion of an employee's income withheld by the employer as partial payment of income tax.

working capital (gross) The sum of the values of a firm's short-term assets.

working capital (net) A firm's short-term assets minus its short-term liabilities.

working-capital facilities Those portions of a company's bank credit agreement usually reserved for the acquisition of working capital such as inventory.

working control   The ownership of sufficient shares to elect a majority to the company's board of directors.

writer (of an option)   One who assumes the short side of a put or call contract and therefore stands ready to satisfy the potential exercise of the long side.

WSW   *See* "Wall Street Week."

yield   The return of an investment expressed as a percentage of its market value.

yield (current)   Current income (dividend, coupon, rent, etc.) divided by the price of the asset.

yield curve   A relationship between yield to maturity and term to maturity (or duration) for equivalent-risk debt securities.

yield curve notes   Debt security whose coupon rate is structured to move inversely with market rates; thus, when the market interest rates decline, the coupon rate on the yield curve notes will rise, and vice versa.

yield to earliest call   The holding-period return for the assumption that the issue is called as soon as the no-call provision expires.

yield to maturity   The yield that takes account of both the coupon return and the principal repayment at maturity.

zero-coupon bond   A bond issued at a discount to mature at its face value.

zero tick   A transaction immediately preceded by a transaction at the same price.

INDEX

Wall Street Computer Review, 150
Wall Street Journal, The, 131, 133,
    144, 153
        quotations, 133, 134, 136–37,
        139–41
"Wall Street Week" TV program, 151
Warrants and rights, 179–80
Washington Document Service, 131
Wilson Foods Corporation, 20

Working capital, 104–5

"Your Money" TV program, 152

Zero-coupon bonds, 162–64
Zeta Services, 194
Zweig, Martin, 147, 151
Zweig Forecaster, 147